# *Spiritual* AWARENESS

*Awakening the Soul*

Larry E. Maugel

ISBN 978-1-63874-977-6 (paperback)
ISBN 978-1-63874-979-0 (hardcover)
ISBN 978-1-63874-978-3 (digital)

Copyright © 2021 by Larry E. Maugel

All rights reserved. No part of this publication may be reproduced, distributed, or transmitted in any form or by any means, including photocopying, recording, or other electronic or mechanical methods without the prior written permission of the publisher. For permission requests, solicit the publisher via the address below.

Christian Faith Publishing, Inc.
832 Park Avenue
Meadville, PA 16335
www.christianfaithpublishing.com

Printed in the United States of America

Scripture quotations marked ESV are taken from the ENGLISH STANDARD VERSION. © 2001 by Crossway Bibles, a division of Good News Publishers.

Scripture quotations marked KJV are taken from the KING JAMES VERSION.

Scripture quotations marked NASB are taken from the NEW AMERICAN STANDARD BIBLE®, Copyright © 1960, 1962, 1963, 1968, 1971, 1972, 1973, 1975, 1977, 1995 by the Lockman Foundation. Used by permission.

Scripture quotations marked NIV are taken from the Holy Bible, New International Version®, NIV®. Copyright © 1973, 1978, 1984, 2011 by Biblica, Inc.® Used by permission of Zondervan All rights reserved worldwide. www.zondervan.com.

Scripture quotations marked NLT are taken from the Holy Bible, New Living Translation. © 1996, 2004, 2007 by Tyndale House Foundation. Used by permission of Tyndale House Publishers, Inc., Carol Stream, Illinois 60188. All rights reserved.

# Contents

Acknowledgments ........................................................................7
Preface......................................................................................9
1. Spiritual Awareness: Introduction to the Devotional Life........11
2. Humility: A Foundational Virtue ..........................................25
3. Openness and Surrender: Doorway to Spirituality..................53
4. Worldview: The Problem of Perception and
   Philosophical Perspective.....................................................69
5. Spiritual Awareness: Awe, Wonder, Reverence ......................85
6. Art and Beauty: Diversity within Design .............................103
7. The Present Moment: The Mystery of Time........................116
8. Practicing Praxis: Intentionality, Affirmation, Choice ..........131
9. Believing the Miraculous: Seeing the Unseen......................149
10. Suffering and Hope: Light in the Midst of Darkness ...........174
11. Grace and Gratitude: Discovering Peace..............................202
12. The Tapestry of Prayer: Prayer within the Fabric of Life .......220
Conclusion............................................................................251
Appendix I. Spiritual Awareness Exercises: Sensitizing the Soul.....253
Appendix II. Spiritual Disciplines..............................................265

# Acknowledgments

This book is really the Lord's work. I have been but a scribe attempting to describe the many blessings that He has brought into my life. Hopefully, that gratitude will flow out into the lives of others in a way that they will draw ever closer to Him. For that is my real purpose and prayer for this book.

My lovely wife Laurel has been instrumental in the preparation of this manuscript. She is the detailed person of the two of us, and I often tease her that this work would have been another ten pages longer had she not removed all of my commas and semicolons! She is a wonderful, loving, and caring person, with whom I could not be more richly blessed!

Laurel is largely credited for our terrific family whom we love and adore: daughter Katherine Fain, son-in-law Tim, and grandchildren Lucas, Jackson, Emma, and Ellie who live in Waxhaw, NC; and son, Michael Maugel, daughter-in-law Laura, and granddaughter Meghan who live in Denver, Co., all of whom love and serve the Lord.

Every person should have a *soul* mate and Bill McDonald has been that to me. I often teasingly refer to him as my "theology professor" because he has been so instrumental in so much of my devotional life, much of which forms the contents of this book. At a little restaurant within a truck stop the two of us would commonly meet. Over our books and coffee refills, our conversations of what it means to live an authentic spiritual, caring life would go late into the night. We jokingly refer to those times as "the Spirituality of the Truck Stop."

And finally all those at Christian Faith Publishing who brought their expertise to bear in taking the original manuscript and bringing it into its final form. Their professionalism is greatly appreciated. They have done a wonderful job and have been a great group of people with whom to work.

# Preface

Is there anything I can do to
make myself enlightened?
As little as you can do to make the
sun to rise in the morning.
Then of what use are the spiritual
exercises you prescribe?
To make sure you are not asleep
when the sun begins to rise.[1]
—Anthony de Mello,
*One Minute Wisdom*

Though this work contains elements of philosophy and theology, it is meant to be primarily a devotional one, whose themes describe observations and reflections on who man is, and where he is going. It is meant to encourage and edify. In addition, it is a work that speaks of spiritual awareness and insights fundamental to spiritual transformation. It intends to challenge one toward a "life worth living."

Over the years, I have enjoyed the reading and studying of topics both "ancient" and "religious." In doing so, I have long ago discovered the delight of finding value and truths anew within the musing of the old scholars. For that reason, I suppose, I am not a subscriber to the contemporary notion that the most recent and more complex thoughts are necessarily the most reliable or valuable. There is much truth still to be gleaned from the familiar adage of "standing on the shoulders of giants."

Furthermore, as I reflect upon the writers I have enjoyed and respected the most, it becomes clear that they are those who write with an honest measure of both curiosity and humility. Their goal is not to indoctrinate or convince, but rather to share their joys of discovery with others. I hope this work will do so as well.

The tenor of this work is meant to be reflective and wistfully philosophical. Though the themes of transcendence and openness initially predominate, the corresponding themes of immanence and actualization are more fully developed as the work progresses…from the abstract to the concrete, if you will.

Furthermore, please don't misconstrue that the author has mastered the degree of awareness this work describes. It has been a work of reflection on how the spiritual life might be lived and enjoyed; though I claim to be no expert in its content. For me, life is still very much a moment-by-moment glimpse of spiritual realities, some of joy and some of struggle, all presented from the loving hand of a benevolent God. It becomes the work of each day to avail myself to His guidance and wisdom.

Like many authors, in some way, this work is an autobiography, for it contains many of the concepts and quotations that shape the person who I am today and who I will be in eternity. It is the material that has chastised me and guided me. For exposure to such rich content of thought I will forever be grateful.

Lastly, I would hope that there will be both some new insights for you to enjoy as you read, as well as some practical examples of how to live this life with more purpose and meaning.

Please forgive the inadequacies in this work. They are many. But pick a few thoughts to ponder and savor, and perhaps you may find some helpful milestones along your journey. My prayer is that you may become more aware of the spiritual realities of each moment, and that a newfound openness to Divine leading may draw you closer to a life of devotion and submission to the will of Christ.

---

[1] "Vigilance" from One Minute Wisdom by Anthony De Mello, 19, copyright © 1985 by Anthony De Mello, S. J. Used by permission of Doubleday, an imprint of the Knopf Doubleday Publishing Group, a division of Penguin Random House LLC. All rights reserved.

# 1

## *Spiritual Awareness*
## *Introduction to the Devotional Life*

> Thirsty hearts are those whose longings have
> been wakened by the touch of God within them.
> —A. W. Tozer[1]

Excited about life? Or do the events of each day flow into an unending sea of gray? Are the sunny days too few and the cloudy days ever threatening? Is there a spring to your step and a twinkle of teasing in your eyes? Does a smile grace your lips and hope shape your vision? The search for a better life, an abundant life, seems to be humanity's ever-constant quest—forcefully driven by some mysterious longing.

We all know individuals who appear to continually express this way of life. They always seem optimistic, energetic, interested, and curious about life. They almost appear to "taste" life deeply each moment. Often, even in the midst of personal misfortune, their spirit shines with grace. Is this just a condition of having a positive attitude or is there something more? How does one find this same richness and meaning? Unfortunately, our personal efforts are more likely laced with moments of uncertainty and ambiguity, and we are found asking ourselves, "What am I to do?"

Usually we start by trying to "patch up" our lives. We begin with the simple and easy things—eating less, exercising more, spending less, giving more, complaining less, smiling more…all the "self-improvement" aids that sell so many books. Sometimes it works for a while, but it seldom leads to where we find a sustaining peace. For in many ways, the path to "self-fulfillment" is pointed in the wrong direction. We are told to patch up the imperfections and to disregard our limitations as we strive for our image of "Renaissance man."

There is this image in each of our minds of who we would like to become. For most of us, it starts with the desire to look good and be good. Soon it becomes a measure of focus as we begin to pursue those desires with greater passion and commitment. Before long, our natural state of imperfection is covered with a cosmetic veneer of poise and beauty, confidence and accomplishments. Our genuine nature is now adorned with the trappings of conventional culture.

So a question confronts each one of us: do we "patch," or do we "transform?"

## PATCHING OR TRANSFORMATION?

> We are not social workers. We are really contemplatives in the heart of the world.[2]
> —Mother Theresa

What is this distinction that Mother Theresa draws between being a social worker and being a "contemplative in the heart of the world"? Of all the wonderful work that social workers do, why is becoming a "contemplative" working amongst the needs of others any different? Perhaps it is the difference between "patching" and "transformation"…between "religion"[3] and "spirituality."[4]

One point that must be made now is that what we are *not* referring to here is a "contemplative" life that is detached and isolated from the suffering of others. Instead, Mother Theresa's life pictures for us a devout, thoughtful, and aware soul who was sensitive and *responsive* to the hunger and pain in our world. She actively *sought out* a place within suffering to perform her works of transformation. She *engaged* suffering and made it her own, to shine a light of love and compassion into the darkness of poverty and suffering.

## SPIRITUAL AWARENESS: INTRODUCTION TO THE DEVOTIONAL LIFE

Yet Mother Theresa identified herself, and those of her order, as "contemplatives." Her desire to be so identified reveals a life deeper than the superficial. It describes a life of awareness to spiritual perspective and forces. It reveres a power and authority beyond any mere human endeavor.

Her life exemplifies a moment-by-moment attentiveness to spiritual inspirations and movements. Yet beyond this, there is also a redemptive aspect of contemplative action. It reaches into my life and yours, to take us from where we are as imperfect persons, constrained by our limitations, to become transformed souls inspired by Divine Presence.

This transformation begins with the desire for something ultimately better, as an innate restlessness constantly stirs this search for meaning and purpose. Aristotle would say that man's greatest desire is for the fulfillment of "happiness." Still other philosophers propose their own opinions of self-fulfillment and identity. Though there may be many ways to describe this ultimate desire, there remains the reality of it being fed by an underlying, innate sense of longing.

*Sehnsucht*

Without doubt, the contemporary author who most vividly described this sense of longing was C. S. Lewis. His word for this was *Sehnsucht*, which is a German word meaning "joy," "longing," or "desire." This concept of innate longing was described by C. S. Lewis and revealed in his writings as a fundamental aspect of his thinking. For Lewis, this desire or longing, which he also described as "joy," was something he experienced at an early age.

> From at least the age of six, romantic longing—Sehnsucht—had played an unusually central part of my experience. Such longing is in itself the very reverse of wishful thinking: it is more like thoughtful wishing.[5]
> [F]or in a sense the central story of my life is about nothing else,…it is that of an unsatis-

fied desire which is itself more desirable than any other satisfaction. I call it Joy...[6]

In some ways, the term *joy* may be a misnomer in today's vernacular. For Lewis, this meant not only a sense of happiness, but a sense of joyful longing embodied in something or someone outside of oneself. Lewis ties this experience with the idea of transcendence. "The human soul was made to enjoy some object that is never fully given—nay, cannot even be imagined as given—in our present mode of subjective and spatio-temporal experience."[7]

And in one of his most famous quoted passages, he uses more figurative language: "If I find in myself a desire which no experience in this world can satisfy, the most probable explanation is that I was made for another world."[8]

Even within these few quotations of C. S. Lewis, one sees that this desire is not for something tangible, nor even possibly something to be possessed. But rather it is to be *experienced*. This notion of Sehnsucht conveys the idea of experiencing an awareness of a greater hope which reaches beyond the immediate images of daily circumstances. It sees life played out on a bigger stage, whose backdrop is one of transcendence. Each person finds themselves within a larger story.

## "Romance"

Brent Curtis and John Eldredge, in their book *The Sacred Romance*, describe their concept of this ineffable desire by using the word *romance*. They describe their perspective of "longing" this way:

> In all our hearts lies a longing for a Sacred Romance.
>
> It will not go away in spite of our efforts over the years to anesthetize or ignore its song, or attach it to a single person or endeavor. It is a Romance couched in mystery and set deeply within us...
>
> Philosophers call this Romance, this heart yearning set within us, the longing for transcen-

> dence; the desire to be part of something larger than ourselves, to be part of something out of the ordinary that is good…
>
> Indeed, if we reflect back on the journey of our heart, the Romance has most often come to us in the form of two deep desires: the longing for adventure that requires something of us, and the desire for intimacy—to have someone truly know us for ourselves, while at the same time inviting us to know them…[9]

In the busyness of today's fast-paced demands, it is easy to become blind to anything but the most urgent. The immediacy of personal responsibilities and tasks force one to focus on the short sound bites of life, rather than the undergirding themes of responsible living. Decisions become based upon the expediency of the moment. Actions follow the path of least resistance. Random emotions and responses clutter the hours of each day. These are the actions that dampen the "romance" of our lives, and leave us less aware of the richness of human experience that could be ours.

Curtis and Eldredge go on to describe their perspective of our post-modern times.

> The central belief of our times is that there is no story, nothing hangs together, all we have are bits and pieces, the random days of our lives. Tragedy still brings us to tears and heroism still lifts our hearts, but there is no context for any of it. Life is just a sequence of images and emotions without rhyme or reason.
>
> So, what are we left to do? Create our own story line to bring some meaning to our experiences. Our heart is made to live in a larger story; having lost that we do the best we can by developing our own smaller dramas.[10]

Our souls were made to live in the Larger Story, but as Chesterton discovered, we have forgotten our part:

"This man walks about the streets and can see and appreciate everything; only he cannot remember who he is. Well, every man is that man in the story. Every man has forgotten who he is… We are all under the same mental calamity; we have all forgotten our names. We have all forgotten what we really are." (Orthodoxy)[11]

So it is that these authors lead us into an awareness of transcendental "longing." Now our journey begins, and we must ask the questions that help us find our way. Who am I? And for what am I longing? …for we have forgotten our names. We have forgotten who we really are.

## THE SPIRITUALITY OF IMPERFECTION

In the exuberance of youth, there is always the notion of becoming the person one wants to be—a more beautiful woman, a stronger athlete, a more accomplished musician. Though reality warns that this may never be the case, aspirations continue to tease one to strive for perfection. It is the hope for something better that drives us. It calls forth courage and sacrifice amongst the possibility of failure. "Renaissance man" embodies the notion that one can become all that one wants to be. But despite all the wonderful actions these attitudes accomplish, disillusionment stands silently in the shadow of the stage.

The midlife years arrive all too soon, reminding us that some of our aspirations will not be met. Career demands, family responsibilities, health constraints place a heavy burden upon accomplishing all that we want. Limitations of time and personal resources frustrate us, and reality hits. We are forced to acknowledge that we will never have enough time, enough energy, enough wealth. Our imperfections stare coldly in our faces. We must reluctantly surrender some of our dreams. Nonetheless, it is from this soil of disappointment that we find the tools of reassessment and revision with which to guide our souls. For even in this barren time of disillusionment, there can be the budding of understanding and growth.

Before we go any farther, let us deal with the concept of trying to be "perfect." In Matthew 5:48 (KJV), we are admonished with these words: "Be ye therefore perfect, even as your Father which is in heaven is perfect." Now to some, this passage of Scripture may mean "without flaw." However, both personal experience and the proper exegesis of Scripture tell us that this is not the case. Reason and experience quickly affirm that no person is without flaw. Furthermore, proper exegesis of Scripture instructs us that the root word for "perfect" used in this passage connotes the idea of "mature." So instead of striving to be a person "without flaw," one is encouraged to work toward "maturity" or the fulfillment of genuine spiritual character. There will be mistakes made and failures to suffer, but one's goal is for the soul to grow in understanding and maturity.

The "spirituality of imperfection" is a phrase that encourages a realistic view of human experience. Failure accompanies success. Imperfection taunts our desire to be flawless. Our limitations shatter our dreams. Yet to be real and genuine is to face these truths.

In their book, *The Spirituality of Imperfection*, Ernest Kurtz and Katherine Ketcham write,

> We are not "everything," but neither are we "nothing." Spirituality is discovered in that space between paradox's extremes, for there we confront our helplessness and powerlessness, our woundedness. In seeking to understand our limitations, we seek not only an easing of our pain but an understanding of what it means to hurt and what it means to be healed. Spirituality begins with the acceptance that our fractured being, our imperfection, simply is. There is no one to "blame" for our errors—neither ourselves

nor anyone nor anything else. Spirituality helps us first to see, and then to understand, and eventually to accept the imperfection that lies at the very core of our human be-ing.[12]

The spirituality of imperfection speaks to those who seek meaning in the absurd, peace within the chaos, light within the darkness, joy within the suffering—without denying the reality and even the necessity of absurdity, chaos, darkness, and suffering.[13]

They, too, like C. S. Lewis, describe this human sense of incompleteness and longing...

The core paradox that underlies spirituality is the haunting sense of incompleteness, of being somehow unfinished, that comes from the reality of living on this earth as part and yet also not-part of it. For to be human is to be incomplete, yet yearn for completion; is to be uncertain, yet long for certainty; to be imperfect, yet long for perfection; to be broken, yet crave wholeness. All these yearnings remain necessarily unsatisfied, for perfection, completion, certainty, and wholeness are impossible precisely because we are imperfectly human...[14]

We have forgotten our names. We have forgotten who we really are. And the questions echo in our minds: Who am I? And for what am I longing?

## WHO IS MAN?[15]

Sometimes it is tempting to think that there are few differences between man and beast. One does not have to look far to see humanity's offense against humanity, for history is filled with the records of human tyranny and oppression. There is the evil inflicted by individuals that we see in the despotism of Adolf Hitler, Karl Marx, Pol Pot.[16] Then there is also the horrific conflict of cultures demonstrated in the bloody battles of the Crusades, the World Wars, and our current endless genocides of Africa. And one is not to forget, our own gory Civil War. The blood of "survival of the fittest" still runs deep in man's veins. Even after so many centuries, man is still not so far removed from his cousin the beast.

But history paints another picture of humanity as well. This is an image that shines with the beauty of humanity reaching outside of and beyond oneself. Man and Woman become someone with an identity, a "name" if you will, and a future. He or she strives to be called "Perfection."

Perhaps no other time in history best exemplifies this than the Renaissance. In many ways, it was a time of some of humanity's greatest achievements. Whether in the fields of science, music, art, or philosophy, man's potential flowered into a demonstration of what mankind could become. There developed a newfound recognition of what a person could be and what a person could create. The Renaissance, more than any other period in history, showcased the distinguishing features of man from the beast: reason, abstract thought, and creativity.

However, in this search for perfection was seeded an individualism from which sprouted a self-centered optimism. Concepts of self-fulfillment and empowerment budded forth from this period like an ornate bouquet. And as the potential of man's intellect and creativity blossomed forth, Divine transcendence became an afterthought. Man, himself, became center stage, and the backdrop of spiritual transcendence was ignored and forgotten.

The *Cambridge Dictionary of Philosophy* aptly describes this Renaissance shift in thought. It describes the shift from the medieval trust in Divine authority to the Renaissance confidence in man's potential in this graphic manner:

> Here [Renaissance], one felt no weight of
> the supernatural pressing on the human mind,

demanding homage and allegiance. Humanity—with all its distinct capabilities, talents, worries, problems, possibilities—was the center of interest. It has been said that medieval thinkers philosophized on their knees, but, bolstered by the new studies, they dared to stand up and to rise to full stature.[17]

Humanism prospered. The reality of Divine grace being the source of man's abilities was abandoned; humanism strode forth to stand upon his self-constructed stage. And the Question shouted louder, "Who is Man?"

This question was played out on a larger stage long ago in a garden. A blessing was given. A prohibition was established. A choice was allowed. A decision was made. A consequence was inherited. Then a burden of imperfection and incompleteness was ingrained in the soul of man...to be carried all its days. Now we have inherited a longing for maturity and fulfillment. We long for a reconciliation between that which we are and that which we may become. And the work of man's spiritual endeavors lies in this very paradox. Through the struggle, he becomes aware of this great need for spiritual reconciliation and for spiritual transformation, and he finds that it must be done in the crucible of paradox. Now amidst our earthly toil, we are still called by the Divine One. But how can we ever return to that garden?

Yet for now we must recognize the struggle: the suffering and toil demanded by man's disobedience. For as man chooses to step out on his own, he takes a step farther from the source of his ultimate peace. Still there is a persistent longing calling him back into relationship. And so the pendulum swings. As man and woman, we are called to eternal relationship with the Divine, while still burdened by our human limitations of imperfection. Man's temporal nature inhibits his rise, and yet in some mysterious way, he nonetheless forges his eternal destiny.

## EXISTENTIAL PARADOX

Kurtz and Ketcham put it this way: "[S]pirituality involves first seeing ourselves truly, as the paradoxical and imperfect beings that we are, then discovering that it is only within our very imperfection that we can find the peace and serenity that is available to us."[18]

A Danish philosopher in the early 1800s eloquently spoke to this paradox between what a person is and what that person can become. He even would go so far as to say that the measure of a person's character is how well he or she pursues this struggle. More than any other, Soren Kierkegaard felt that the genuineness of personal meaning is defined by the quality of his or her struggles. Though Kierkegaard's philosophy of man is found throughout his voluminous writings, it is most prominent in his work which he published in 1849, *The Sickness unto Death.*

Kierkegaard proposes that every individual lives within existential paradoxes that consist of "dialectically related tendencies."[19] By this, Kierkegaard posits dialectic or contrasting pairs of encounters between which every person struggles. For Kierkegaard, these primarily consisted of those of "finitude/infinite," "temporal/eternal," and "necessity/possibility."

The dialectic pair of finite/infinite is the most general and predominant in Kierkegaard's thought. In it, the "self" is envisioned as a synthesis of the limited and the unlimited, the bound and the boundless. A person perceives the world as it actually exists but also imagines the world as it could possibly become. To be an authentic person involves living realistically in the factual present yet also living creatively in the infinite possibilities of the imagination.

Similarly, the temporal/eternal pairing contrasts an individual's perspective of time and priorities. Those items most desirable in the temporal realm may not at all be of value in eternal existence. These choices between immediate and delayed gratification, material and spiritual priorities, allocation of time and resources between a fulfilling earthly life and a blessed eternal one, all serve to shape the "self" into an authentic being.

In the instance of the necessity/possibility dialectical, Kierkegaard places this in the striving for a future better than the current one. John Douglas Mullen describes this concept thus:

> To live only in necessity is to live as if I am what I am and can be no different. To live only in possibility is to live as if I can be whatever I imagine. The problem is to hold together a synthesis of the pair.[20]

Perhaps more so than the dialectical pairs themselves, Kierkegaard was concerned with the process within the paradox, the "working out" of the paradox that was so essential to the formation of a truly authentic human being. For him, it is a process both necessary and strenuous—necessary for the growth and development of the individual, and strenuous because of the ever-constant "negotiation" of the will between conflicting dialectical possibilities.

> It is sustained by the constant imposition of the non-natural power of spirit (will). This means that human life involves constant effort, vigilance, and courage to maintain itself as distinctly human, that is, as genuinely or authentically human. The facts that anxiety exists, that human life is not easy, is painful, are not consequences of circumstances but of the very nature of human life itself. To have broken with nature (to be free) involves, as the necessary other side of the coin, tension, anxiety, constant effort.[21]

Furthermore, Kierkegaard believed that in this process toward authenticity, there would be "no permanent solution." That is to say that each decision carries with it a degree of ambiguity resulting in uncertainty and anxiety. There are no clearly defined rules and no definite permanent conclusions. Nonetheless, the struggle is worth the effort toward personal fulfillment and spiritual transformation.

## SPIRITUAL AWARENESS: INTRODUCTION TO THE DEVOTIONAL LIFE

What shall I do with my life? What kind of person can I be?

This meditation is about just this. The ongoing struggle and redefinition of what it is to be truly human, finite yet facing an eternal destiny. The devotional life is a life focused on pursuing the means of clarifying the realities of life and practicing the principles of spiritual experience that allow one to become more truly "human." It is a life based on the sobering understanding of what one is, yet buoyed by the hope of what one can become.

The devotional life is by necessity a strenuous life. It demands a rigorous and truthful examination of one's current attitudes and priorities. It calls for a willingness to change, to let go of idols which hold our attentions, and to trust in things unseen and unknown. It requires one to leave the comfort of concepts and enter the moment-by-moment struggles of practicing what we hold to be genuinely true.

So we have man and woman both faced with an intrinsic longing for something beyond themselves. Yet they find themselves in the midst of a dilemma, a struggle between that which one is, and that which he or she can become. It is a paradox between their physical finite limitations and their spiritual infinite destiny.

We are left with a pivotal question, "How does one begin?"

---

[1] From *The Sacred Romance* by Brent Curtis and John Eldredge, 1. Copyright © 1997 by Brent Curtis and John Eldredge. Used by permission of Thomas Nelson. www.thomasnelson.com.

[2] The writings of Mother Teresa of Calcutta © by the Mother Teresa Center, exclusive licensee throughout the world of the Missionaries of Charity for the works of Mother Teresa. Used with permission.

[3] Excerpt from *The Spirituality of Imperfection* by Ernest Kurtz, 1992 by Ernest Kurtz, Ph.D. And Katherine Ketcham, 23. Used by permission of Bantam Books, an imprint of Random House, a division of Penguin Random House LLC. All rights reserved.

*Spirituality is not religion:* "Those who consider themselves 'spiritual' and those who consider themselves 'religious' seem to agree that there are differences between them, but those differences are only broadly delineated.

Viewing religion, 'the spiritual' see rigidity; viewing spirituality, 'the religious' see sloppiness. Religion connotes boundaries, while spirituality's borders seem haphazard and ill-defined. The vocabulary of religion emphasizes the *solid*; the language of spirituality suggests the *fluid.*"

4. Excerpt from *The Spirituality of Imperfection* by Ernest Kurtz, 1992 by Ernest Kurtz, Ph.D. And Katherine Ketcham, 15. Used by permission of Bantam Books, an imprint of Random House, a division of Penguin Random House LLC. All rights reserved.

"What is spirituality? To have the answer is to have misunderstood the question. Truth, wisdom, goodness, beauty, the fragrance of a rose—all resemble spirituality in that they are intangible, ineffable realities. We may know them, but we can never grasp them with our hands or with our words."

5. *Narrative Poems* by C. S. Lewis, 4. Copyright © C. S. Lewis Pte. Ltd. 1969. Extracts reprinted by permission.
6. *Surprised by Joy* by C. S. Lewis, 17-18. Copyright © C. S. Lewis Pte. Ltd. 1955. Extracts reprinted by permission.
7. *The Pilgrim's Regress* by C. S. Lewis, Preface, 10. Copyright © C. S. Lewis Pte. Ltd. 1933. Extracts reprinted by permission.
8. *Mere Christianity* by C. S. Lewis, 121. Copyright © C. S. Lewis Pte. Ltd. 1942, 1943, 1944, 1952. Extracts reprinted by permission.
9. Taken from *The Sacred Romance* by Brent Curtis and John Eldredge, 19. Copyright © 1997 by Brent Curtis and John Eldredge. Used by permission of Thomas Nelson. www.thomasnelson.com.
10. Ibid., 41.
11. Ibid., 94–95.
12. Excerpt from *The Spirituality of Imperfection* by Ernest Kurtz, 1992 by Ernest Kurtz, Ph.D. And Katherine Ketcham, 2. Used by permission of Bantam Books, an imprint of Random House, a division of Penguin Random House LLC. All rights reserved.
13. Ibid., 2.
14. Ibid., 19.
15. Psalm 8:4: "Who is man that Thou art mindful of him?" (KJV, paraphrased)
16. Pol Pot, the Khmer Rouge rule of Cambodia (1975-1979), was responsible for the deaths of millions.
17. "Humanism," *The Cambridge Dictionary of Philosophy.*
18. Excerpt from *The Spirituality of Imperfection* by Ernest Kurtz, 1992 by Ernest Kurtz, Ph.D. And Katherine Ketcham, 28. Used by permission of Bantam Books, an imprint of Random House, a division of Penguin Random House LLC. All rights reserved.
19. John Douglas Mullen, *Kierkegaard's Philosophy, Self-Deception and Cowardice in the Present Age* (New York, Scarborough, Ontario: Meridian, New American Library, 1981), 46.
20. Ibid., 50.
21. Ibid., 47.

# 2

# *Humility*
# *A Foundational Virtue*

> Are you thinking of raising the great
> fabric of spirituality? Attend first of
> all to the foundation of humility.[1]
> —Augustine

Like the warm, dark loam of a summer's garden, composed of the gentle and gradual broken-ness of the earth and fallen leaves, humility forms the fertile soil of spiritual living from which the beauty and bounty of spiritual awareness can flourish. In a very real way, our limitations and vulnerabilities, our disappointments, our sufferings all merge, like so much compost, to form the deep soil of humility. Gradually, our moments of submission and honest reflection begin to create the nourishment necessary for a "self-forgetfulness" to form, out of which will grow the fruits of an enriched spiritual life.

## HUMILITY AS A FOUNDATIONAL VIRTUE

Even before Plato, the Greek philosophers were espousing concepts that would later be regarded as the four "cardinal virtues." Initially, these were those of prudence, justice, temperance, and courage—often translated as wisdom, fairness, restraint (or moderation), and fortitude. These were the secularly derived virtues that were to be aspired to by every person for the happiness of the individual and the efficient functioning of a just society.

Subsequently, there would be added the "theological virtues," consisting of those of faith, hope, and charity, which were viewed as given to humanity from God.[2]

From these virtues would flow a profusion of various classifications designed to give additional clarity to other attitudes (or sub-virtues) in their relationship to each specific cardinal and theological virtue. Humility's place in this schema was the cause of some disagreement, which centered upon the debate between whether humility was a subset of "temperance" or a virtue in its own right.

One of the first to take a stance for humility being a virtue in its own right was St. Thomas Aquinas, a thirteenth-century theologian, who took an analytical approach to the concept of humility in his work, *Summa Theologica*. Catholic philosophy at that time held that humility was not a true cardinal virtue but was contained within the cardinal virtue of temperance.

Because temperance has to do with restraint of one's appetites, Aquinas has this to say of humility as he proposes it as a true virtue in its own right:

> Wherefore a twofold virtue is necessary with regard to the difficult good: one, to temper and restrain the mind, lest it tend to high things immoderately; and this belongs to the virtue of humility: and another to strengthen the mind against despair, and urge it on to the pursuit of great things according to right reason; and this is magnanimity. Therefore it is evident that humility is a virtue.[3]

Aquinas continues his thoughts on humility:

> It is contrary to humility to aim at greater things through confiding in one's own powers: but to aim at greater things through confidence in God's help, is not contrary to humility; especially since the more one subjects oneself to God, the more is one exalted in God's sight.[4]

## HUMILITY: A FOUNDATIONAL VIRTUE

And from the Gospel of Luke:

> For everyone who exalts himself will be humbled, but he who humbles himself will be exalted. (Luke 18:14 NASB)

Not only can humility be considered a true virtue, but it may very well be considered a foundational virtue, in which other virtues are rooted. Though charity may be regarded as the highest virtue, humility certainly could be regarded as the most basic and foundational one, in which others could be justifiably seen as being grounded.

Long before St. Thomas Aquinas, another Church Father, St. Augustine (436 BC) had written: "Are you thinking of raising the great fabric of spirituality? Attend first of all to the foundation of humility."[5]

One might legitimately ask why St. Augustine would regard humility so highly. What is there about this virtue that would cause him to describe it as a "foundational" virtue? Let us start by first examining what others of faith have written about humility.

- Humility presupposes a condition of imperfection and limitations.

> I knew Jesus, and He was very precious to my soul, but I found something in me that would not keep sweet and patient and kind. I did what I could to keep it down, but it was there. I beseeched Jesus to do something for me, and when I gave Him my will He came to my heart, and took out all that would not be sweet, all that would not be kind, all that would not be patient, and then He shut the door.[6] (George Fox, founder of the Society of Friends, the Quakers)

- Humility presupposes an acknowledgment of submission to a higher authority.

    But humility, considered as a special virtue, regards chiefly the subjection of man to God, for whose sake he humbles himself by subjecting himself to others.[7] (Thomas Aquinas)

- Humility opens the conduit for Divine attendance through spiritual surrender and receptivity.

    I often pray to God that He would keep you in the hollow of His hand. And this He certainly will do if you remember to keep a humble and obedient spirit. Humility is good in every situation, because it produces that teachable spirit which makes everything easy.[8] (Fenelon)

Semantics aside, it is readily apparent that humility is the root of experience from which many other virtues sprout. Therefore, humility should be regarded as indeed a profound and foundational virtue. This is important because many of the topics later to be explored in this work germinate vitally from this grounding within humility's rich soil.

## HUMILITY ALLOWS FOR HONEST SELF-EXAMINATION

Spiritual awareness begins with self-awareness. Humility provides the groundwork for honest self-examination.

   Spirituality involves first seeing ourselves truly, as the paradoxical and imperfect beings that we are, then discovering that it is only within our very imperfection that we can find the peace and serenity that is available to us.[9]

Ingrained with a longing for something more, yet constrained by their limitations and imperfections, man and woman still search for a more genuine existence and a more hopeful future. This struggle is one that demands an honest look at the attitudes and priorities that move one either closer to these ideals or farther away. Though abstract in nature, they have powerful impact in shaping the choices one makes and the person one is to become. As layers of artificial behaviors are peeled away, an awareness of deeper, more intrinsic truths is born. These birth pains are rooted in an understanding of humility.

Honestly examining my life demands looking beyond the delusions and masks that have accumulated over a lifetime. It necessarily involves being confronted by my inadequacies and intentional wrongs. It involves recognizing the self-centered pride that continually calls to be satisfied. Nor are the appetites and desires of the moment exempt from a consideration of the motives behind each choice and each action. This is sobering work, but to quote a familiar phrase of Socrates, "The unexamined life is not worth living."

Yet this process does not have an end in a degrading self-condemnation. Instead, its purpose is to give clarity for how a person can best step from the mire of "self" onto a firmer footing of spiritual engagement with Someone More. This transitioning from honestly acknowledging the delusions of life to aspiring a growth toward "perfection" or spiritual maturity is the work of each moment. It is redemptive work. It is work that can only be realized by the grace of Another. And this is when humility is born from the roots of honest self-examination. The realization and acceptance that there is a greater One that is required for this process to be possible is the mark of true humility. Humanity struggles between the finite and the infinite, between that which one is, and that which one may become, but it is only possible through the presence and benevolence of God. It is in the darkness of life's struggles with loneliness, uncertainty, and fear that one sees the Burning Bush. And as one finds themselves before the great "I AM," one is allowed to see his or her genuine humanness and future destiny with unique spiritual awareness and clarity.

## HUMILITY IS A SELF-FORGETFULNESS

> Humility does not mean thinking less of yourself than of other people, nor does it mean having a low opinion of your own gifts. It means freedom from thinking about yourself at all.
> —William Temple

Qualities of being modest and unassuming stem from an even deeper experience of a life built upon reverence and submission. This reverence is expressed in an appreciation of the beauty and diversity of creation. It values the uniqueness and potential of each person and experiences a genuine desire to reach out benevolently to the needs of others. The attitudes of selflessness blossom to form the fruits of patience, kindness, and compassion.

Another characteristic of humility is the attitude of submission. Submission stems from an acknowledgment that there is a higher authority than oneself. There is a code of conduct that guides our choices for the best. And there is a Divine Law Giver that provides this natural law[10] for humanity out of His personal Love for His creation. Interestingly enough, this moral code of conduct is not meant to enslave, but to allow us to experience a spiritual freedom from the confines of this earthly life.

A snapshot of humility is provided by David Jeremiah, in his little book, *The 12 Ways of Christmas*. He describes humility this way:

> "There are two kinds of people in the world—those who come into the room saying, 'Here I am!' And others who enter a room saying, 'There you are!'"[11]

> "Be completely humble and gentle; be patient, bearing with one another in love." (Ephesians 4:2 NIV)

Another picture of humility can be appreciated in the Amish concepts of *Demut* (humility) and *Gelassenheit* (calmness, composure, placidity). This Anabaptist religious framework, even today, places an emphasis on demonstrating in the conduct of everyday activities the attitudes of submission or "letting be." They discourage self-assertion and promote the needs of the community over those of the individual. They abide in a poised acceptance before God.

Of interest is that the German philosopher, Heidegger, would use this same term, *Gelassenheit*, in the context of his thought to mean serenity, "meditative thinking," or listening to the "truth of being."[12]

This "poised acceptance before God" is a wonderful image of humility for it conveys the concepts of submission and acceptance before God; amplifying by comparison, both the insignificance and also the infinite value of every human being. For it is within this paradox, each person throughout their lives will search to find authenticity and meaning for each day.

## THE DECEIT OF FALSE HUMILITY

Pride never surrenders. We constantly fight this battle with pride even as we strive for some simple measure of humility in our lives. The Gospel of Luke paints this powerful image of false humility.

Prayers of the Pharisee and the publican: Luke 18:9–14 (NIV).

> To some who were confident of their own righteousness and looked down on everyone else, Jesus told this parable: "Two men went up to the temple to pray, one a Pharisee and the other a tax collector. The Pharisee stood by himself and prayed: 'God, I thank you that I am not like other people—robbers, evildoers, adulterers—or even like this tax collector. I fast twice a week and give a tenth of all I get.' But the tax collector stood at a distance. He would not even look up to heaven, but beat his breast and said, 'God,

have mercy on me, a sinner.' I tell you that this man, rather than the other, went home justified before God. For all those who exalt themselves will be humbled, and those who humble themselves will be exalted."

Thomas Aquinas has this to say on the idea of false humility:

As stated (ad 1), humility, in so far as it is a virtue, conveys the notion of a praiseworthy self-abasement to the lowest place. Now this is sometimes done merely as to outward signs and pretense: wherefore this is "false humility," of which Augustine says in a letter (Ep. cxlix) that it is "grievous pride," since to wit, it would seem to aim at excellence of glory.[13]

Once a person feels he or she has obtained humility, it is gone. False humility eases into one's life stealthily to satisfy rather than to submit. False humility is not a true "self-forgetfulness." Instead it concentrates upon how one can appear as spiritual without the sacrifice. It does not truly accept God's authority over oneself, nor others' needs over those of one's self. Actions flow from a desire for acknowledgment, rather than from a genuine concern for others.

## HUMILITY AND SUBJECTION IN CONDITIONS OF OPPRESSION

One cannot discuss the virtue of humility without the troubling questions confronting us, "How does humility respond to the conditions of radical injustice and oppression?" "Just what does humility look like when a person or community is persecuted?" "How does one preserve the spirit of humility when coercion reigns and hope fades?"

Every day we see examples of this in our world. Whole cultures are subjected to the genocide of African warlords. Governments grow in wealth and power upon the shoulders and sufferings of the hungry and poor. Economies thrive in the same cities where there are many underserved and undervalued. Communities struggle daily with the violence upon the innocent by gangs and drug cartels. When does one fight back against the oppression and injustice? Or perhaps, more importantly *how* does one respond to such misery?

*Responding Individually: Job*

As an individual unjustly treated or persecuted, humility reminds us that any wrong done to us is a wrong against God's moral code. That is not to excuse the perpetrators' evil nor regard a person's pain and suffering lightly. But the reality is that all injustice stands as evil before the moral code of a benevolent, but just and omnipotent God. And this same righteous God will demand a penalty for that sin in His due time. It may not be a time of our choosing or even in our life on this earth, but God's righteous justice will prevail for all eternity. My suffering is not lessened by this understanding, but perhaps it is consecrated through my personal choice to remain true to my Lord and personal Savior in moments of extreme pain and misery… when I, like Job can only cry out, "Naked I came from my mother's womb, And naked I shall return there. The Lord gave and the Lord has taken away, Blessed be the name of the Lord. Through all this, Job did not sin nor did he blame God" (Job 1:21–22, NASB).

*Responding as a Faith Community*

As a faith community, humility compels us to respond with acts of benevolence, but not violence. A familiar passage of Scripture reminds us with these difficult words:

> Love must be sincere. Hate what is evil; cling to what is good. Be devoted to one another in love. Honor one another above yourselves. Never be lacking in zeal, but keep your spiritual fervor, serving the Lord. Be joyful in hope, patient in

affliction, faithful in prayer. Share with the Lord's people who are in need. Practice hospitality. Bless those who persecute you; bless and do not curse. Rejoice with those who rejoice; mourn with those who mourn. Live in harmony with one another. Do not be proud, but be willing to associate with people of low position. Do not be conceited. Do not repay anyone evil for evil. Be careful to do what is right in the eyes of everyone. If it is possible, as far as it depends on you, live at peace with everyone. Do not take revenge, my dear friends, but leave room for God's wrath, for it is written: "It is mine to avenge; I will repay," says the Lord. On the contrary: "If your enemy is hungry, feed him; if he is thirsty, give him something to drink. In doing this, you will heap burning coals on his head." Do not be overcome by evil, but overcome evil with good. (Romans 12:9–21 NIV)

There is a time and place in our hearts in which we as individuals, and as a faith community must relinquish the desire for retribution. We must abandon our desire for vengeance and place that decision in God's hands.

## HUMILITY AND LEADERSHIP OF RESOLVE: NONVIOLENT CIVIL RESISTANCE

Perhaps two of the most significant leaders of our time who exemplified humility and nonviolence in the midst of great resolve were Gandhi and Martin Luther King Jr. Ironically, both died from assassination, yet the fruit of both leaders' commitment to nonviolent resistance remains today. Though thousands of miles apart, their thought and ethical positions would be found to be deeply inter-woven. Both were deeply influenced by their respective religious beliefs, as well as the writings of Henry David Thoreau and Leo Tolstoy. Both Gandhi and King would propose and personally exemplify the thoughts and beliefs to bring hope and liberation to the masses of underserved and oppressed.

*Mahatma Gandhi (1869–1948)*[14]*: Humility in the face of cultural and political oppression*

Perhaps no one is more associated globally with the notion of humility and passive resistance to oppression than Mahatma Gandhi. At the time of his birth in 1869, India was a colony of the British Empire and very heavily under its autocratic rule. His mother, Putlibai, was deeply religious, worshipping the Hindu god, Vishnu. Her influence can be seen prominently as Gandhi was likewise raised as a Hindu with a Jainism lifestyle. The Jainism religion, believing that everything in the universe was eternal, promoted "ashima"[15] or the nonviolence to all living things. This upbringing emphasized the disciplines of nonviolence, fasting for purification, vegetarianism, tolerance, and meditation, which would so prominently influence Gandhi in later life.

His father was a government administrator and was instrumental in altering Gandhi's original desire to pursue a career in medicine, to that of a career in law instead. Therefore, in 1888, at the age of eighteen, Gandhi traveled to London, England, to enter law school. After graduating with his law degree, he returned to India in 1891, but because of difficulties finding work, in April 1893, he accepted a contract to provide legal services in Natal, South Africa, which was also at that time still a part of the colonial British Empire.

Upon his arrival in South Africa, Gandhi was soon met with discrimination from British authorities. It was this crucible of discrimination that would be instrumental in developing his views of nonviolent resistance within a culture of racial prejudice and oppression. During the more than twenty years spent in South Africa, he worked with several organizations to confront and reject the unfair and oppressive laws, which restricted the rights of racial and cultural minorities, especially those of the Hindu faith. While there Gandhi organized his first nonviolent protests, which he called "satyagraha," meaning "holding onto truth" or "truth force." Moreover, he edited his own newspaper, *The Indian Opinion*, which promoted his political and social convictions, running contrary to the ruling British authorities time and again. He would be imprisoned for the first time for his noncompliance to the taxation and restrictions of the British ruling class, but during his lifetime, Gandhi would be imprisoned at least six times for his acts of noncompliance with authorities.

Gandhi returned to India in 1915 to find the British colonial rule still oppressing the rights of the poor and impoverished masses there. Because of his experiences with rejecting the unjustly ruling elite while in South Africa, he soon rose to be recognized as a leading figure in the movement for India's self-rule.

During this time, he would deepen a Jainist lifestyle of simplicity, which centered upon prayer, fasting, and meditation, becoming known as "Mahatma," which means "great soul."[16] He would further advocate this nonviolent movement for change through encouraging mass boycotts from British products and taxes, nonparticipation in British educational and governmental institutions, and even withdrawal from the military. His most famous actions were his peace walks, or "satyagraha," whose three principles affirmed truth, refusal to do harm to others, and self-sacrifice for a cause or ideal. He would organize these marches to oppose the injustices of those in power. Perhaps the most famous walk of civil disobedience was the "Salt March" of 1930, which he organized as a 240-mile march to the Arabian Sea to oppose the imposition of additional restrictions upon Indians for the collection and purchase of salt. Overall, approximately sixty thousand Indians, including Gandhi, were jailed in their opposition to the Salt Acts. Still, it symbolized the influence of civil disobedience in opposition to an oppressive regime, which was the most remarkable result of Gandhi's personality and leadership. That same year (1930) *Time Magazine* would name him "Man of the Year." Over his lifetime, Gandhi was nominated for the Nobel Peace prize five times but was never awarded that honor.

Gandhi's religious and philosophical principles were heavily influenced by his Hindu and Jainism beliefs, which emphasized the importance of nonviolence, fasting, simplicity, and meditation. Shrimad Rajchandra, known as a Hindu intellectual, became Gandhi's spiritual mentor. His ethical thinking was also influenced by his familiarity with the writings of Plato *(Apology)*, Mohammed, Bhagavad Gita, and the New Testament narratives, especially the Sermon on the Mount. In a more contemporary mode, he greatly valued the writings of John Ruskin (*Unto this Last*), William Salter (*Ethical Religion*), Henry David Thoreau (*On the Duty of Civil Disobedience*), and Leo Tolstoy (*The Kingdom of God Is Within You*).

Gandhi would go on to develop a friendship with Leo Tolstoy and wrote to Tolstoy requesting his advice regarding nonviolent resistance. He was also influenced by Tolstoy's book, *A Letter to a Hindu*. While both agreed regarding opposing oppressive political structures with civil disobedience and nonviolent confrontation, Gandhi was much more inclined to become politically involved than Tolstoy.

In 1945, negotiations began between India and Great Britain for India's independence. Gandhi pleaded for a unified India, but instead the subcontinent was divided along religious lines—India predominantly Hindu, and Pakistan predominantly Muslim. This would lead to a violent conflict between Hindus and Muslims, and an increasing frequency of rioting and bloodshed. Gandhi would attempt to calm this antagonism but was increasingly identified as a traitor, too often expressing sympathy toward Muslims. On January 30, 1948, a Hindu extreme nationalist knelt before Gandhi then shot him three times at point-blank range, killing the one whose life had been so committed to nonviolence and who had done so much for his people.

Though his life resulted in a legacy in and of its own right, his influence would go on to inspire the ethical and philosophical beliefs of both Martin Luther King Jr. in the United States and Nelson Mandela of South Africa.

# SPIRITUAL AWARENESS

*Dr. Martin Luther King Jr. (1929–1968): Humility in the face of racial oppression*

Dr. Martin Luther King Jr. is without doubt the champion of racial equality most recognized and admired in the United States. Through his powerful personality and eloquent speech, he was able to change the political structure of a stubborn and biased nation. And he did so with a personal magnanimity and compassion that would add a sense of truth and genuineness to his insightful words.

It should be no surprise that Dr. King's personal ethical and philosophical perspectives stemmed from his strong family and religious upbringing. As an American Baptist minister, his Christian beliefs demanded a charitable yet firm response to the degradation and inequality of his African American people. He would be the one to stand strongly upon his Christian principles to demand they be recognized and respected by the oppressive culture in which he lived.

His belief in nonviolent means in which to effect positive change not only stemmed from his religious convictions, but from some of his closest advisors and acquaintances. African American civil rights activist Bayard Ruskin was one of Dr. King's earliest advisors to introduce him to a nonviolent process toward social and political change. Two white activists, Harris Wofford and Glenn Smiley, were also influential in his thinking. Both Ruskin and Wofford were of the Christian pacifist tradition and Wofford and Ruskin had both studied the teaching of Gandhi and shared those principles with King. Mahatma Gandhi's success in India with the use of peaceful civil disobedience against the British authorities' oppression was of particular interest to Dr. King, and he was exposed to some of Leo Tolstoy's thinking directly through the influence of Gandhi. It is said that all three, Gandhi, King, and Tolstoy were greatly affected by Jesus's Sermon on the Mount. As a student, he read Henry David Thoreau's *On Civil Disobedience* and later was influenced greatly by the writings of Reinhold Niebuhr, Paul Tillich, and Walter Rauschenbusch's *Christianity and the Social Crisis*.

In April of 1959, with financial assistance of his friends and supporters, Martin Luther King Jr. was able to travel to India to visit

## HUMILITY: A FOUNDATIONAL VIRTUE

Mahatma Gandhi's birthplace in India to deepen his understanding of using nonviolent means to effect social and political change. Dr. King, on his final night in India, during a radio address stated, "Since being in India, I am more convinced than ever before that the method of non-violent resistance is the most potent weapon available to oppressed people in their struggle for justice and human dignity."

In 1955, Martin Luther King Jr.'s involvement in the civil rights movement catapulted upon the events of Rosa Parks's incident of Montgomery, Alabama. Upon boarding a city bus, Rosa Parks, a forty-two-year-old worker, sat down in the "colored" section of the bus. When the bus driver saw that several white men were standing because of a lack of seats, he asked Ms. Parks to get up and give one of the white men her seat. She refused. Because of this action, she was arrested and fined for violating the Montgomery City Code. The response of the local NAACP and other local civil rights activists resulted in a 382-day bus boycott, which ultimately resulted in the city of Montgomery rescinding the law of mandated segregated public transportation.

This soon led, in 1957, to the formation of the Southern Christian Leadership Conference, which was composed of Dr. King, Ralph Abernathy, and sixty other ministers and civil rights activists.[17] This organization served as a focus and resource to provide nonviolent resistance and protests to further the civil rights movement. Furthermore, it also was instrumental in encouraging the African American community to become actively involved in the political and voting process.

Years later after being jailed following a demonstration in Birmingham, Alabama in 1963, King would declare his theory of nonviolence: "Nonviolent direct action seeks to create such a crisis and foster such a tension that a community, which has constantly refused to negotiate, is forced to confront the issue."

On August 28, 1963, the historic March on Washington drew more than two hundred thousand people in the shadow of the Lincoln Memorial. It was here that King made his famous "I Have a Dream" speech, emphasizing his belief that someday all men could be brothers. "I have a dream that my four children will one day live in a nation where they will not be judged by the color of their skin but by the content of their character" (Martin Luther King Jr., "I Have A Dream," August 28, 1963).

In 1964, a growing public sentiment supporting the civil rights movement culminated in passage of the Civil Rights Act of 1964, which authorized the federal government to enforce desegregation of public facilities. This was also the year in which Martin Luther King Jr. received the Nobel Peace Prize for his leadership of nonviolent protest in opposition to the racial injustices of the time.

Another march, which occurred in March of 1965, proved to have pivotal consequences. A civil rights march from Selma to Montgomery initially encountered a violent outbreak with authorities while attempting to cross the Edmond Pettus Bridge. Though Martin Luther King Jr. was not at the initial conflict, he would return two days later with a group of 2,500 black and white protestors. Upon again encountering barricades, Dr. King asked his marchers to kneel in prayer, and then they turned back. It is said that this show of nonviolent, but persistent resistance to oppression was instrumental in the support and eventual passage of the Voting Rights Act of 1965.

By 1965, not all in the civil rights movement were in step with Martin Luther King Jr.'s nonviolent resistance. Among the young black activists developed a complaint that Dr. King's approach to social change was too passive, and change was occurring too slowly. A more militant and strident movement began to develop to challenge Dr. King's leadership. In addition, as the civil rights movement gathered momentum, a greater hatred and violent reaction amongst whites developed to suppress the rights of the black community.

In the spring of 1968, a labor strike brought Martin Luther King Jr. to Memphis, Tennessee. On April 3, he would declare, "I've seen the promised land. I may not get there with you. But I want you to know tonight that we, as a people, will get to the promised land." The next day, while standing on a balcony outside his room at the Lorraine Motel, Martin Luther King Jr. was struck by a sniper's bullet at the hands of a malcontent drifter and former convict named James Earl Ray.

## HUMILITY: A FOUNDATIONAL VIRTUE

There is an evil perhaps even more heinous than those of racial and cultural oppression...that of systematic genocide. It begs the question of what threshold, if any, does one actively and purposefully respond in a violent manner to such a great evil. As the Jewish persecution grew under the regime of Adolf Hitler, it was a question that Dietrich Bonhoeffer wrestled with his entire adult life, until Hitler ordered his death by hanging just before the end of WWII.

*Dietrich Bonhoeffer (1906–1945): Humility and Response to Evil/ Genocide*

A lesser-known individual of passivist character who faced the forces of terror and evil was Dietrich Bonhoeffer.[18] He was born as a twin to sister Sabine in Breslau, Germany on February 4, 1906 of an aristocratic family with a strong German heritage. His father, Karl Bonhoeffer, was a professor of psychiatry and neurology, who would later assume a leadership position within the Department of Neurology in Berlin. His mother, Paula was of the von Hase family and is described as a "stimulating and indefatigable mother" who provided much of the children's education within their home. Born into a large family that would consist of eight children, Dietrich was quick to express his keen intellect in his love for chess, music, and puzzle games. Yet he was known for his warm and friendly personality who listened intently to the thoughts and ideas of others. Tall and blond, Dietrich was also energetic and athletic, and is described as intense and competitive in anything in which he was involved.

As a child Dietrich was precocious in his studies and was especially accomplished in music, causing his family to encourage him to pursue study to become a concert pianist. But Dietrich longed for more and chose to enter his father's *alma mater* at the University of Tubingen to study theology. Later he would transfer to Berlin University. There, in 1927, he would complete his dissertation, *Sanctorum Communio,* which presented the concept of "Christ existing as church-community"[19] and graduate summa cum laude.

Bonhoeffer would soon go on to become a prominent leader amongst the evangelical state Church of Germany. However, in

1933, Hitler took over the leadership of the German government, and subsequently continued to promote his National Socialist political agenda into all aspects of German society. It was a time of political turmoil, and after the Reichstag was burned to the ground, Hitler issued his famous decree which abolished nearly all personal rights:

> Therefore restriction of personal freedom, of the right of free speech, including the freedom of the press, of the right of association and of public assembly, intervention in the privacy of post, telegraph and telephone, authorization of house searches and of the confiscation and restriction of property, beyond the hitherto legal limits, will henceforward be admissible.[20]

The Church of Germany was not spared. It, also, came increasingly under the pressure of the National Socialists to accept the doctrines of Aryan superiority and Jewish persecution. Through church elections, Hitler gradually placed his candidates in positions of authority…later followed dismissals of established church leaders, censorship of opposition church leaders, oppression of the Jews, intimidation by the Gestapo, and marginalization of the Evangelical church by the State Church of Germany. In May of 1934, in Barmen, Germany, Dietrich Bonhoeffer, and others broke from the Church of Germany to form the Confessing Church. They posited the Barmen Declaration which expressed their opposition to the principles imposed by Hitler's German Christian faction and its desire to form an overarching "Reich Church" supportive of National Socialist doctrine.

Having many associates and several family members who were Jewish, Bonhoeffer was always sensitive to the plight of the Jews, and actively worked to protect their rights individually and within the church. His efforts placed him in a unique and dangerous position. As he traveled outside of Germany to promote ecumenical cooperation between church leaders of other countries and the Confessing

## HUMILITY: A FOUNDATIONAL VIRTUE

Church, he also attempted to convey to them the growing aggression and oppression within Nazi Germany.

Though of passivist temperament, Dietrich Bonhoeffer found himself gradually drawn into the German resistance movement, and ultimately into the very plot to assassinate Hitler at the Zeughaus in Berlin. Eric Metaxas furnishes this quote of Eberhard Bethge that describes Bonhoeffer's struggle with Christian principles in the circumstances of great evil.

> Bonhoeffer introduced us in 1935 to the problem of what we today call political resistance…The escalating persecution of the Jews generated an increasingly hostile situation, especially for Bonhoeffer himself. We now realize that mere confession, no matter how courageous, inescapably meant complicity with the murders.[21] (Eberhard Bethge)

After the failed assassination attempt on Hitler's life, the Gestapo quickly closed in on Bonhoeffer and his co-conspirators. Initially imprisoned in Tegel Prison in Berlin, Bonhoeffer was later transferred to Buchenwald concentration camp. On April 5, 1945, Hitler ordered the execution of Dietrich Bonhoeffer, and on April 9, Dietrich Bonhoeffer was executed by hanging in Flossenburg, less than one month before the end of World War II.

Metaxas summarizes Bonhoeffer's legacy upon his book's[22] inside cover:

> Bonhoeffer gives witness to one man's extraordinary faith and to the tortured fate of the nation he sought to deliver from the curse of Nazism…a man determined to do the will of God radically, courageously, and joyfully—even to the point of death…a life framed by a passion for truth and a commitment to justice on behalf of those who face implacable evil.

"Silence in the face of evil is itself evil. God will not hold us guiltless. Not to speak, not to act is to act." (Dietrich Bonhoeffer)

It is estimated that during the Holocaust nearly 6 million Jews were systematically murdered at the hands of Hitler during World War II.

## HUMILITY IN DAILY LIVING

"Humility is the bloom and beauty of holiness."[23]

"Learn from me, for I am gentle
and humble in heart…"
—Matthew 11:29 (NIV)

We are all too familiar with this fellow called Pride. He is our constant companion along life's way, and he is all too eager to direct our steps. Sometimes his voice shouts to us; at other times, his nudging comes as a subtle whisper. But he is always there. And in many ways he has different voices. In circumstances of pain and suffering, he calls us to focus on our need above the needs of others. At times of indecisiveness, he tells us to rely on our own strength and ingenuity. In our moments of confidence, he teaches us the mantra, "Because I can, I will!"

Pride is a strong adversary, made stronger each day by our reliance on our own perspectives and strength of will. Furthermore, Pride has many cousins, all sired by self-absorption. Impatience states, "My time is more important than yours." Discourtesy demands, "My desires are more important than yours." Egotism proclaims, "My importance is greater than yours." "I'm worth it."

Surrounded by a world that values the powerful and self-sufficient, humility is hard pressed to have a voice. Humility is often drowned out by the clamor for possession, personal desire, and influence. One is confronted with the question, "How can one escape these influences to find humility in living out the events of each day?"

## HUMILITY: A FOUNDATIONAL VIRTUE

*Humility is not something to be contrived or constructed…but to be found in a spirit of receptivity and surrender.*

Humility is not an attribute that can be created or manufactured. It is more likely to be found in an awareness of the spiritual dimensions of humanity's struggles. As a person experiences the conflicts of living this life of imperfection, he or she is faced with the decision to casually ignore and walk away, or humbly acknowledge and respond to the reality of spiritual living. Spiritual living requires an awareness of the unseen and under-appreciated dimensions of life. It is in these venues one finds genuine humility amidst the clamor of culture.

*We find humility in recognizing the fragility and brevity of life.*

Humility starts when we remember that the day is not ours. It is a moment of time given to us to honor our Lord. One does not need to consider very long to see around us the lives of young children and adults maimed or taken "long before their time." In an instant, one's future can change from promise to tragedy. It is in this recognition of life's fragility and brevity that one is reminded that our earthly lives are but only a speck of eternity.

*We find humility in our moments of brokenness and vulnerability.*

There are those circumstances in life from which we can find no escape. Each person's life carries the scars of the unwanted experiences of failed expectations, broken relationships, and shattered dreams. Within these chapters of life, in the pain and disappointment of attitudes and actions, one is confronted with his or her profound insignificance and impotence. From the trauma of our suffering, humility begins to seep from the fractured vessels of our brokenness. "To believe in suffering is pride: but to suffer, believing in God, is humility"[24] (Thomas Merton).

## SPIRITUAL AWARENESS

*We find humility in the suffering of others.*

Humility can grow out of an experience of serious injury or illness of a loved one. Humility is the soil from which tenderness and sensitivity grow and produces the fruits of nourishment and genuine healing... True humility bears the fruits of loving others in an empathetic and compassionate way.

*We find humility in our search for hope and purpose.*

True humility creates an attitude of openness and surrender to the desires of God (that "poised acceptance before God"). Humility is the understanding that one's time and opportunities of the moment are not one's own, but are given by Another. Our moments of time are to be held in reverence and experienced with gratitude, as Divinely offered gifts, to be used and enjoyed within God's will and purpose...for it is in this attitude that one finds true hope and confidence. In humility one finds not only a selflessness, but a surrender to a higher ethical principle or authority. Humility also creates a receptivity and response to that higher authority with acts of lovingkindness toward others.

*Humility demands daily decision...*

On the back side of humility are the contrary forces that drive one into oneself ...the pace of life demands one's moment-by-moment attentions, the harshness and disappointments cause one pain and suffering, the uncertainties of the future call one to feelings of anxiety and restlessness...one desires more, searches for satisfaction, strives for peace. Ambition rules. Life becomes self-absorbed and humility becomes a dwindling dimension of one's soul.

> For by the grace given me I say to every one of you: Do not think of yourself more highly than you ought, but rather think of yourself with sober judgment, in accordance with the faith God has distributed to each of you. (Romans 12:3 NIV)

> This lesson is one of deep significance. The only humility that is really ours is not that which we try to show before God in prayer, but that which we carry with us, and carry out, in our ordinary conduct.[25] (Andrew Murray)

The daily decision that humility gently forces upon us is how we will choose to view the events of each moment. That, in some way, is the focus of this whole enterprise, that of *spiritual awareness within the present moment of our encounter with the world as we live out a spiritual destiny.* It is learning to "hold every thought captive" to the insights of spiritual truths. That means every thought and action is to be taken as though "poised in acceptance before God." It means learning to deal with distractions and desires, and learning to see into the beauty of spiritual encounter, even in the daily clamor of culture. It desires a willingness to risk an openness and a surrender unto a benevolent God, and to cultivate a spiritual perception which leads to true spiritual awareness. Instead of ruled by daily ambition, humility asks me to see the needs of those around me. It is a truism that genuine, compassionate living always germinates from humility's deep fertile soil.

Thomas A'Kempis writes in his famous work, *The Imitation of Christ*:

> A true understanding and humble estimate of oneself is the highest and most valuable of all lessons. To take no account of oneself, but always to think well and highly of others is the highest wisdom and perfection.[26]

Regina Brett in her book, *God Never Blinks,* shares this anonymous quote on humility that she noticed on the desk of an Alcoholic Anonymous counselor, whom she refers to as "Capt. Bob":

> Humility is perpetual quietness of heart.
> It is to have no trouble.

> It is never to be fretted or vexed, irritable or sore; to wonder at nothing that is done to me, to feel nothing done against me.
>
> It is to be at rest when nobody praises me, and when I am blamed or despised, it is to have a blessed home in myself where I can go in and shut the door and kneel to my Father in secret and be at peace, as in a deep sea of calmness, when all around and about is seeming trouble.[27]

There is a gentleness about this thing we call humility. It is formed by an unassuming attitude of acceptance and appreciation, and an acknowledgment of the brevity of life and the value of others. Reverence attends here too, reminding us of both our insignificance, but also our infinite value in the sight of our Creator.

## HUMILITY REVEALED AND MODELED IN THE INCARNATION AND LIFE OF CHRIST

> [T]he grace for humility is also greater and nearer than we think. The humility of Jesus is our salvation, and Christ Jesus Himself is our humility. Our humility is His care and His work. His grace is also sufficient for us to meet the temptation of pride. His strength will be perfected in our weakness.[28]
> —Andrew Murray

> Do nothing out of selfish ambition or vain conceit. Rather, in humility value others above yourselves, not looking to your own interests but each of you to the interests of the others. In your relationships with one another, have the same mindset as Christ Jesus: Who, being in very nature God, did not consider equality with God something to be used to His own advantage; rather, He made himself nothing by taking the

> very nature of a servant, being made in human likeness. And being found in appearance as a man, He humbled himself by becoming obedient to death—even death on a cross!
> —Philippians 2:3–8 (NIV)

A person's humility lies in the example and work of Jesus Christ. Perhaps no greater example of Jesus's humility before His crucifixion can be found, than that demonstrated as He washed the disciples' feet before the Last Supper in anticipation of His persecution and death upon a Roman cross.

> Jesus knew that the Father had put all things under His power, and that He had come from God and was returning to God; so He got up from the meal, took off His outer clothing, and wrapped a towel around His waist. After that, He poured water into a basin and began to wash His disciples' feet, drying them with the towel that was wrapped around Him.
> When He had finished washing their feet, He put on His clothes and returned to His place. "Do you understand what I have done for you?" He asked them. "You call me 'Teacher' and 'Lord,' and rightly so, for that is what I am. Now that I, your Lord and Teacher, have washed your feet, you also should wash one another's feet. I have set you an example that you should do as I have done for you. Very truly I tell you, no servant is greater than his master, nor is a messenger greater than the one who sent him. Now that you know these things, you will be blessed if you do them."
> (John 13:3–5, 12–17 NIV)

In Jesus's washing of the disciples' feet, we see His never-ending lovingkindness demonstrated in the simplest of everyday tasks.

## SPIRITUAL AWARENESS

As Christ kneels before the feet of His disciples, He demonstrates a humility and brokenness, which foreshadows the reality of His broken body upon the Cross. As the Living Water washes the filth and dirt from the human condition, He introduces the New Covenant that will be ushered in soon by the spilling of His precious blood. Do we fully realize what it means to give one's life for another? Can we ask ourselves when we last gently served others on bended knee?

## A PRAYER FOR HUMILITY

Lord, help me understand this thing called Humility…not that I may create it or try to mimic it…but that I may walk within its presence and graces…may its virtue touch my soul in a way that changes me a bit…in a way that opens my life's experiences to spiritual realities beyond myself…may I be melded into Your Presence as humility teaches me of selflessness and surrender…may patience and gentleness be my guides and may compassion be my staff…Shield me from the subtle seduction of Pride so that my path might be sincere and obedient to Thy will and fruitful in Thy work.

---

[1] Augustine (De Verb. Dom., Serm. [*S. 10, C[1]]): Quoted in *Summa Theologica*. "Of Humility," Article 5, Obj 2, by Thomas Aquinas.

[2] The cardinal virtues are the four primary moral virtues. The English word cardinal comes from the Latin word *cardo*, which means "hinge." All other virtues hinge upon these four virtues. Unlike the theological virtues, which are gifts of God through grace, the cardinal virtues can be practiced by anyone…

The four cardinal virtues are prudence, justice, fortitude (or courage), and temperance (or moderation).

Unlike the cardinal virtues, which can be practiced by anyone, the theological virtues are gifts of grace from God, and the object of the virtues—what the practice of the virtue aims at—is God Himself.

The three theological virtues are faith, hope, and charity.
(http://catholicism.about.com/od/beliefsteachings/tp/Cardinal_Virtues.htm)

3. Thomas Aquinas, *Summa Theologica*, "Of Humility," Article 1, "I answer that."
4. Thomas Aquinas, *Summa Theologica*, "Of Humility," Article 2, "Reply to Objection 2."
5. Augustine, (De Verb. Dom., Serm. [*S. 10, C[1]]): Quoted in Summa Theologica. "Of Humility," Article 5, Obj 2, by Thomas Aquinas.
6. George Fox, quoted in *Humility* by Andrew Murray, 49. Permission granted from Bridge Logos, Inc. Newberry, Florida for quotes used from *Humility* by Andrew Murray and revised by Harold J. Chadwick. ISBN: 9780882708546, www.bridgelogoscom.
7. Thomas Aquinas, *Summa Theologica*, "Of Humility," Article 1, "Reply to Objection 5."
8. Francois Fenelon, *Let Go* (New Kensington, PA: Whitaker House, 1973), 1. "The Advantages of Humility," paraphrased version of "Spiritual Letters."
9. Excerpt from *The Spirituality of Imperfection* by Ernest Kurtz, 1992 by Ernest Kurtz, Ph.D. And Katherine Ketcham, 28. Used by permission of Bantam Books, an imprint of Random House, a division of Penguin Random House LLC. All rights reserved.
10. C. S. Lewis calls this "natural moral law."
11. David Jeremiah, *The 12 Ways of Christmas* (Nashville: Thomas Nelson, 2008), 34.
12. Barbara Dalle Pezze, Heidegger of Gelassenheit, *An Internet Journal of Philosophy* 10 (2006).
13. Thomas Aquinas, *Summa Theologica*, "Of Humility," Article 1, "Reply to Objection 2."
14. www.britannica.com article written by B. R. Nanda, author of *Mahatma Gandhi: A Biography.*
15. Louis Fischer, *Gandhi: His Life and Message for the World* (New York: New American Library Classics: A Signet book, 2010).
16. Ronald Stuart McGregor, *The Oxford Hindi-English Dictionary* (Oxford University Press, 1993), 799. ISBN 978-0-19-864339-5. Retrieved 31 August 2013. Quote: (mahā—(S. "great, mighty, large, …, eminent") + ātmā (S. "1. soul, spirit; the self, the individual; the mind, the heart; 2. the ultimate being."): "high-souled, of noble nature; a noble or venerable man."
17. www.biography/people/martin-luther-king-jr.
18. Eberhard Bethge, *Dietrich Bonhoeffer: A Biography* (Minneapolis: Fortress Press, revised edition, 2000).
19. Ibid., 81ff.
20. Werner Hofer, *Der Nationalsozialismus: Dokumente 1933–1945* (1957), 53. Quoted in Bethge, Eberhard, *Dietrich Bonhoeffer: A Biography* (Minneapolis: Fortress Press, revised edition, 2000). p. 263.
21. Taken from *Bonhoeffer—Pastor, Martyr, Prophet, Spy* by Eric Metaxas, 358. Copyright © 2010 by Eric Metaxas. Used by permission of Thomas Nelson www.thomasnelson.com.

## SPIRITUAL AWARENESS

[22] Taken from *Bonhoeffer—Pastor, Martyr, Prophet, Spy* by Eric Metaxas, inside cover. Copyright © 2010 by Eric Metaxas. Used by permission of Thomas Nelson www.thomasnelson.com.

[23] Permission granted from Bridge Logos, Inc. Newberry, Florida for quotes used from *Humility* by Andrew Murray and revised by Harold J. Chadwick, 52. ISBN: 9780882708546, www.bridgelogoscom.

[24] Excerpts from *No Man Is an Island* by Thomas Merton, 78. Copyright © 1955 by The Abbey of Our Lady of Gethsemani and renewed 1983 by the Trustees of the Merton Legacy Trust. Reprinted by permission of Houghton Mifflin Harcourt Publishing Company. All rights reserved.

[25] Permission granted from Bridge Logos, Inc. Newberry, Florida for quotes used from *Humility* by Andrew Murray and revised by Harold J. Chadwick, 42. ISBN: 9780882708546, www.bridgelogoscom.

[26] Thomas a'Kempis, *The Imitation of Christ* (London: Penguin Books, 1952), 29.

[27] Regina Brett, *God Never Blinks* (New York: Grand Central Publishing, 2010), 135–136.

[28] Permission granted from Bridge Logos, Inc. Newberry, Florida for quotes used from *Humility* by Andrew Murray and revised by Harold J. Chadwick, 90. ISBN: 9780882708546, www.bridgelogoscom.

# 3

## *Openness and Surrender*
## *Doorway to Spirituality*

> Generally speaking, we are more firmly
> convinced by reasons that we have
> discovered for ourselves, than by those
> which are given to us by others.
> —Blaise Pascal

### OPENNESS

Humility prepares the heart by means of a greater capacity for openness and receptivity to "Divine breathings." It is in humility that one takes a first step away from personal desires and preoccupations. Individual opinions and strongly held attitudes are now subjected to the insights of Divine revelation and relationship. What were once held as nonnegotiable may now be surrendered in the light of a greater Authority.

This willingness to allow the Holy Spirit to enter and guide one's soul is essential in moving toward that sense of spiritual awareness we desire. It entails relinquishing personally chosen structures of security and gratification. It also demands a frank and honest look at the areas of sin in our lives that still reside within us, those areas of sin we have been unwilling to address and abandon.

Therefore, a spirit of openness is not only an attitude of receptivity, but it includes an openness to examine the aspects of one's life still abiding in sin, and to honestly deal with that sin. That is to say that openness should not be considered an entirely passive and thoughtless experience. Rather, it requires an initial attentiveness and discernment before insight can occur. As such, this attitude of awareness allows for both more sound perception and evaluation.

It should be made perfectly clear here, that what we speak of as spiritual "openness," is *not* the open-mindedness to anything and everything characterized by the mystical religions of the East. It is *not* a mindless emptying to any thought or emotion to which I am exposed, or to that which I desire. On the contrary, Scripture encourages us to "take every thought captive to the obedience of Christ."[1]

Furthermore, it must *not* be an endeavor without Christian spiritual grounding and discernment. For to be "open" in prayer can be a time of great vulnerability if pursued in a naïve manner. It is not a task to be attempted lightly or without preparation, for even the most well intended can be misled into false and harmful perceptions.

Scripture admonishes us with the following warning:

> Now when the unclean spirit goes out of a man, it passes through waterless places seeking rest, and does not find it. Then it says, "I will return to my house from which I came"; and when it comes, it finds it unoccupied, swept, and put in order. Then it goes and takes along with it seven other spirits more wicked than itself, and they go in and live there; and the last state of that man becomes worse than the first. That is the way it will also be with this evil generation. (Matthew 12:43–45 NASB; also, Luke 11:24–26)

Moments of "openness" and spiritual receptivity can be a time of vulnerability to misperceptions and delusion. Perhaps, for this reason, the monastic traditions assign a "spiritual director" to the young proselytes striving for spiritual maturity. Many are the dangers of opening the mind indiscriminately to spiritual forces and personal imagining. In the contemplative tradition of prayer, one focuses upon a portion of Scripture, an image of Christ, or the "Jesus Prayer" as means for staying grounded and protected during moments of receptivity or listening prayer. It creates focus upon traditional Christian traditions and truths in which to ground the contemplative.

Another means of protection is that of the longstanding tradition of the Sign of the Cross. In apostolic times, and still in the Catholic community today, the sign of the cross is used as not only a recognition of the Triune God, but for protection from evil.[2] It serves as a reminder of the reality and authority of the Godhead as provider and protector and redeemer.

> And then you bless yourself with the sign of the holy cross… And in this blessing you begin with your hand from the head downward, and then to the left side and after to the right side, in token and belief that our Lord Jesus Christ came down from the head, that is from the Father into the earth by his holy Incarnation, and from the earth into the left side, that is hell, by his bitter Passion, and from thence unto his Father's right side by his glorious Ascension. (Mirror of Our Lady, fifteenth century)[3]

> "As soon as you get out of bed in the morning, you should bless yourself with the sign of the Holy Cross and say, 'May the will of God, the Father, the Son and the Holy Spirit be done! Amen.'"[4] (Martin Luther, *The Small Catechism*)

Bert Ghezzi, in his book, *The Sign of the Cross*, continues with these insights.

> Making the sign [of the Cross] with the invocation of the Trinity has a multilevel spiritual significance. On one level, it serves as a mini-creed that we can frequently use to affirm our faith. On another level, it corrects our misimpressions of God and welcomes us into the presence

of the Trinity. And on still another, it elevates our prayer, allowing us to pray with Godpower instead of mere humanpower.[5]

Spiritual "openness" must be accompanied by an undergirding of the Trinity in order for these moments to be Divinely prepared and protected. This avenue of spiritual receptivity is no undisciplined or nondiscriminating attitude. Instead, it is an attitude that requires a healthy portion of spiritual focus and discernment in order for it to be spiritually authentic and Divinely endorsed.

## OPENNESS AND SURRENDER

Openness and Surrender are both words which probably initially evoke impressions of vulnerability from most of us. There is a sense of exposure and loss of autonomy, which can be perceived as threatening to today's self-sufficient and self-determining culture.

Openness is likely the less troublesome notion to us, since there is still a sense of control or "filtering" which can be readily at hand to restrain undesired expectations or impulses. There is a kind of conditionality or partially retained control, and the simple act of "opening" implies a retained right and capacity to "close."

Surrender on the other hand requires an acknowledgment of, and submission to, another's independent authority…that authority's priorities, constraints, and demands. Surrender can be conditional or unconditional, but in a spiritual context of submission to a Divine Being, it is in most cases considered an unconditional one…a total relinquishment.

## SPIRITUAL DISCIPLINES AS "ATTITUDES FOR OPENING"

Developing a sense of receptivity to spiritual insights is a gradual process for most. Though certainly some persons will experience an abrupt, dramatic, and total receptivity to spiritual presence, that is not the case for most of us. Most journals and letters of spiritual mentors describe a gradual and episodic journey of increasing awareness to spiritual movements. This process is not characterized by a discreet "step by step" like progression, but rather more like a wax and waning, or ebb and flow that gradually and gently leads toward a sense of increasing spiritual enlightenment.

Despite there not being any single or sure-fired paths to spiritual openness, there have been time-honored disciplines practiced by the saints to allow for a greater capacity for spiritual encounter. These "disciplines" are simply viewed as "tools" to be used in various ways and to different degrees by each individual. They are not to be envisioned as a quick "three-step" program, but rather a preparation initiated by grace and assisted by the Holy Spirit …the disciplines are seen as a variety of stepping stones toward awakening the soul.

This perspective is perhaps best conveyed by the quote of Anthony de Mello shared in the Preface:

> "Is there anything I can do to make myself enlightened?"
> "As little as you can do to make the sun to rise in the morning."
> "Then of what use are the spiritual exercises you prescribe?"
> "To make sure you are not asleep when the sun begins to rise."[6] (Anthony de Mello, *One Minute Wisdom*)

## SPIRITUAL DISCIPLINES[7]

A full discussion of the Spiritual Disciplines is beyond the scope of this study, but in an effort to give some insight into their role, perhaps the following will be of some benefit. Keep in mind, this is only an abbreviated list of some of the more commonly referenced Spiritual Disciplines. There are many others (See Appendix II).

- Awakening the soul:
    - o Solitude: being alone; separated from the support and companionship of others; alone before God

- Silence: being quiet; free from the distractions and demands around us; receptive to the Spirit's leading
- Listening Prayer, Meditation: being attentive; listening to God's "still small voice"
- Fasting: being detached; stepping away from immediate gratification
- Scripture study and meditation (*Lectio Divina*): being focused upon absolute truths; finding instruction for attitudes and actions
- Vulnerability Moments: death, loss, depression—being vulnerable; finding tenderness and compassion within suffering

It should be emphasized again that this is only a skeletal outline of some of the more commonly described Spiritual Disciplines. The numerous approaches to spiritual receptivity are as varied as the hues of an autumn sunset. St. Ignatius, in his use of spiritual exercises, would use Scripture and visual imagery to become open to spiritual reflection and insight.[8] The "exercises" are composed of a series of prayers and meditations led by a spiritual guide. In the Christian mystical tradition, one can identify both the apophatic and kataphatic approaches to unity with God. Those of the apophatic tradition emphasize that God cannot be known through the intellect, but only through entry into the uncertainty of a silent love (St. John of the Cross). Contrarily, those of the kataphatic tradition emphasize finding God in all things, in relationships with people and the world (St. Teresa of Avila).[9] Richard Foster of the Quaker faith favors the disciplines of meditation, prayer, fasting, study, simplicity, solitude, submission, service, confession, worship, guidance, and celebration.[10]

A word of caution is demanded here. There are two dangers that can undermine and distort one's participation in this aspect of spiritual growth. The first is that of *naiveté*: of *indiscriminately opening one's mind and heart* in moments of openness and surrender. If there is a lack of discernment and Christian focus, a person can easily be led astray into counterfeit concepts and perceptions.

The second is the danger of *legalism*: of using the Spiritual Disciplines as rigid and legalistic *rules required* for authentic religious maturity. An understanding and participation in the Spiritual Disciplines do not make a person a "better Christian." They do not impart additional value upon an individual and should never become a source of pride. The spiritual disciplines have no "trophies" as rewards. Rather, they should be regarded as a means of preparing the soul, a means of surrendering personal desires and distractions in order to provide the soil for spiritual receptivity, awareness, and discernment.

Here it may be appropriate to consider what safeguards exist to protect one amidst the fluid movements of spiritual encounter... from both the dangers of *naiveté* and that of *legalism*.

## THE PROVISION OF GRACE

As one considers the use of Spiritual Disciplines as various means to more deeply open our lives unto Divine inspiration, it is important to also consider the provision that Grace allows. With grace, a person can enter into his or her spiritual journey gently and compassionately. There is a kindness and sense of preparation to its presence which comforts and consoles. Grace is not acquired, but rather received, as a gift of Divine love.

This "unmerited favor," which we call grace, flows freely into our lives from the benevolent hand of God. It is an expression of God's deep and ever abiding Love for us. It touches our deepest yearnings and our most painful wounds. It comforts and heals, yet also inspires us into profound gratitude. It seems these two, grace and gratitude, enjoy dancing together to the rhythm and beat of a Divine Love. Within this harmony, these two complement one another to form a resonance of encounter. Grace guides us with her gentle outstretched arms with insight and protection, as gratitude in turn, flows from this Divine embrace, into the awaiting arms of our Lord.

Another point worth making is that it is grace which prevents these Spiritual Disciplines from becoming rigid and legalistic. It is far too tempting to regard the Spiritual Disciplines as the end all and be all…to be mastered and pinned like so many merit badges upon our breasts. But grace will not allow for codifying these practices into confining rules for religion; instead grace facilitates the movement of the Spirit into Divine spiritual encounter. It is only by grace that one can make this passage, and only by grace can one truly be guided by the Spirit.

> "Therefore let us draw near with confidence to the throne of grace, that we may receive mercy and find grace to help in time of need." (Hebrews 4:16 NASB)

> "Do not be carried away by varied and strange teachings; for it is good for the heart to be strengthened by grace…" (Hebrews 13:9 NASB)

## THE GUIDANCE AND PROTECTION OF THE HOLY SPIRIT

As grace and gratitude perform their dance, it is the Holy Spirit that guides our steps. The Holy Spirit acts as a maestro before the symphony, directing a new rhythm while a previous one gradually fades to later return again…now softening the percussion while the reeds bring forth their trill. So it is with deep prayer that one requires a leader, one who keeps us focused upon the Divine score…for in those moments of quietness and surrender we desperately need a guide…one to grant us discernment amidst our spiritual impressions…one to guard our minds from distraction, our hearts from undue desire, and our souls from discord.

> Yet we do speak wisdom among those who are mature; a wisdom, however, not of this age nor of the rulers of this age, who are passing away; but we speak God's wisdom in a mystery, the hidden wisdom which God predestined before the ages to our glory; the wisdom which

none of the rulers of this age has understood; for if they had understood it, they would not have crucified the Lord of glory; but just as it is written, "THINGS WHICH EYE HAS NOT SEEN AND EAR HAS NOT HEARD, AND which HAVE NOT ENTERED THE HEART OF MAN, ALL THAT GOD HAS PREPARED FOR THOSE WHO LOVE HIM." For to us God revealed them through the Spirit; for the Spirit searches all things, even the depths of God. For who among men knows the thoughts of a man except the spirit of the man which is in him? Even so the thoughts of God no one knows except the Spirit of God. Now we have received, not the spirit of the world, but the Spirit who is from God, that we may know the things freely given to us by God, which things we also speak, not in words taught by human wisdom, but in those taught by the Spirit, combining spiritual thoughts with spiritual words. But a natural man does not accept the things of the Spirit of God, for they are foolishness to him; and he cannot understand them, because they are spiritually appraised. But he who is spiritual appraises all things, yet he himself is appraised by no one. For "WHO HAS KNOWN THE MIND OF THE LORD, THAT HE WILL INSTRUCT HIM?" But we have the mind of Christ. (1 Corinthians 2:6–16 NASB)

## ESSENTIAL BENCHMARKS: SCRIPTURE

The Scriptures form an anchoring to absolute truth and ultimate reality from which to base one's spiritual perceptions. As mentioned previously, in moments of spiritual openness, various impressions and thoughts may occur, and it is essential to hold those insights up to the light of biblical truth as a judge of the authenticity of Divine spiritual experience. Those perceptions, if not consistent with God's Word, are to be discarded without further consideration.

> All Scripture is inspired by God and profitable for teaching, for reproof, for correction, for training in righteousness; so that the man of God may be adequate, equipped for every good work. (2 Timothy 3:16–17 NASB)

> For the word of God is living and active and sharper than any two-edged sword, and piercing as far as the division of soul and spirit, of both joints and marrow, and able to judge the thoughts and intentions of the heart. (Hebrews 4:12 NASB)

## SURRENDER

Surrender is our *response* to this movement of open-ness and examination. It is the acknowledgment of a greater authority for our lives, and a greater provision for our spiritual destiny. It is a decision made and a subsequent action taken.

Faith is the process by which a person decides to what authority he or she will surrender. In what person or institution will I place my ultimate confidence and trust? On what bedrock will I build the faith principles that will shape my priorities and guide my decisions? Faith requires surrender…the loss of ultimate control. And it is this concept to which we now focus.

It is tempting not to use the word "surrender" here. A word like "submission" seems a little more kind and gentle. Submission implies a *conditional* relinquishment of autonomy. Perhaps in this setting, at this time, to this person I will submit to another's authority. But I still retain my right to withdraw that decision or perhaps to modify it further at some later date.

But "surrender" has a much more directness to it. The word connotes more a sense of completeness and finality that places reconsideration or renegotiation out of the question. There is no going back. It is a done deal. We "cross the Rubicon." And as if this was not restrictive enough, our minds soon associate surrender with another unpopular concept, that of "obedience." There are perhaps no two less attractive words in the course of our spiritual lives than those of "surrender" and "obedience."

For most of us, this is a very uncomfortable position…unconditional surrender. The cost to my own happiness and freedoms seems too great. My autonomy is threatened. I still want to be in control. Uncertainty looms large over the horizon. What is to become of me? What does my future hold?

Yet the call by Christ is very direct.

> Anyone who loves their father or mother more than Me is not worthy of Me; anyone who loves their son or daughter more than Me is not worthy of Me. Whoever does not take up their cross and follow Me is not worthy of Me. Whoever finds their life will lose it, and whoever loses their life for My sake will find it. (Matthew 10:37–39 NIV)

Still, our feelings of anxiety are captured in this quotation from *The Sacred Romance*:

> So much of the journey forward involves a letting go of all that once brought us life. We turn away from the familiar abiding places of the heart, the false selves we have lived out, the strengths we have used to make a place for ourselves and all our false loves, and we venture forth in our hearts to trace the steps of the One who said, "Follow me"… The freedom of heart needed to journey comes in the form of detachment. As Gerald May writes in Addiction and Grace…[11]

> "*Detachment* is the word used in spiritual traditions to describe freedom of desire. Not freedom *from* desire, but freedom *of* desire... An authentic spiritual understanding of detachment devalues neither desire nor the objects of desire. Instead, it 'aims at correcting one's own anxious grasping in order to free oneself for committed relationship to God.' According to Meister Eckhart, detachment 'enkindles the heart, awakens the spirit, stimulates our longings, and shows us where God is.'"[12]

Now just for a moment, let's step away from the emotional impressions we carry with us about these two words, "surrender" and "obedience," and consider those concepts from a more spiritual context. In the quotation of Gerald May above, it is interesting that he uses the expression "detachment" to describe a condition of heart that engenders "Not freedom *from* desire, but freedom *of* desire." So in surrender, can one find the freedom *of* desire that allows for a deeper, more genuine relationship with Christ...a relationship that steps from the bondage *of* our personal desires into a relationship of freedom which "enkindles the heart...and shows us where God is?"

So the natural question is how this all happens. First of all, we need to get some baggage off the table, for there are some false notions of "detachment" or self-denial that can be quite misleading and need to be dispelled.

*Self-denial is not self-hatred or self-contempt.*

An honest examination of one's soul soon reveals our inadequacies and failures. We all too quickly are confronted with our willful pride and selfish decisions. Yet it is not to say that our response should be solely to sit in our mire of self-depreciation, but to recognize our sinfulness for what it is, and to allow repentance to provide the pathway to restoration. Surrender not only includes the detachment from our desires of possessions and privilege, but it demands a detachment from our old ways of thinking. In a spirit of repentance, we are instructed to "put on the new self" of a redeemed soul birthed by the sacrifice of Christ.

*Self-denial is not loss of identity.*

Genesis tells us that we are made "in the image of God." We are His "workmanship" Ephesians 2:10 (NASB). God values the individual person, for we are all created unique and special by the Creator Himself. And furthermore, He values us so much as to send His Son to die for us, so that we may be reunited with Him. In this redemptive relationship with God, a person not only finds an authentic identity, but finds a new purified and consecrated identity of meaning and purpose. "That you be renewed in the spirit of your mind, and put on the new self, which in the likeness of God has been created in righteousness and holiness of the truth" (Ephesians 4:23–24 NASB).

*Self-abandonment of De Caussade.*

Another term used to describe this attitude of spiritual surrender is that of "self-abandonment," used by Jean-Pierre De Caussade (d. 1751). Rather than speaking of "self-denial," which can be misleadingly perceived as self-punishment or self-degradation, he chooses to speak of "self-abandonment" in a manner that infers a sense of self-release or self-forgetfulness. In his classic work, *The Sacrament of the Present Moment*, De Caussade describes this moment-by-moment self-abandonment to Almighty God:

> So these souls are by their nature solitary, free, and detached from everything, in order that they may contentedly love the God who possesses them in peace and quiet, and faithfully fulfil their duty to the present moment according to his wishes.[13]

# SPIRITUAL AWARENESS

And the following additional quotations of Fenelon expand on this notion "self-abandonment" just described by De Caussade:

> My desire is that you might have an absolutely settled surrender to the Lord Jesus—a surrender which does not size itself up as being "pretty good"—a surrender which is complete, with nothing held back, no matter how dear it might be...
>
> Also, you must determine to be just as humble and simple when you are out in society as you are in your own prayer closet. Never do anything just because it seems logical, or because it's what you like to do. Whatever you do must be done under submission to the Spirit of life... Let us accept everything God sends in humility of mind, never asking questions, and always dealing sternly with self. Let God do His work in you, and concentrate on living a selfless life in each and every moment, as though each moment was the whole of eternity.[14]

## A MONASTERY IN THE MALL?

This segment would probably have best been written by a monk in a monastery. All those notions of silence, solitude, time in listening prayer, and sacrificial detachment seem to work well within the cloister of monastic life. But how do they work within the busyness and noisiness of the mall? That is to say, "I don't live in a monastery! I live in a frantic, chaotic, ambition-driven world with expectations of social responsibility much different than the monastic life." As I write these words, I realize they are my life-long cry. I have always struggled with finding balance between serving in my profession and surrendering to spiritual servanthood. Daily I would combat the clamor of the urgent in an attempt to find the "still small voice" of spiritual insight, and I would wonder what a monk's life would be like. I still find myself asking, "Can we find monasteries within the busy malls of our lives?" Surrounded by desire and consumption, can we find the quiet moments and the gentle whisperings of the Spirit's leading? Can we carve out the moments of solitude and silence necessary for meditation and worship? Awareness of the spiritual dimension of each moment allows us to begin to understand. It is not about the *effort* of spirituality; it is about learning to confidently rest in the loving arms of our Creator.

Perhaps we can find some final comfort and assurance in these closing words by Fenelon:

> Sometimes we are tempted to believe that weakness and humility are not compatible with the surrendered life. This is because we tend to think of surrender as that great thing we do when we want to show God how much we love Him, and how heroically we are willing to sacrifice everything. But a true surrender to God has nothing to do with such a flattering description as that.
>
> Let me tell you what real surrender is. It is simply resting in the love of God, as a little baby rests in its mother's arms...[15]

---

[1] 2 Corinthians 10:5 (NASB).
[2] Bert Ghezzi, *The Sign of the Cross* (Chicago: Loyola Press, 2004). Used by permission of the author.
[3] Herbert Thurston, *The Sign of the Cross*, in the *Catholic Encyclopedia* (New York, the Universal Knowledge Foundation, 1907), 13:786-87; quoted in Bert Ghezzi, *The Sign of the Cross* (Chicago: Loyola Press, 2004), 17.
[4] Martin Luther, *Luther's Little Instruction Book* (*The Small Catechism of Martin Luther*), trans. Robert E. Smith (Project Wittenberg: http://www.iclnet.org/

pub/resources/text/wittenberg/luther/little.book/web/book-appx.html) app. I, quoted in Bert Ghezzi, *The Sign of the Cross*, (Chicago: Loyola Press, 2004), 17.
5. Bert Ghezzi, *The Sign of the Cross*, (Chicago: Loyola Press, 2004), 29–30. Used by permission of the author.
6. "Vigilance" from *One Minute Wisdom* by Anthony De Mello, 19, copyright © 1985 by Anthony De Mello, S. J. Used by permission of Doubleday, an imprint of the Knopf Doubleday Publishing Group, a division of Penguin Random House LLC. All rights reserved.
7. For a more extensive discussion of *Spiritual Disciplines*, see appendix II.
8. Louis J. Puhl, S. J., *The Spiritual Exercises of St. Ignatius* (Chicago: Loyola University Press, 1951).
9. Harvey D. Egan, S. J., *Christian Mysticism* (New York: Pueblo Publishing, 1984), xvii–xviii.
10. Richard J. Foster, *Celebration of Discipline: The Path to Spiritual Growth* (New York: Harper & Row, 1978).
11. Taken from *The Sacred Romance* by Brent Curtis and John Eldredge, 149. Copyright © 1997 by Brent Curtis and John Eldredge. Used by permission of Thomas Nelson. www.thomasnelson.com.
12. Gerald May, *Addiction and Grace* (San Francisco: Harper San Francisco, 1988). Taken from *The Sacred Romance* by Brent Curtis and John Eldredge (1997), 149. Copyright © 1997 by Brent Curtis and John Eldredge. Used by permission of Thomas Nelson. www.thomasnelson.com.
13. Jean-Pierre de Caussade, *The Sacrament of the Present Moment*, trans. Kitty Muggeridge (Harper San Francisco, 1989), 9.
14. Fenelon, "Letter 33: The Will of God Our Only Treasure," in *Let Go* (New Kensington, PA: Whitaker House, 1973), 11. This is a compilation of letters written by Francois de Salignac de La Mothe Fenelon, the archbishop of Cambrai, France, during the seventeen century, 74–75.
15. Fenelon, "Letter 34" "Surrender Is Not a Heroic Sacrifice, but a Simple Sinking into the Will of God," in *Let Go* (New Kensington, PA: Whitaker House, 1973), 11. This is a compilation of letters written by Francois de Salignac de La Mothe Fenelon, the Archbishop of Cambrai, France, during the seventeen century, 76.

# 4

# *Worldview*
# *The Problem of Perception and Philosophical Perspective*

## THE PROBLEM OF PERCEPTION

*Illusions/Delusions*

I have long been fascinated by visual illusions…those intriguing diagrams and images that can cause one to perceive sense experiences quite different from that which is really true. You've all seen them, the straw appearing bent as it passes through the surface of water in a clear glass; the image of urn or bust dependent upon one's view; the parallel lines which look convergent. How is it that our perceptions can fool us so easily? What does that imply about other images and imaginings that we perceive as true? Could these be just as wrong? Are there cultural norms and philosophies that "sound right" but are "truly wrong?" Could cultural deceptions produce delusions that distort our view of the world and its principles as well?

*The Deception of Language*

Of primal necessity is to ask, "What shapes one's sensitivity and perception of 'reality?'" Eastern religion might shape the question as, "Does a tree falling in an empty forest have a sound?" There is the reality of the event, but does the event have a "sound" if there is no presence to "hear?" Communication has frequently been analyzed as a tripartite process, the content (intended meaning), the voice (expression, word, language, medium) and that which is heard (understanding, perception). Because perception is shaped by multiple factors, many of which are outside of an individual person's control, it always carries with it a measure of ambiguity. So when one speaks of "reality" in any general sense, that concept could be understood in various and very different ways. One then needs to use other more specific words, with a narrower, well-defined meaning, and with more universal understanding, in order to clarify or elaborate genuine intent. For example, if a person were to state, "You should always be polite with others." Though the statement may have been intended as a general expression of politeness, as in "everyone should be polite"; a spouse might take that statement personally as meaning, "You, Henry, should be more polite." It becomes readily apparent that the proper use of language is fundamental to accurate communication if it is desired that a specific content is to be conveyed. The expression of a word or phrase, to be effective, requires specificity. However, in current culture, language is instead commonly used to intentionally distort, obscure or deceive.

Borrowed from the culture of artistic expression is the heresy that truth and reality are in the perception (or "eye") of the beholder. Communication through the art forms of sculpture, music, dance, are often intentionally designed with a great deal of ambiguity in order for the observer to perceive content uniquely shaped by his or her own personality and prior experience. One's attitudes, emotions, and sensuality become the letters that shape the language of understanding and opinion in an individually unique and personal way.

Culture today has now gradually adopted this art form of ambiguity to include that of the written and spoken word. Stepping away from the intent to clearly communicate exactly the same content between giver and receiver, we now are bathed in a culture of language that feels at home with conditions of ambiguity and uncertainty. The result of which is that a speaker's original intent (or purposed meaning) can be conformed or distorted into whatever interpretation is desired by the receiver, whether by innocent or nefarious intent.

## WORLDVIEW: THE PROBLEM OF PERCEPTION AND PHILOSOPHICAL PERSPECTIVE

Of course, this now allows the receiver to justify his or her perception, belief, and actions based upon *their own preferred understanding*, rather than that genuinely intended by the giver (sender). Instead of searching for the originator's true intent of the expression, one can now comfortably choose to perceive as one desires. It becomes clear that this "misunderstanding" now leads to an even greater disparity of meaning between individuals as they communicate between one another in our increasingly diverse culture. Unfortunately, there has been little attention or attempt to clarify and effectively correct this problem, and we drift more and more apart from learning and sharing with one another. One need only glance at the many social issues that experience such radically varied support or denial to see how ineffectual contemporary communication has become. As ambiguity increases, so do misunderstandings and mistrust between us. To some, the phrase "illegal aliens" is an offensive phrase (though factually accurate). Others would use the term "undocumented immigrants" as a means to soften the term. Violent football players become "chippy"; lies become "short-circuits." Intentionally derogatory and degrading comments about others on the internet are now referred to as "dissing" or "trolling."

The use of euphemism, guilt by association, illogical reasoning, comments edited without context, partial truths, or misrepresentation…all form the "spin" we are subjected to each day. Before long, we begin to believe that the straw in the glass of water is truly bent.

*Perception of Personality*

This process of misrepresentation and misperception, unfortunately, also commonly affects how we view other people and, how they view us. Without an awareness that our perceptions of others may be imperfect, it becomes easy to evaluate and judge others through our own lens of belief and bias. We forget that *every* perception of others is incomplete and imperfect at best, and distorted and discriminatory at its worst. Spiritual sensitivity begins with this sense of awareness. An awareness in personality that there are realities in myself and others that I do not see.

It is helpful to remind ourselves of the need to view others with a compassionate and empathetic lens, for there is much about each person, including ourselves, that we fail to see. The Ahari diagram reminds us that there are various aspects of personality that are apparent to oneself, and also to others, and there are also those aspects which remain unseen to both.

Ahari Diagram

| My self that I can see<br>My self that others see | My self that I can see<br>My self that others cannot see |
|---|---|
| My self that I can not see<br>My self that others see | My self that I can not see<br>My self that others cannot see |

This realization, that each person is an amalgam of that perceived and that not perceived, is something to carry with us as we interact with one another. Like a murder mystery, we struggle with that which is known and that which is unknown in an effort to comprehend. Viewed and hidden, we each live out our earthly days as persons of light and shadow. This should cause us to pause and reflect. C. S. Lewis stated it this way:

> It is a serious thing to live in a society of possible gods and goddesses, to remember that the dullest most uninteresting person you can talk to may one day be a creature which, if you saw it now, you would be strongly tempted to worship, or else a horror and a corruption such as you now meet, if at all, only in a nightmare. All day long we are, in some degree helping each other to one or the other of these destinations. It is in the light of these overwhelming possibilities, it is with the awe and the circumspection proper to them,

## WORLDVIEW: THE PROBLEM OF PERCEPTION AND PHILOSOPHICAL PERSPECTIVE

> that we should conduct all of our dealings with one another, all friendships, all loves, all play, all politics. There are no ordinary people. You have never talked to a mere mortal…it is immortals whom we joke with, work with, marry, snub, and exploit—immortal horrors or everlasting splendors.[1] (C. S. Lewis, *The Weight of Glory*)

It is clear that one's opinions of persons and events are shaped a great deal by our own emotions and preconceived notions of propriety. How we choose to perceive often has little to do with truly understanding the person or circumstances, and much more to do with what we desire to believe, or that which is most convenient or most conventional to believe. As subtle as serpents, our presuppositions powerfully shape our opinions of others into distortions of reality, and all empathy for others is dismissed.

Though I've long ago forgotten the source, I have forever been influenced by this story of a woman on the subway (paraphrased below). It speaks to the value of choosing to see from a spiritually sensitive perspective.

> It had been a long, hectic day and I was almost looking forward to the forty-five minute subway ride home. Hopefully this transit time would give me a few moments in which to have some peace and quietness…some moments to "de-stress." I chose a seat somewhat removed from others and closed my eyes. Before me paraded the events of the day, all my frustrations and disappointments, and I flowed into a prayer for the Lord's peace and wisdom to touch my weary soul.
>
> Soon, several subway stops later, a man with three young boys got on the subway car and sat across the aisle from me. The boys were quickly running from one seat to another and noisily chasing one another while the father just sat qui-

etly, seemingly paying no attention to their boisterous behavior.

"Why did he have to sit next to my place of solitude and meditation?" I found myself thinking irritably. "Can't he at least see that his children behave themselves and not trouble other passengers? Why can't he be more sensitive to those sitting around him?" Yet he sat silently, as though in a trance.

As a paper wad hit me, thrown by one of the young children, my frustration rose. But just as I was about to ask the man to control his children's behavior, he turned to me and spoke these words I'll never forget:

> "I'm sorry my children are out of control. I'm stunned myself," the young man responded. "We've just come from the hospital. My wife just died."
>
> How my perspective now changed...and my attitude was turned upside down...from judgment to compassion...from self-absorption to empathy.

Once this woman became aware of the realities of another person's tragic circumstances, her own life changed. Now this woman prays on the subway, amidst the noise and turbulence, for those she does not know, for the struggles and suffering she cannot see. This degree of sensitivity grows out of an appreciation for the lives of others...it requires a sense of "otherness" in how one envisions the conditions and events of the day. And in this process, the Holy Spirit becomes a constant companion on the way...revealing and guiding one's sensitivities to spiritual perceptions.

## WORLDVIEW: THE PROBLEM OF PERCEPTION AND PHILOSOPHICAL PERSPECTIVE

> The moment of grace comes to us in the dynamics of any situation we walk into. It is an opportunity that God sews into the fabric of a routine situation. It is a chance to do something creative, something helpful, something healing, something that makes one unmarked spot in the world better off for our having been there. We catch it if we are people of discernment. (Lewis Smedes in *A Pretty Good Person*)

*Discernment*

What does it mean to be a person of discernment? How does this spiritual discernment, this "awareness," occur? Grace arrives to reveal the fenestrations within personal experience which prepare one for spiritual comprehension and insight. To some extent it must depend on seeing and listening well. With a sense of humility, one gains the attitudes of openness and surrender which allow for the sensitivity of experience required for proper discernment. A receptivity is then available for one to perceive the "still small voice" amidst the storm.

However, affective experiences are only the building blocks for this life of awareness, for the intellect has much to say as well. While our affections register the perceptions of experience, the intellect plays conductor. Most of us are familiar with the experience of having several persons view the same auto accident or a crime committed, only to have different versions of the events later from the various witnesses.

The intellect shapes our understanding by guiding how we interpret the perceptions provided by our senses. It assigns significance, decides fact from fallacy, and evaluates the congruence and continuity with one's preconceptions. It is the "maestro" of this symphony of discernment.

SPIRITUAL AWARENESS

# THE PROBLEM OF PHILOSOPHICAL PERSPECTIVE

It is commonly agreed that discernment is a blend of sense perceptions and the intellect in distinguishing the reality and value of an event or idea. Furthermore, to a large extent, the intellect uses its own preconceptions in evaluating and differentiating. These preconceptions are shaped by a person's philosophical positions, or what is commonly called one's "worldview."

*Perspective Shaped by One's View of Universals: "Worldview"*

If discernment is shaped by one's worldview, then it is imperative to examine some of the various worldviews that are commonly encountered today. As we read the subsequent definitions of nominalism and realism, it may be helpful to keep several questions foremost in our minds.

Is it possible to comprehend reality? Is there any value in comprehending partial reality, or derivative reality, even though total and all-encompassing reality cannot be fully appreciated?

Are there any principles one can use to confirm the authenticity and truth of one's beliefs? If so, what might they be?

Are there discreet realities independent of my awareness? Or are all realities confined to culturally defined norms? Who decides which cultural norms to promote and exercise? What would some of the consequences be to a society, based solely upon culturally and generationally defined norms, if taken to their logical natural conclusions? Or as Francis Schaeffer would ask, "What happens when 'culture' becomes absolute?"

*Dealing with Universals: Establishing a "Worldview"*

On a spiritual plane, insight involves developing a sensitivity to abstract reality…beyond the realm of social construct. This is an area of thought commonly neglected or overlooked in our contemporary conversation. Or if it is addressed at all, it is left as a muddled view consisting of confusion and contradiction. Is there such a reality as abstract universal truths, or is our concept of reality limited to that "in our minds" as constructed by culture or personal experience?

Since this is meant to be primarily a devotional work, this discussion will not delve deeply into the many and varied philosophical opinions of reality, but it is a fair question to ask, "What is it that shapes my view and understanding of the world around me?"

The concept of one's "world-view" is in vogue in Christian circles today, but an even more basic consideration is that of one's view of ultimate reality, or the reality of universals. In philosophical circles, the term, "universals" is used in various contexts, but can generally be understood to convey the concept of an overarching abstract ideal, such as "truth," "justice," "equality," etc. that is common to a large body of persons or circumstances. Obviously, how (and even *if*) a person can comprehend such abstract ideals is a topic of fervent debate. Typical of philosophy, there are many varied positions on the reality of universals. Some of the more prominent ones are to be discussed now.

*Ethical Perspectives*

One approach to an understanding and establishment of one's worldview is to examine how one goes about making ethical or moral decisions. Which values are subordinate to others? Which is more important, the *process* or the *goal*? At the risk of oversimplification, the approach of making moral decisions can be classified as *teleologic* or *deontologic* approaches.

A teleologic approach is one whose primary mantra is "the end justifies the means." It is an approach in which the primary focus is on actually accomplishing a specified goal, the *means* or *process* of which is secondary. It is therefore utilitarian in its nature.

A deontologic approach rather, is one in which the primary attention is placed upon the *process* of decision-making. It values one's "*duty*" to make proper ethical choices all along the path to the goal, even if it may jeopardize the actual hope at arriving at the specified goal.

The difference in these two approaches, in the context of ethics, is readily apparent, and one can easily see what a person chooses in moral decision-making is shaped by his or her ethical worldview.

*Metaphysical Perspectives*

Metaphysics is the study of knowledge, or how one "knows." As one can surmise, there are many different metaphysical perspectives, and it is certainly beyond the scope of this discussion to fairly discuss them all.[2] However, I would like to focus on two of the most important and pivotal concepts that we see consciously or unconsciously utilized in current cultural thought; those being *nominalism* and *realism*. The concept of realism is then distinguished further between that of Platonic realism vs. Aristotelian realism.

To paraphrase, *nominalism* recognizes no reality that is not of the material world. Universals are *properties* of an object or person and are found only in the material features of things within the same class. However, there is no reality outside of that which is tangible or can be confirmed by our senses. For instance, the *essence,* or *property*, of a ball is its roundness. But "roundness" does not *exist* independently of a spherical object. Therefore, extended to an ethical sense, an individual person would not be motivated in any way to consider an external abstract principle of "duty" to decide moral action for lack of any corresponding material property to "duty." Instead, the nominalist would be guided only by what would be envisioned as the best way to accomplish his or her goals. From a societal perspective, it becomes the utilitarian mantra of "what is the greatest good [i.e., "tangible benefit"] for the greatest number of people?"

On the contrary, *realism* asserts that all entities can be divided into either universals or particulars. Furthermore, universal realities exist outside and separate from the particulars in which they are found. Plato proposed that there were "forms" like goodness, truth, and beauty that exist independently in the abstract and are apprehended through the use of deduction by means of an innate "recollection" from prior existence. Aristotle, instead, promoted an inductive approach which encompassed studying particulars to arrive at the conclusion that universal abstract realities must exist. Those of a realism mindset approach ethical decisions in a completely different manner than those of a nominalist. Adherence to the abstract universals like goodness, truth, and justice define a fundamental "duty" to exhibit fidelity to those universals. As moral considerations are experienced, even though an eventual goal or result may be undermined in doing so, the realist acknowledges a responsibility, both individually and corporately, to posit decisions and actions upon these abstract universals. To those persons the *process* is as important as the prize.

So why is this discussion important? One's worldview determines the framework upon which issues of belief and ethics take place. In a culture of ambiguity, it provides valuable tools with which to evaluate and understand the significance of various moral positions. It determines through what lens one chooses to view concepts like "rights," "truth," "freedom," "equality," or "justice." Furthermore, it establishes the uniform and timeless parameters for responsible and equitable social action that shape a person's actions and relationships with others.

As our culture becomes more individualistic, yet interdependent, we are increasingly confronted by the concepts of individual versus communal responsibility. In an affluent society, how should wealth be accumulated and shared with those underprivileged in an ethical manner? What is the best way to offer equality of opportunity to all? How can justice be meted out to those of markedly different moral upbringing and persuasions? What is best for the individual? What is best for the community of others, or should one even care?

## HOW THEN, DO I LIVE? A WORLDVIEW PERSPECTIVE

*Compassion and Community*

Most people readily acknowledge the fact that truly caring about an ideal, cause, or relationship involves personal expenditure of one kind or another. Though we can freely choose into what we invest our time and attention, ultimately those choices are shaped by our priorities and values. Some of these values will be foundational, while others are superficial and expedient. Our problem in contemporary culture, I would argue, is that our foundational universals remain muddled in our minds. By forfeiting to concepts more easily accessible, those that are most superficial and expedient, we lose the clarity needed to make appropriate moral decisions.

How then, do I live? Upon what principles do I place my confidence? What beliefs determine my priorities? Do my decisions and actions reflect my bedrock foundational beliefs, or are they constructed from the fleeting delusions of a superficial life? Throughout our lives we go through this process of value clarification. We design, we construct, we remodel this belief structure, and as we do so, we shape the person we will be. For it is this value structure, our "worldview," that will determine the type of house in which we live.

> Therefore everyone who hears these words of Mine and acts on them, may be compared to a wise man who built his house on the rock. And the rain fell, and the floods came, and the winds blew and slammed against that house; and yet it did not fall, for it had been founded on the rock. Everyone who hears these words of Mine and does not act on them, will be like a foolish man who built his house on the sand. The rain fell, and the floods came, and the winds blew and slammed against that house; and it fell—and great was its fall. (Matthew 7:24–27 NASB)

Upon what type of foundation does my present life and eternal destiny rest? For we all have an eternal destiny, either that of "nothing" or that of "something." If there is "nothing" of existence after this life, then why not practice "survival of the fittest?" Why not live in such a way as to subjugate others? Why respect any ethical codes of equality, freedom, or respect? Or is there in fact some other "natural law" which constrains us? Is there in reality, "something other" than that which we can control? If so, from whence does this ethically-imparting source flow? Is it possible that this "something or someone other" and our relationship with it determines in any way my eternal destiny?

The flooring of our convictions, resting upon our foundational beliefs, forms the basis of decision-making as we step into the day-to-day activities of our lives. These convictions form the basis of how we view ourselves and our relationships with others. They shape our attitudes and behaviors. They support an individual's "moral code" if you will, upon which one can develop meaningful priorities and make beneficial choices. Joists undergird these convictions by providing strength and consistency within our worldview. For example, in my decision-making toward a defined goal, what governs my choice making? Does acquiring the goal justify any means, or does one's "duty" to always do the right thing in the pursuit of a goal take preference over actually reaching the desired goal? Convictions may change from time to time, but these (and other) philosophical beliefs will still serve to support the decisions we make on our daily walks.

The common room calls us into relationship and fellowship… to a sense of community. In contrast to the harshness of the winter outdoors, the hearth of love and affection shares its healing warmth. Decorated in the tones of hospitality, acceptance, and joy, this is the room of safety and delight. It is the place of family and friends; of relationships formed from encouragement and also from forgiveness… memories filled with happiness and also those shared in sorrow. It is a room of authenticity. Because of this, we enjoy this "living" room in which experiences of personal investiture and bonding are found. It becomes a favorite room in which to dwell.

Then too, there remain the walls of separation that stand sternly, partitioning off one from another. Sometimes constructed from timbers of resentment or bitterness; at other times from rejection or abandonment. Like so many kinds of lumber, one's constructed partitions come in many varieties…unforgiveness, disappointment, envy…all serving to isolate one from another. Adding another wall here and another there, we soon find that we are existing in a very small room alone. These walls of separation now confine us. What we have constructed to separate us from others encloses and hedges us in...making us very small people indeed. Perhaps it is time to tear down some of these walls of resentment and isolation between one another...between races and cultures? Perhaps it is time to take a fresh look at what it means to live in community beyond one's self-constructed one.

An aroma of nourishment emerges from a nearby room, promising the enjoyment of one's fruitful labors. Out of the agency of effort and work stem forth the products of bounty and provision. Physical sustenance surely, but also emotional and spiritual sustenance as well. What does one feed upon? Television, materialism, success, social media? Or good literature, Scripture, prayer, acts of kindness, compassionate living? I have heard it said that we become that which we eat. What we feast upon, soon becomes a part of who we are. We may be wise to heed that warning.

But what is a house without its decorations of delusion? We all have them...those polished portraits, framing mask-like busts of influence over the poverty of their character. Famous paintings, mimicking the originals, but all copies, forgeries, worthless...satisfying in casual appearances only. There are also the adorning draperies that cover the dusty windows of our lives...those delusions we care not to face. We want them to remain hidden behind the drapes... shielded from truthful examination and insight. Instead, we desire the protection and concealment offered in delusion...though forever false and fleeting.

Perceptions matter, for they are what form one's convictions and emotions. But perceptions, and memory for that matter, can be easily misconstrued. Our minds sometimes construct images and stories which are false in an effort to ease a painful event or in an effort to see ourselves in a more favorable light. Research psychologists have found that between 25–35 percent of individuals will recall in great detail a falsely presented memory when offered amongst a group of true ones.

In a way, they construct a false memory out of what they *want* to believe, in order to bolster themselves.[3] Perhaps, in the best of days, we will be able to see clearly and to become aware of both false and true perceptions as we labor to construct a meaningful and authentic worldview.

So is our house built on a rock of substance, or the shifting sands of superficiality? Are we to choose to live a life of self-absorption and self-gratification, or one that perceives value in an awareness beyond self…of relationships within community?

To genuinely care requires a deeper understanding of, and commitment to, some view of universal reality. Otherwise, what difference does it make for ethical vs. unethical choice? For how one chooses to view ethical propositions (one's constructed worldview) not only affects one's view of personal choice, but also of one's responsibilities within community.

The notion of community has changed a great deal in the last several decades. Once shaped by where a person lived, it now has become more likely shaped by a person's preferences. The "neighborhood," once including one's home and family, were powerful influences that defined and fashioned a person's morals and sense of culture. Often it would be the impact of a close relative or appreciation of a cultural norm that would become the guiding principle of a person's life. Outside influences were minimal, and often discouraged and shunned. Whether African-American, Jew, Italian, or Irish, one grew up in a cauldron of particular languages, traditions, and attitudes that were directly shaped by the physical environs in which he or she lived.

The concept of community has now more likely morphed from that of one's immediate home environment to that created by that of one's personal preferences. One can now choose to step from the influences of their immediate neighborhood and familial ties to create for himself or herself a community that is composed of work associates, faith community, or social circles. Social media now opens the doors to the global community. Rather than being imposed by close family and neighbors of a national culture, it is self-created. Rather than externally shaped morals and a sense of mutual dependency and culture, community can be self-defined and comfortable. Instead of the conflict between cultural mores and desire, one can, to a large extent, choose to step outside of that into a community which is self-created and self-defined. His or her "community" becomes what they want it to be. A person can now say, "If I don't know, I don't have to care."

To a large extent, what one chooses to do with this sense of community reveals what his or her desires and values are. Sensitivity is composed of caring, and caring demands responsiveness to the events of each day. It requires time and effort. It eventually calls for personal investiture.

There can be a newfound sense of freedom in this shift in community from that of a strictly defined set of mores in the home to those chosen by oneself. However, as in so many cases, with freedom comes its conjoined twin, responsibility. To live a life of fullness and awareness, one must be careful not to construct a myopic life of self-delusion. There is a great need to live in a genuine community in which one can sincerely care and be cared for; a community that views reality clearly and is guided by a healthy worldview. For community calls us out of our individual particulars, and beckons us into a realm of universal truths. It beckons us to examine what it means to be "Genuinely Human." Perhaps the initial realization begins with an appreciation that one is part of something much bigger than oneself; an awareness of an overarching reality of which one is only a tiny part. On occasion, we are reminded of this fact within our experiences of awe, wonder, and reverence, to which we will now turn.

---

[1] *The Weight of Glory* by C. S. Lewis, 39. Copyright © C. S. Lewis Pte. Ltd. 1949. Extracts reprinted by permission.

[2] An important principle to mention, though not expressly discussed here, is that of the Correspondence view of Truth, which asserts that which we sense or consider is related to Ultimate Truth in some corresponding way; although incomplete and derivative in nature.

[3] Will Storr, *The Unpersuadables* (New York: The Overlook Press, 2014), 166–169.

# 5

## *Spiritual Awareness*
## *Awe, Wonder, Reverence*

### AWARENESS

Let us not look back in anger or forward
in fear, but around in awareness.[1]
—James Thurber, American writer
and humorist (1894–1961),
*The New Yorker*

The ultimate value of life depends upon
awareness and the power of contemplation
rather than upon mere survival.[2]
—Aristotle (384 BC–322 BC)

*The Garden of Awareness*

*Humility* is that deep garden bed well dug…which empties us of the clutter and debris of self-absorption and pride. Humility creates this space of self-forgetfulness in which a spirit of openness can dwell. *Openness* in turn is the dimension of our lives that provides acceptance for the soil of surrender to be placed. And it is in this very precious soil of *surrender* that our souls will find the nourishment in which to grow. That nourishment, like fertile loam, is the *perspective* taken toward how our souls face the events of life. Though unseen, and often unappreciated, it is essential for the growth needed to become the person the Lord wants us to be. The bed has been dug, good soil has been laid down, and now the seedlings and young plants arrive.

Why is this place of awareness so important? It is because awareness is that moment-by-moment connectedness to that "Something Other"…that spiritual dimension which flows eternally, but which we can, even in the here and now, presently sense. Awareness allows us to see and appreciate a deeper and more profound dimension of spiritual life. This awareness shifts our attentions and affections from the trivial and banal, toward the significant and eternal. It is this awareness that leads to more genuine and loving relationships through its fruits of awe, wonder, and reverence.

*Awareness Reveals a New Reality*

Developing a sense of spiritual awareness allows one to experience a clearer and deeper understanding of that which is genuinely significant. It assists us in seeing the events of each day with a perspective prepared by "deep… prayer and Divine attendance." It allows us to refocus our priorities and to actively respond to those spiritual insights with empathy and compassion. Here is where a person is most genuine; in the interplay of finiteness and infinity, of the temporal and eternal, of the actual and the potential "being."

Thomas Kelly describes this awareness with these words:

> There is a way of ordering our mental life on more than one level at once. On one level we may be thinking, discussing, seeing, calculating, meeting all the demands of external affairs. But deep within, behind the scenes, at a profounder level, we may also be in prayer and adoration, song and worship and a gentle receptiveness to Divine breathings.
>
> The secular world of today values and cultivates only the first level, assured that *there* is where the real business of mankind is done, and scorns, or smiles in tolerant amusement, at the

cultivation of the second level—a luxury enterprise, a vestige of superstition, an occupation for special temperaments. But in a deeply religious culture men know that the deep level of prayer and of Divine attendance is the most important thing in the world. It is at this deep level that the real business of life is determined. The secular mind is an abbreviated, fragmentary mind, building only upon a part of man's nature and neglecting a part—the most glorious part—of man's nature, powers and resources.

Between the two levels is fruitful interplay, but ever the accent must be upon the deeper level, where the soul ever dwells in the presence of the Holy One. For the religious man is forever bringing all affairs of the first level down into the Light, holding them there in the Presence, reseeing them and the whole of the world of men and things in a new and overturning way, and responding to them in spontaneous, incisive and simple ways of love and faith. Facts remain facts, when brought into the Presence in the deeper level, but their value, their significance, is wholly realigned. Much apparent wheat becomes utter chaff, and some chaff becomes wheat.[3] (Thomas R. Kelly, *A Testament of Devotion*)

*Awareness Confronts Us with our Imperfections and Limitations*

We are all flawed people. Continually confronted by our imperfections of form and attitude, we aspire to be something else, only to be frustrated by our limitations of time and resources.

Awareness does not teach one to accept his or her flaws; only to acknowledge them as an aspect of humanness...and to see them clearly. To do so is an aspect of being genuine and real. Spiritual awareness does not make us perfect, but instead allows us to view ourselves honestly. For out of this truthfulness is sown the seeds of authenticity which allows us to live accepted by One who loves us despite who we are. We can then remove our masks of pretense; to experience the safety and peace of genuine acceptance in relationship with God and with one another.

Great truth is revealed in the conversations of the toys within the nursery described in the children's book, *The Velveteen Rabbit*. The stuffed Velveteen Rabbit begins the dialogue and discovers a wisdom from the Skin Horse, unmatched by many philosophers, when he asks the Skin Horse, "What is REAL?"

> "Real isn't how you are made," said the Skin Horse. "It's a thing that happens to you. When a child loves you for a long, long time, not just to play with, but REALLY loves you, then you become REAL."
>
> "Does it hurt?" asked the Rabbit.
>
> "Sometimes," said the Skin Horse, for he was always truthful. "When you are Real you don't mind being hurt."
>
> "Does it happen all at once, like being wound up," he asked, "or bit by bit?"
>
> "It doesn't happen all at once," said the Skin Horse. "You become. It takes a long time. That's why it doesn't often happen to people who break easily, or have sharp edges, or who have to be carefully kept. Generally, by the time you are Real, most of your hair has been loved off, and your eyes drop out and you get loose in the joints and very shabby. But those things don't matter at all, because once you are Real you can't be ugly, except to people who don't understand."[4]

Real love transcends the imperfections revealed within our authenticity. We can earnestly become "Real," because we can no longer be ugly, except to people who don't understand.

## SPIRITUAL AWARENESS: AWE, WONDER, REVERENCE

*Awareness Leads to Change*

> "To become different from what we are, we must have some awareness of what we are"[5] (Eric Hoffer, American writer, 1902–1983).

The insight of awareness, in which we are confronted with our imperfections, and cradled in a spirit of safe authenticity, allows for the opportunity for personal growth. The spirit can now fly from the limitations of ignorance and self-deception. Now a sense of freedom drifts across our faces and inspires us to "become."

The attitudes of openness and surrender now allow a person to perceive concepts and events with a new sensitivity. Released from the conditioned responses shaped by personal desires or societal expectations, a fresh awareness of spiritual insight and purpose becomes more available. A person senses a deeper dimension of experience underlying first appearances. Spiritual possibilities and consequences are entertained in the events of everyday life, and a heightened desire to participate in Divine "breathings" is born.

But what is it that causes us to lose the sensitivity toward life and toward others? Why is it so commonplace to disregard the needs of those around us and in the world at large? How can we become more caring and more giving in the midst of busy and chaotic lives?

One problem is that we are continuously assaulted by the hardships and injustices of the everyday, and we soon are inclined to develop a callousness to the pain and suffering of our world. We hear of the heinous crimes of African genocide between tribes, and of the mutilation, rape, and enslavement of thousands…crimes too horrible to even imagine. We try to forget. Orphaned and malnourished children, without even clean water, struggle and perish hourly. We choose to look the other way. In our own communities are the homeless and underprivileged existing amongst the affluence of personal and corporate America. We distract ourselves with our ambitions. Insulated walls of indifference now protect us from the pain and suffering around us and in our world. Compassion and empathy become marginalized in the busyness of our own personal lives.

Constant exposure to the oppression and misery of others can soon lead to a casual indifference. Insensitivity germinates neglect, and neglect yields eventually to callousness. We forget. We turn the other way. It becomes the way we live our days. Now, only the dramatic and tragic will move us to interest or emotion. The daily helplessness and hopelessness of others become merely a wearisome distraction. The commonplace and subtle movements of spiritual dimensions are ignored. Now our attentions are captured only by the unique and entertaining.

Another cause of our lack of spiritual sensitivity is the haze of our busyness. In our desire and drive to acquire, to provide for, to obtain, we become distracted and preoccupied with our efforts. The sensitivity to spiritual movements and opportunities is abandoned to neglect as the cloud of busyness obscures momentary glimpses of tenderness and insight. Life's intimacies of awe, wonder, reverence, are sacrificed to our daily demands.

Then, how can we regain the spiritual awareness which leads to a heightened sensitivity to "Divine breathings?"

*Spices of the Garden of Awareness*

Like cinnamon and cloves, there is a fragrance and seasoning to life that can easily be passed by in the rapid pace of our days. Being small and seemingly insignificant and shaded by the large oak tree, they are easily overlooked. Yet these tiny and brief spices of experience add the precious richness of novelty and mystery to our lives. To be aware is to be *available* for these moments and to celebrate their fleeting intrusions into our preoccupations. Brief moments of insight and inspiration, unexpected as they may be, tease our appetites away from the mundane toward the splendorous realm of "Something Other."

## AWE

In contemporary conversation the words surprise, awe, and wonder are often used interchangeably, but there is a significant difference to be distinguished in each of these words.

*Surprise* is a reaction to the unexpected... a variation from the regular and routine. It is simply a sudden exposure to that which is out of the common expectations of the moment or circumstance. It is a reaction to something that is known, but surprise is generated because of its unusual or sudden presentation.

*Awe*, rather, is the reaction of amazement to something far beyond easy comprehension. It engenders a sense of the unexplainable. It is an *initial* step into an experience of that which is beyond our imagination or comprehension. Awe unexpectedly springs upon us; to startle us with a sudden awareness of a vast reality, beyond the familiar, which challenges our convictions of ourselves and the world around us.

While religious and philosophical scholars have long mused over the emotion known as "awe," the more recent interest in the topic of awe can properly be attributed to the work in 2003 of Dacher Keltner and Jonathan Haidt. From the University of California at Berkley and the University of Virginia respectively, their co-authored article, "Approaching Awe, a Moral, Spiritual, and Aesthetic Emotion," generated a sudden explosion of interest in the empirical psychological aspects of awe.

After studying numerous persons in various situations, they proposed that there are two main themes that distinguish awe from its cousins of joy and surprise...those being a sense of "vastness" and a necessity for "accommodation." They present their definition of awe as "the feeling of being in the presence of something vast and greater than the self, that exceeds current knowledge structures."[6]

Vastness refers to anything experienced as greatly larger than oneself, or a sense of transcendence. Though it may be of physical dimensions as in the awe of nature; it can also be experienced within the dimensions of aesthetic expression or admiration of a rare personality trait or ability. Common events described by participants as inciting awe were those of the seemingly limitless complexity and expanse of nature, spiritual communion, the profound beauty of art or musical composition, or the inspiration of a person of unique skill or virtue.

Accommodation refers to an adjustment in perspective from that previously held. These experiences of accommodation can sometimes challenge strong convictions, often resulting in emotions of confusion or threat. Combined with that of vastness, one finds oneself as a "small" item within a "vast" realm of reality. Though accommodation is confrontational in nature, it can often result in feelings of new insight and renewal, or a revision of perspective in a very positive manner.

Alongside the two main themes of vastness and accommodation, Keltner and Haidt found what they described as five additional sub-themes that alter or "flavor" the experience of awe by means of their unique and varied circumstances. These include threat or danger, beauty, ability, virtue, and the supernatural.

Of additional interest is that subsequent studies have discovered various possible beneficial physical and psychological aspects of experiencing awe:

- *Awe may lead to improved health.* Some studies have reported an increased release of adrenaline in the midst of an "awe" experience, resulting in increasing heart rate, mental alertness and attentiveness. Also, markers for acute inflammation have been found to be reduced in those experiencing awe.[7]
- *Awe increases the capacity for both creative and critical thinking.* Studies have suggested an increased capacity for fluency, flexibility, and elaboration[8] in creative thinking when measured by improvement tests. Furthermore, there is an apparent increase in critical thinking as individuals experiencing awe have been observed as being less susceptible to weak arguments put forth by others.
- *Awe creates the concept of what researchers call the "small-self."* Confronted with emotions of vastness and accommodation, one experiences a diminution of self, resulting in a decreased focus upon oneself and a greater awareness of transcendence. A whole range of studies have found that this newfound humility results in numerous practical and beneficial personality traits.

- *Awe's "small-self" effect can result in a sense of slowed time.* Much like Csikszentmihalyi's description of "Flow," individuals report a slowing in time as they consider the near timelessness of the Grand Canyon or the myriad of mysteries still to be discovered and understood within the universe. This re-setting of time perspective allows for a person to envision their moments in a different manner. Studies have revealed a tendency for reduced materialism, and a greater capacity to volunteer with acts of kindness and generosity toward others.
- *Awe's "small-self" emphasizes our interconnectedness with others.* There is a sense of being part of a "greater whole" amidst the vastness one discovers in awe. As such, one finds a greater appreciation for others as community, and a greater recognition for the importance of cooperation and mutual interdependency. Self-sufficiency is paused in order to consider the value of helping one another within a culture of community.[9]

Ways to find awe in everyday life:

1. Ask yourself, when was the last time you experienced a sense of awe.
2. Disengage from your devices and practice listening and seeing the beauty of nature which surrounds us.
3. Sit upon the beach at sunrise and quietly appreciate the sun peek over the deep blue horizon as the gulls dive for their morning feeding.
4. Regularly visit a park or museum and quietly ponder what you experience.
5. Study and enjoy the great masterpieces of art and music such as Claude Monet's French Impressionism, Auguste Rodin's sculpture of "The Thinker," Vivaldi's "Four Seasons," the cello performances of Yo Yo Ma, Beethoven's 'Fifth Symphony," Shakespeare's *King Lear* or *MacBeth*.

## SPIRITUAL AWARENESS

# WONDER

> The most beautiful thing we can experience
> is the mysterious. It is the source of all
> true art and science. He to whom this
> emotion is a stranger, who can no longer
> pause to wonder and stand rapt in awe, is
> as good as dead; his eyes are closed.[10]
> —Albert Einstein

How is it that…

The innocent smile of a child proclaims goodness within a world of senseless violence?

A long-ago memory instantly rekindles the love and affection for another even amidst our deepest grief?

A wrinkled, leather-worn face of an elder silently speaks of the wisdom of the ages?

Brief notes of melody arouse such an array of response: sadness, joy, grief, hope, sorrow, inspiration, courage, humility?

*Wonder* introduces one to the mysterious…as awe does within the unexpected and the unexplainable. Like a revolving door it reveals to us, even in the commonplace, the surprise and delight of novelty, then beauty, then courage, now kindness. If only one can pause to see and appreciate, wonder has much to share. But unlike awe, the mystery revealed in wonder is most like meeting another sentient Being. It demands a response from which a conversation, and interchange of experience may flow with the Everlasting Father. The mystery of wonder is a beckoning that is purposeful, intimate and beautiful. Arthur Gordon describes it this way:

### Prayer of a Writer[11]

Lord of all things, whose wondrous gifts to man
Include the shining symbols known as words,
Grant that I may use their mighty power

## SPIRITUAL AWARENESS: AWE, WONDER, REVERENCE

> Only for good. Help me to pass on
> Small fragments of Your wisdom, truth, and love.
> Teach me to touch the unseen, lonely heart
> With laughter, or the quick release of tears.
> Let me portray the courage that endures
> Defiant in the face of pain or death;
> The kindness and the gentleness of those
> Who fight against the anger of the world;
> The beauty hidden in the smallest things;
> The mystery, the wonder of it all....
> Open my ears, my eyes; unlock my heart.
> Speak through me, Lord, if it be Your will.
> Amen.
> —*A Touch of Wonder* by Arthur Gordon

Appetizers. I love appetizers. They tantalize my mind toward what soon will be, and build an appetite for something that is bigger and better yet. I think of wonder a bit like that. Small morsels of spontaneous discovery that tease us with what is yet to come... that which is bigger and better. Life serves many tables... Some barren and others of bounty... Some tasteless and others of delicacies...and wonder is ever-present, moving from table to table teasing our hunger with a touch of mystery for that which is beyond this course.

But wonder is something other than curiosity. It seems sentient and intentional...as though wonder contains a touch of the miraculous as it weaves its unbidden presence within the concrete events of the commonplace... calling forth a sense of awareness out of our complacency... to find delight even within the mundane or perilous. Wonder is a summons to spiritual dialogue, into spiritual relationship and companionship. Like a mysterious messenger, it takes us from our temporal sense of awe to introduce us to the spiritual realm of reverence.

Wonder reminds us that the best is yet to come... in the "here and now" we are reminded of "that which will be."

... Order out of chaos
... Joy out of sorrow
... Hope out of despair

Awe declares, "This is amazing!"
Wonder asks, "How can this be?"
Reverence simply kneels in prayerful adoration.

The noted Jewish theologian, Abraham Joshua Heschel writes[12]:

> To pray is to take notice of the wonder, to regain a sense of the mystery that animates all beings, the Divine margin in all attainments. Prayer is "our" humble "answer" to the inconceivable surprise of living. It is all we can offer in return for the mystery by which we live... Only one response can maintain us: gratefulness for witnessing the wonder, for the gift of our unearned right to serve, to adore, and to fulfill. It is gratefulness which makes the soul great.

Wonder springs forth into worship, for within one's gratitude is a desire to come before the Lord in thanksgiving and praise; to experience His Presence in the intimacy of prayer.

While surprise and awe are both reactions to a circumstance or condition, wonder is a "participation" in something beyond the comprehensible. It is to become aware of participating in a mystery beyond that which we can fully sense. Wonder enters the spiritual. Wonder participates in spiritual awareness.

As such, wonder as *participation* encapsulates the early stages of surprise and awe but goes beyond to confront conviction and response within mystery. Wonder impels response. It is not only an "existential posture," but an existential conversation within a realm of metaphysical mystery. It is a mystery that searches for meaning within the mundane, insight within uncertainty, a voice within the silence.

I very much like Heschel's concept of wonder as "existential posture,"[13] (Shai Held's words) as it engenders the concepts of searching, spiritual attentiveness, and expectancy. But I would offer that true wonder goes beyond "posture" to include the idea of response. If I understand Heschel's thought properly, our response of reciprocity is born out of a sense of "indebtedness" to God.

For the Jewish mindset, that may very well be the case. I personally would not use the word "*indebtedness*" because, to me, it implies that there is something that I can do of value in response—a present unpaid debt, so to speak…an unfulfilled obligation that remains. I would prefer to view my response of wonder as purely compelled by profound gratitude with the understanding that there is nothing that I can do worthy of that which has been given. Gratitude is more than emotion. It is also a mental acknowledgment of that which has been freely given. Perhaps that is a difference between a Jewish and Christian perspective. Because of the Christian's personal relationship with Christ, God does not expect a payment of our "indebtedness." Christ has paid that once and for all. Therefore, I propose that profound gratitude from a repentant heart is sufficient if expressed reverently before the Holy of Holies. It is gratitude for what God has provided through the sacrifice of Christ that allows for a personal relationship with Almighty God because the veil has been torn down that now allows us to approach the Holy of Holies. The sacrifice has been made…the indebtedness paid once, for one and all who accept Christ, forever. I believe it was Meister Eckhart who once said regarding prayer: "Sometimes it is enough to simply say 'Thank You'."

It is participation in Wonder that propels my gratitude toward an ever expanding insight into this mysterious thing we call Divine love. Though I may be *grateful* to my earthly father for what he has *done* for me, I even more so *love* him for *who he is*. Likewise, though I will always be *grateful* for what the Lord has *done* for me, I *love* Him for *Who He is*, as His Divine love beckons me further into a place of holiness.

Wonder teases of that which is beyond the veil… that which is the Source of all being and goodness… that which offers purpose and hope within confusion, and order to be brought forth out of chaos. It introduces us to the beauty of Divine love.

Therefore, wonder becomes the mysterious pathway to reverence… the grateful honoring and adoration of Almighty God. Is this not when we first are allowed to approach the Holy of Holies? Can we really begin to comprehend holiness without first participating deeply in a sense of wonder of God's mercies and lovingkindness, His authority and justice?

And is it not reverence that brings us to a place of confidence in knowing that there is an omnipotent, omniscient, and omnipresent God that cares for each one of us personally and tenderly? Is it not this awareness that causes us to fall on bended knee in prayer before God… to find comfort in the one we call Wonderful Counselor, Mighty God, Everlasting Father, Prince of Peace?

## REVERENCE

> Gratitude bestows reverence, allowing us to encounter everyday epiphanies, those transcendent moments of awe that change forever how we experience life and the world.
> —John Milton, English poet, historian, and scholar (1608–1674)[14]

Reverence then flows out of our gratitude and wonder to express our praise and honor to God, for who He is and for the benevolence of His creation. This reverence is also expressed for the preciousness of life within His magnificent design.

*A Reverence for God*

> "But as for me, by Your abundant lovingkindness I will enter Your house, At Your holy temple I will bow in reverence for You." (Psalm 5:7 NASB)

*A Reverence for God's Benevolent Design*

> Sing to the LORD new song; sing to the LORD, all the earth.
>
> Sing to the LORD, bless His name; proclaim good tidings of His salvation from day to day.
>
> Tell of His glory among the nations, His wonderful deeds among all the peoples.
>
> For great is the LORD and greatly to be praised; He is to be feared above all gods.
>
> For all the gods of the peoples are idols, but the LORD made the heavens.
>
> Splendor and majesty are before Him, strength and beauty are in His sanctuary.
>
> Ascribe to the LORD, O families of the peoples, ascribe to the LORD glory and strength.
>
> Ascribe to the LORD the glory of His name; bring an offering and come into His courts.
>
> Worship the LORD in holy attire; tremble before Him, all the earth.
>
> Say among the nations, "The LORD reigns; Indeed, the world is firmly established, it will not be moved; He will judge the peoples with equity."
>
> Let the heavens be glad, and let the earth rejoice; let the sea roar, and all it contains;
>
> Let the field exult, and all that is in it. Then all the trees of the forest will sing for joy before the LORD, for He is coming, for He is coming to judge the earth.
>
> He will judge the world in righteousness and the peoples in His faithfulness. (Psalm 96:1–13 NASB)

# SPIRITUAL AWARENESS

*A Reverence for Life*

God values life and cares for me intimately…

> "O LORD, You have searched me and known me.
> You know when I sit down and when I rise up; You understand my thought from afar.
> You scrutinize my path and my lying down, and are intimately acquainted with all my ways.
> Even before there is a word on my tongue, behold, O LORD, You know it all.
> You have enclosed me behind and before, and laid Your hand upon me.
> Such knowledge is too wonderful for me; it is too high, I cannot attain to it.
> Where can I go from Your Spirit? Or where can I flee from Your presence?
> If I ascend to heaven, You are there; if I make my bed in Sheol, behold, You are there.
> If I take the wings of the dawn, if I dwell in the remotest part of the sea,
> Even there Your hand will lead me, and Your right hand will lay hold of me.
> If I say, 'Surely the darkness will overwhelm me, and the light around me will be night,'
> Even the darkness is not dark to You, and the night is as bright as the day. Darkness and light are alike to You.
> For You formed my inward parts; You wove me in my mother's womb.
> I will give thanks to You, for I am fearfully and wonderfully made; Wonderful are Your works, and my soul knows it very well.

> My frame was not hidden from You, when I was made in secret, and skillfully wrought in the depths of the earth;
>
> Your eyes have seen my unformed substance; and in Your book were all written the days that were ordained for me, when as yet there was not one of them.
>
> How precious also are Your thoughts to me, O God!" (Psalm 139:1–17 NASB)

Reverence is a deep respect for something or, more likely, some One. It flows from an appreciation and honor for the character of another. In Christianity, it reflects a gratitude within wonder for the character of God and all that He has done for mankind in the past, and that which He continues to do in each of our lives in the present. It reveres God's omniscience, His omnipotence, and His omnipresence, and from that mysterious sense of wonder flows our reverence for Him, for He is like no other.

## PRAYER FOR AWARENESS

> Dear Lord, grant me the grace of wonder. Surprise me, amaze me, awe me in every crevice of Your universe. Delight me to see how your Christ plays in ten thousand places, lovely in limbs, and lovely in eyes not His, to the Father through the features of men's faces. Each day enrapture me with Your marvelous things without number. I do not ask to see the reason for it all, I ask only to share the wonder of it all.[15] (Abraham Joshua Heschel)

# SPIRITUAL AWARENESS

1. James Thurber Quotes. BrainyQuote.com, BrainyMedia Inc, 2020. https://www.brainyquote.com/quotes/james_thurber_106488, accessed September 14, 2020.
2. Aristotle Quotes. BrainyQuote.com, BrainyMedia Inc, 2020. https://www.brainyquote.com/quotes/aristotle_132267, accessed September 14, 2020.
3. From *A Testament of Devotion* by Thomas R. Kelly, 35-37. Copyright © 1941 by Harper & Row Publishers, Inc. Renewed 1969 by Lois Lael Kelly Stabler. Used by permission of HarperCollins Publishers.
4. Margery Williams, *The Velveteen Rabbit* (New York: Doubleday & Co. Garden City, n.d.), 17.
5. Eric Hoffer Quotes. BrainyQuote.com, BrainyMedia Inc, 2020. https://www.brainyquote.com/quotes/eric_hoffer_152406, accessed September 14, 2020.
6. Dacher Keltner and Jonathan Haidt, "Approaching Awe, a Moral, Spiritual, and Aesthetic Emotion," *Cognition and Emotion* 17, no. 2 (2003): p. 297.
7. J. E. Stellar, J. E., et al., "Positive Affect and Markers of Inflammation: Discrete Positive Emotions Predict Lower Levels of Inflammatory Cytokines," *Emotion* 15, no. 2 (2015): 129–133.
8. Alice Chirico, et al., "Awe Enhances Creative Thinking: An Experimental Study," *Creativity Research Journal* 30, no. 2 (2018).
9. Paul K. Piff, et.al, "Awe, the Small Self, and Prosocial Behavior," *Journal of Personality and Social Psychology* 108, no. 6 (2015): 883–899.
10. *Einstein:* Albert Einstein, "What I Believe," in *Forum* (Oct. 1930), quoted in Philip Yancey, *Rumors* (Grand Rapids: Zondervan, 2003), 13.
11. Arthur Gordon, *A Touch of Wonder* (New York: Jove Books, 1974), Introductory Prayer. Reprinted with permission from the estate of Arthur Gordon.
12. Abraham Joshua Heschel (source unknown), quoted in Brennan Manning, *The Ragamuffin Gospel* (Sisters, Oregon: Multnomah Publishers, 1990, 2000), 103.
13. Shai Held, *Abraham Joshua Heschel: The Call of Transcendence* (Bloomington and Indianapolis: Indiana University Press, 2013), 29. Note: I am indebted to my long-time friend, Bill McDonald for introducing Shai Held's works to me.
14. John Milton Quotes. BrainyQuote.com, BrainyMedia Inc, 2020. https://www.brainyquote.com/quotes/john_milton_400414, accessed September 14, 2020.
15. Abraham Joshua Heschel (source unknown), quoted in Brennan Manning, *The Ragamuffin Gospel* (Sisters, Oregon: Multnomah Publishers, 1990, 2000), 103.

# 6

# *Art and Beauty*
# *Diversity within Design*

*Is beauty truly "in the eye of the beholder?"*

## AWARENESS AND BEAUTY

We all share beauty. It strikes us
indiscriminately...There is no end to beauty
for the person who is aware. Even the cracks
between the sidewalk contain geometric
patterns of amazing beauty. If we take pictures
of them and blow up the photographs,
we realize we walk on beauty every day,
even when things seem ugly around us.
—Matthew Fox, *Creation Spirituality*[1]

The nature of beauty is one of the most
enduring and controversial themes in
Western philosophy, and is—with the nature
of art—one of the two fundamental issues
in philosophical aesthetics. Beauty has
traditionally been counted among the ultimate
values, with goodness, truth and justice.[2]
—Stanford Encyclopedia of Philosophy

## SPIRITUAL AWARENESS

## ART AND BEAUTY

*What is "art"?* Art *stirs one from complacency.*

Foremost art is arbitrary, based upon the beliefs and desires of the artist. The art form is not necessarily contingent upon any universal value, but rather only the personal desire of the artist. While beauty may be expressed in art (and often is in traditional forms); not all art speaks of beauty. Art can be an instrument to express beauty, or instead an instrument of adulteration. Needless to say, we will soon see that traditional art and contemporary art often have much different intentions.

*What is "beauty"?* Beauty *inspires.*

The Merriam-Webster Dictionary gives this definition:[3] "*the quality or aggregate of qualities in a person or thing that gives pleasure to the senses or pleasurably exalts the mind or spirit.*" This is a particularly accurate definition, over that of others, because it describes the two-fold aspect of the concept of "beauty." To be sure, there is the temporal gratification of pleasure that is experienced as one perceives objects and experiences. However, there is also the aspect of "beauty" that is found in the experience which "exalts the mind or spirit." This speaks to a more eternal value, one grounded in consistent and reliable universal values which are timeless. That is why the above quote includes beauty with the "ultimate values" of "goodness, truth, and justice."

The Arts (*tapestry of man*) vs. Beauty (*tapestry of God*).

*The Arts: That which stirs one from complacency*

Art challenges our preconceptions; it teases our curiosity and stirs our emotions. Varied of form and message, art reaches into our staid and comfortable home, and like a whirlwind, topples all the furniture. Condensed and poignant, it can instantly move our emotions with the rush of pathos.

However, contemporary art often has different views of artistic expression from that of the past. It has a clear distinction from the traditional forms and concepts of the past, and strives to give current social circumstances expression by unconventional and sometimes startling means.

If one were to ask, "What is the goal/role of art today?" multiple answers would come to the fore. Historically a list might include the aspects of conceptualizing beauty, revealing reality, eliciting pleasure, or demonstrating creativity and novelty. On the contrary, often the predominant modes of art in contemporary culture would stem from a strong social commentary and social agenda bias. The role of contemporary art in that instance becomes a tool for societal confrontation and change (of course, only consistent with the ideology of the artist).

While traditional art forms expressed realistic forms of beauty, tragedy, pleasure, and pain; contemporary art forms focus on confrontational and abstract modes aimed at reshaping ideas and concepts. Implicit in the art form is a goal to alter societal principles and priorities according to a specific ideology.

An ever-increasing use of artistic expression is in promoting these specific social agendas. This aspect of "art" uses persuasion to power a move toward a self-defined ideology of social change. In the movement from simply expressing opinion and social commentary, we now witness presentation of social agendas as socially accepted and even idolized ways… outside of the reality of traditional cultural norms. This is especially seen in the manner that contemporary art portrays time-honored cultural norms such as religion, civil discourse, and authority. What once was normative can no longer be acceptable; and furthermore, even open to derision.

*Beauty: That Which Inspires*

Art can anger, challenge, tease, placate, or soothe, but only beauty can universally inspire.

In a lecture of Francis Schaeffer entitled "Art Forms and the Loss of the Human,"[4] Schaeffer rebuts the notion that "art is for art's sake." Instead, he makes a forceful argument that art should be much more than that. Schaeffer asks, "Is art just a 'style' or does it 'say something?' Is art to be arbitrary, or is there to be universal content and meaning in the form of the artistic expression?" To substantiate his viewpoint, he quotes Sullivan, a pioneer of modern architecture, who once stated that architecture, as art form, "is a record of human belief and aspiration." Schaeffer goes on to declare that modern art has rejected this notion of universal content and meaning. In doing so, he would argue that some modern art is thereby also rejecting the forms of morality created by God, and consequently rejecting and ridiculing God's ultimate design. The central question posited is whether artistic expression is to be formed by the arbitrary desires and opinions of individuals, or formed by an underlying conviction of universally held values. Is it to be utilized to tear down, or to "exalt the mind or spirit?"

Few modern artistic works can compare with the Greek tragedies or Shakespearian dramas, but all can strive to remind us of the joys and sorrows of life, of the gentle touch of kindness and forgiveness, of the fidelity of genuine love, of the heartaches of suffering and loss...then, too, there is the joy of creativity and the beauty of diversity.

Life's lessons are condensed within the precious chrysalis of natural and artistic expression in forms that grant a newfound insight into the drudgeries of everyday living. How is it that a favorite melody can suddenly transform monotony into a dance; or, how can a uniquely colored sunset majestically transform our chaotic and turbulent mind into one of peace and tranquility? How is it that a perfectly crafted phrase can instantly inspire and encourage?

One answer may be that whether by nature's magnificent design, or by man's artistic expression, there lies a realization and awareness of something greater than ourselves. And it is this insight that resonates so profoundly within the sensitivities of our souls. Is this not the task of the artist? It should not be to debase and defile the intrinsic patterns and beauty of our existence, but rather to inspire one toward transcendence, even within the tragedy of human suffering.

## ART AND BEAUTY: DIVERSITY WITHIN DESIGN

The photograph of the starving child, the tortured African woman, the broken-ness of poverty all serve to sensitize us that we can do better, we can be better, we can give "better" to others. Art is not to tear down, but rather to build up. To ridicule and deride serves no purpose other than self-serving ones of notoriety. However, to inspire and challenge leads to responsive efforts to make the world a little better than yesterday; perhaps one more candle now burns amongst the darkness.

Caring and responding to suffering is the greatest form of beauty. Here is where beauty transcends the sculpture or painting and reaches its highest expression and fulfillment. It is where experience "exalts the mind or spirit." This is true universal beauty, the expression of lovingly caring for another in their hours of suffering. Of sharing in their suffering. Of participating in their pain. It is the beauty of the quiet sacrifice, to those beyond family and friends, without any recognition or chance of repayment. The beauty lies in the act of the tired Traveler washing the dusty feet of his fellow companions. Most of us realize that beauty is more than glamor. It is a melding of compassion, goodness, truth, and justice into something beyond ourselves.

There are those who would proclaim that "beauty is in the eye of the beholder." Paraphrased, this is to say that each person can have his or her own concept of "beauty." Though perhaps some truth can be made in a temporal sense, there can be no place for the position that universal absolute beauty is shaped by man's imaging or imaginings.

Universal values and truths are fundamental to any discussion of ethical or moral conceptualization and conduct. They are not shaped by human desires and opinions, and are not conditioned by era or culture. Creation itself shouts the reality and necessity for ethical human existence based upon the pre-existing universal absolutes established by God. True beauty is that which inspires by means of expressing great diversity within a grand design.

# SPIRITUAL AWARENESS

*Diversity within Design*

While art may be the tapestry of man, certainly nature is the tapestry of God. Upon His tapestry of humanity, God reveals to humankind universal truths upon which to confidently trust and upon which to find genuine hope. Within the design of God's creation, there is found a *grounding* that gives confidence in the value of trusting and loving relationships, of the value of sacrificial conduct, of the tenderness of forgiveness.

### The Beauty of Humankind's Design: The Uniqueness of "Human-ness"

As created in the "image of God," humankind is created as a unique being.

- Humankind is first and foremost a spiritual being, with a *spiritual destiny*, and as such, has infinite worth. It is the recognition of this fact that not only allows for, but even promotes the notion of human equality. As each person is created by God as a unique, spiritual being, each person, therefore, has a uniquely defined spiritual capacity here amidst our earthly existence. To value such is to value one another with an appreciation of that person's individual worth and potential even in the here and now.
- Humankind is unique from the rest of nature in being given *unique abilities*: reason, creativity, spirituality, imagination, and abstract thought. It is within the capacity of abstraction that we generate our concepts of ethics, morality, truth, freedom, equality, etc. These concepts become the beams we use to build the structure of societal values… its freedoms and its constraints, which can potentially lead to a just and fair environment for every individual.
- Humankind is to be a *responsible* being. Genesis 2:15— uniquely created, with special gifts, calls for a unique responsibility. It is this responsibility of stewardship which

## ART AND BEAUTY: DIVERSITY WITHIN DESIGN

calls forth our need to care for and preserve our environment, and relate to and nurture one another. In so doing, each of us exercises his or her free will to mobilize the agency given to us by God that leads to individual and communal meaning and value. Furthermore, it is in this process of responding to this responsibility that we discover genuine and effectual purpose for living.

Interestingly enough, it is just because of these universal absolutes, that humanity can find and experience the beauty of novelty, mystery, and variety. For only out of God's creative design can flow the true freedom for meaningful diversity.

God's design for gravity was to be a consistent force of cohesion.
Yet within gravity's force, witness the diversity of size and distance of the suns and planets scattered throughout the vast universe.
God's design is for a predictable cyclical pattern of days and seasons.
Yet within each cycle is a uniqueness of temperature, wind, and rainfall.
God's design was for each one to mate with "one of their own kind."
Yet within this design is a myriad of different races and creatures.

Not diversity *without* design, but *within* design. Though Art may choose to break from structure and form into wild and exotic expressions; Beauty instead finds its value in its diversity *within* the design of ultimate truths. As Beauty showcases the wonder of diversity, it remains rooted in the universal truths of reality. Genuine Beauty, then, reveals something beyond this temporal existence, perhaps even into another dimension of novelty or mystery, yet it remains grounded into a reality that is consistent and upon which one can rely to be true.

Diversity of creation stems from the structure of design, but design flows from the Creator. William Paley famously stated that where there is a watch, there is a watch maker. So it is not too far a leap to conceive that where there is design, there is a Designer. And the beauty of the design speaks of the character of the Creator.

This grounding of diversity within design can also be expressed with a musical metaphor. In musical composition, the German phrase of "Grundton" was used by Dietrich Bonhoeffer to describe the "tonic" or "key note" of the composition. It *"is the first degree of a major or minor scale or the main note of the key…after which the key is named."*[5] So before a single note can be written, the fundamental key has to be established; upon which the whole composition rests. Bonhoeffer's musical metaphor for the reality of the Godhead is expressed in a letter to his friend, Eberhard Bethge.[6] His conviction is that all rests upon the benevolence of a personal Godhead that establishes design through universal truths. These truths, in turn, allow for the expression of genuine diversity enabled by the freedom granted by the structure and confidence of that God-given design or "fundamental key." As Bonhoeffer developed his metaphor further, he used the musical term, *cantus firmus*, to describe the foundational design;[7] while using the term "polyphony" to describe the variation of musical movements allowed, and even encouraged, by the fundamental key of the musical composition.

Perhaps there is no better way of expressing this concept than to consider how it plays out in considering the realm of man's "humanness." What does it look like to experience life as genuinely "human?" Are there principles at play which allow one to enjoy the fullness of individual personal expression, yet to do so in a manner that fulfills one's responsibilities to others? Are there patterns of living which value one's unique insights and abilities, as well as his or her innate responsibility to live civilly in community? How does the *cantus firmus* of one's design express itself in the polyphony of one's diversity of talents and inclinations?

*The Beauty of Humankind's Diversity: The Uniqueness of Nature*

Nature, to some degree, reflects humanness in its similar diverse forms. The snowflake falling, then melting upon the mountain granite reminds us of the brevity of life, our vulnerability and frailty.

There is the harshness of the winter which plays upon our memories of our selfishness and apathy, our angers and biases. Yet as seasons change the mountain meadow comes once again alive in an explosion of color as wildflowers burst forth in their splendor of hope; soon to herald the warmth of summer's compassionate abundance. Autumn ushers in moments of restfulness and preparation for winter's returning bitterness.

We are all a part of this unending cycle of life. Created to move in our various ways, made tall and short, domineering and passive, selfish and generous; we all dance this cycle of existence within our so many different colors and cultures. There are the seasons of our lives which pass ever fleetingly from youth to maturity. There is beauty in this diversity of humanness, this ever-changing expression of personality and actions that teaches us the value of one another. Yet the polyphony of the music to which we dance is grounded upon a greater design for humanness, a "*cantus firmus*" providing the measure and beat to guide our steps and sway, our posture and our actions. This "*cantus firmus*" is the beauty found in humankind's Divine design.

*To What End Does Beauty Inspire?*

Beauty calls us from dullness and complacency to a realm of hope and inspiration. Though humanly constructed art can do so as well, it does not do so exclusively. Art instead is a human construct, and as such contains the imperfections of contrary and sometimes adulterated forms and expressions. On the contrary, Genuine Beauty universally and authentically inspires us to reflect upon what it is to be a genuine human being.

*Beauty of Form and Function*

Beauty expresses itself in various forms and functions. The masterpieces of Michelangelo's *David*, Van Gogh's eerie *Starry Night*, Handel's *Messiah*…all find beauty in the manner in which they inspire one to perfection. In some mysterious manner, they reach deeply into the human soul to arouse the pathos of life's battlefields—joy and suffering, victory and defeat, forgiveness and vengeance, loving-kindness, and hatred.

There are those objects that are clearly not as beautiful in form or appearance, but are impressively beautiful in their function. From ancient forms of architecture one appreciates the symmetry and strength of the Greek Ionic columns, the Roman arches, and the intricacies of the Egyptian pyramids (which we are yet to fully understand today). From the simplicity of the wheel, to the intricacies of the computer, their beauty is expressed in their respective functions.

*Beauty of Nature*

Then there is the wild beauty of nature. The yawning Grand Canyon, Australia's Great Barrier Reef, the towering snow-covered Rockies, the tap-tap of the woodpecker, the delicacy and fragrance of a budding red rose, the mystery of a spider's web… all designed with uniqueness and diversity of which one can only experience a sense of awe.

*Beauty of Personhood*

The innocence of a newborn baby, the delight of a child's eyes, the courage and self-sacrifice of first responders… A smile and the joy accompanied by laughter. Kindness across cultures, empathy born out of lovingkindness, respect generated by responsibility, the forgiveness which recognizes the dignity of each person. Who cannot marvel at the value of second chances?

*Beauty of Character*

In our heroes and heroines, we find beauty in their character. We find integrity in Martin Luther King Jr.'s eloquence, wisdom in the Psalms of David, honesty in the literature of Dostoyevsky and Solzhenitsyn, courage in the war-worn soldier.

Yet more beautiful are those who reveal the character of their lives amidst their own personal battlefields:

- The single parent who courageously strives to provide for and to care for their family.
- A child of disability who ambles upon deformed limbs with a victorious smile upon his face.
- One bearing the scars of ridicule and rejection who finds value in serving others.
- Those bearing the inevitable fear and anguish of terminal illness.

Though there is certainly no beauty in their circumstances, each expresses Beauty out of the strength of their own personal character. They are our true heroes and heroines.

- Each inspires us to see ourselves as part of something greater which we do not fully understand.
- Each inspires us to appreciate that a relationship with that "Someone Other" is valuable and to be desired because it gives meaning and purpose to life.
- Each inspires us to use our capabilities (our "agency") to find relationship and purpose with God and with others… to add the touch of healing or encouragement, to make a difference, to light one candle, to make tomorrow a better day.

This Awareness of diversity within design is a fundamental principle upon which to understand and appreciate the value of each person…which is in itself an expression of genuine Beauty.

*Beauty's Symphony*

What is a garden without its sounds? From the gentle whisperings of the wind rustling playfully amongst the leaves, to the bass-like percussion of the thunder as it ushers in the promise of life-giving

## SPIRITUAL AWARENESS

raindrops. Enjoy the tweets and chirps of the cheerful birds searching for their next treat and the hum of the bees tasting the nectar from the palette of multi-colored flowers. What is a garden without the music of Beauty?

*Participate with Beauty*

- Write a love poem or note to your spouse.
- Sing a favorite song of inspiration.
- Remember an act of courage.
- Create a flower arrangement.
- Eat an apple slowly and appreciate it as a unique experience.
- Send a "thank you" note to a new or life-long friend.
- Meditate on an enlightening portion of Scripture or poetry.
- Appreciate your favorite color, food, music…enjoy them slowly.
- Find an endearing characteristic in a person not a close friend.
- Make a grocery check-out person smile with a kind word.
- Intentionally "build a bridge" with a person of a different race or culture.
- Practice kindness and generosity.
- Practice healing (of emotions, relationships, disappointments, etc.).
- Choose an anonymous sacrificial gift for another.
- Send a "Thank you" note to a soldier, sailor, police officer, or first responder.

## A PRAYER FOR BEAUTY

As the scarlet leaf lazily drifts downward, back and forth, back and forth, from the giant oak to gently rest upon the glistening dew-covered grass, nature's beauty whispers its message of God's design…a design that allows for and values diversity within its realm of Divine purpose…Dear Lord, help me see and appreciate true beauty of diversity within your design in each moment of each day that I may share hope with another.

[1] Matthew Fox, *Creation Spirituality: Liberating Gifts for the Peoples of the Earth* (HarperCollins Publisher Inc., 1991) 48.
  Frederic and Mary Ann Brussat, *100 Ways to Keep Your Soul Alive* (San Francisco: Harper San Francisco, 1994), 33.
[2] Crispin Sartwell, "Beauty," in *The Stanford Encyclopedia of Philosophy* (Winter 2017 Edition), Edward N. Zalta (ed.), URL = <https://plato.stanford.edu/archives/win2017/entries/beauty/>.
[3] www.merriam-webster.com/dictionary/beauty.
[4] Francis Schaeffer: www.labri-ideas-library.org; "Art Forms and the Loss of the Human" Part 1 lecture; this was brought to my attention by my close friend, Bill McDonald.
[5] Robert O. Smith, "Bonhoeffer and Music Metaphor," *Word and World* 26, no. 2 (Spring 2006): 202.
[6] Dietrich Bonhoeffer, "Thoughts of the Day of the Baptism of Dietrich Wilhelm Rudiger Bethge," *Dietrich Bonhoeffer: Letters and Papers from Prison*, First Paperback Edition, ed. Eberhard Bethge (New York: Macmillan Publishing Company, 1972), 308.
[7] I am deeply indebted to my life-long friend, Bill McDonald for introducing me to Bonhoeffer's concepts of the Cantus Firmus as a musical metaphor for the notion of diversity within design.

# 7

## *The Present Moment*
## *The Mystery of Time*

> But do not let this one fact escape your
> notice, beloved, that with the Lord
> one day is like a thousand years, and
> a thousand years like one day.
> —2 Peter 3:8 (NASB)

> All we have to decide is what to do
> with the time that is given us.
> —JRR Tolkien, *Fellowship of the Ring*

> We are merely moving shadows, and all
> our busy rushing ends in nothing.
> —Psalm 39:6 (NLT)

### THE CONCEPT OF TIME

Long ago astronomers measured the movement of the Earth circling the Sun. These sages recorded our planet's regular rotation, then diced these observations up into so many pieces and called it "Time." These pieces we now name "days" or "hours" or "minutes," as though we can somehow define and control their portion of reality. But that will prove not to be the case, for Time is as elusive and fleeting as the wind. His presence is an enduring mystery to us…so intimate to our every moment, yet so far from our understanding.

Yet we can observe his play as Time has a way of teasing with us. We will speed past a slow-moving vehicle (in order to save time), only to find it pull beside us at the next stoplight. We have gained nothing. And we can hear Time's laughter. He can make a minute into an eternity or reduce a day into only a moment of memory.

Time's mystery puzzles even the wisest of the philosophers. Is time linear or cyclical? Is time only within one's mind or does it exist independent of oneself? Can one trace the origins of time? What was once, has gone, and what is envisioned, may never be.

> "The timeless in you is aware of life's timelessness. And knows that yesterday is but today's memory and tomorrow is today's dream" (Kahlil Gibran, *The Prophet*).

So far we have been referring to what the Greeks would call "chronos" time. That which is measured and referenced from day to day. It is a part of our natural cycles of sunrise and sunset, of season upon season, our birth and our death. It is impersonal to each of us, not tarrying to allow us to affect its relentless march. However, the Greeks also referred to a measure of time they considered much differently, that of "kairos" time or an "opportune time" or a "season."[1] It is used often to refer to a time of harvest, an opportunity to do something, a time of discharging one's duties, or sometimes even that of a time for punishment. "*Chronos* marks quantity, *kairos*, quality."[2]

The Greek concept of *kairos* time is perhaps expressed somewhat in the well-known Hebrew passage of Ecclesiastes 3:1–8 (NASB).

> There is an appointed time for everything.
> And there is a time for every event under heaven—
> A time to give birth and a time to die; A time to plant and a time to uproot what is planted.
> A time to kill and a time to heal; A time to tear down and a time to build up.
> A time to weep and a time to laugh; A time to mourn and a time to dance.

A time to throw stones and a time to gather stones; A time to embrace and a time to shun embracing.

A time to search and a time to give up as lost; A time to keep and a time to throw away.

A time to tear apart and a time to sew together; A time to be silent and a time to speak.

A time to love and a time to hate; A time for war and a time for peace.

*Kairos* has this connotation of a time of "actualization," or "an appointed time." It infers a pivotal point or culmination of events within human experience. It is within this *kairos* time that one can find "the present moment." This "Present Moment" is the concept of a moment in the *now* that briefly awaits a decisive choice or action…a decision which may never occur again.

## THE PRESENT MOMENT

Exhaust the little moment. Soon it dies.
And be it gash or gold, it will not come
Again in this identical disguise.
—Gwendolyn Brooks[3]

This is a pivotal chapter. Moving from a consideration of the foundational virtues of humility, openness, surrender, and sensitivity, then examining the tools of awareness; we now focus our attention upon the "Present Moment." We shift from the conceptual to the practical. Intentionally, we weave the concepts of our faith into the daily practice of spiritual living. Attitudes now blossom into Actualization.

Most of the following chapters will be very pragmatic in nature, and this shift is first experienced here as we begin a consideration of what it means of live in the "here and now." The "Present Moment" is an expression with a very rich and meaningful history. It has long been used in the spiritual literature to re-orient our attentions upon that which we can experience most intimately and profoundly. It calls us to shift our preoccupations from the regrets of the past and from the anxieties of the future. For we are reminded, neither past nor future can we control as we would like. But we *can* act in the present moment. We can choose how to approach the choices and decisions of each moment. Moreover, *how* we respond to those choices shapes who we will become. It is in the work of the present moment that we are transformed into the souls prepared for eternity. Because of this, we can sense what a powerful opportunity learning to live in the moment presents for each one of us.

It is true that the past still holds us within its grip, for it is those past experiences that have shaped the person we are presently. We still carry with us all the wounds and joys of our past. They still call out to us and dramatically affect our attitudes and decisions.

Likewise, our concerns for the future continue to enter into every day. We worry about the years ahead, and we yearn for a future that sees our dreams fulfilled. Each day's efforts become focused on accomplishing those desires. It is for the future we strive. Present awareness is sacrificed for our hopeful vision of the future.

It is in this struggle between our past and future that the present moment plays such a pivotal role. For it is in this struggle that man and woman define who they genuinely are and who they will ultimately become. It is a place of profound transformation. The present moment is as transient and fleeting as the wind, yet it results in permanent and irrevocable consequences. One might even say eternal consequences. Perhaps it is this dimension of "time" that so intrigues the mind to ponder it so. It is here that one sees the spiritual in the ordinary moments of time.

In that light, it is no small wonder that the "present moment" has drawn such interest amongst spiritually focused individuals for centuries. It is a topic with a rich heritage. And it is in its history we shall begin.

Much of the reflection and writings upon the present moment come from the monastic community. Theirs was, and still is, a culture very much attentive to the process of spiritual transformation. Through the study of Scripture, prayer, and meditation their literature would begin to speak of these moments of time of profound spiritual intimacy.

## SPIRITUAL AWARENESS

Though there are many, we will only touch on a few writers who have perhaps most clearly described this action of living in the present moment. There are more intellectual and more devotional tomes, but those chosen to be discussed in this chapter are chosen for their simplicity and clarity.

One of the classics of Christian spiritual literature is a work by the title of *The Sacrament of the Present Moment* by Jean-Pierre De Caussade. In this small book, De Caussade describes his experience of prayerfully living in the present moment:

> God speaks to every individual through what happens to them moment by moment…
>
> There remains one single duty. It is to keep one's gaze fixed on the master one has chosen and to be constantly listening so as to understand and hear and immediately obey his will…the only condition necessary for this state of self-surrender is the present moment in which the soul, light as a feather, fluid as water, innocent as a child, responds to every movement of grace like a floating balloon.[4]

Awareness of the spiritual dimension of the present moment is apprehended by practicing an attentiveness to Divine movements within our daily lives, even in the most trivial of moments. How many of us have not felt the occasional urging to do a mundane task for someone, perhaps even anonymously, to find that the task had a benefit to that person far beyond anything we had imagined? Can we not wonder that the Spirit was at work there? Attentiveness and listening have a fundamental way of assessing spiritual movements.

Brother David Steindl-Rast addresses this notion in his book, *A Listening Heart:*

> [I]t is time, not our time.
> The moment we let go of our time, all time is ours. We are beyond time, because we are in

the present moment, in the now which transcends time. The now is not in time. If any of us know what now means, we know something that goes beyond time...And so we find that in time there is only the seam between a past that is no more and a future that is not yet; and the now is not in time at all. Now is beyond time.[5]

If Steindl-Rast is correct and the present moment, the *now* is beyond time, it must touch eternity in some manner. If eternity exists, how can there be such a thing as time unless it is somehow contained *within* eternity? And if so, would not each moment of "*kairos* time," each "present moment," have an eternal dimension? Is it not reasonable, then, to ask if the present moment has eternal significance and consequences? And if so, what a profound reality that would be!

Here it may be wise to remember that each person, made "in the image of God" is created as a *spiritual being*, existing temporally in a finite material form, yet enjoying an eternal destiny. As a spiritual being, we are wired for communion with eternal Spirit. This Holy Spirit, this "parachlete" is our companion along this earthly journey, our guide and protector. As such, is it not reasonable to expect to encounter the Holy Spirit's (beyond time) influence in the events of each day, and perhaps even the events of each "present moment" in *kairos* time?

To most Christians, this is not such profound insight, for the work of the Holy Spirit is a fundamental aspect of Christian theology. However, is it fair to ask if we actually "live out" our days in such a manner that we exercise this belief in a consistent way? Have distractions dulled our senses to spiritual insights? Has affluence allowed complacency to undermine our attentiveness to spiritual inspirations and guidance? How can we become more spiritually "aware" amidst the busyness of everyday living? Even though we have introduced fundamental attitudes which can prepare us for these encounters (i.e., humility, openness and surrender, clear perception and appropriate philosophical worldviews, sensitivity and appreciation of awe, wonder, reverence, and beauty), Steindl-Rast shares an additional concept that can heighten our awareness to spiritual movement in the "Present Moment." He speaks of spiritual "asceticism."

The word "asceticism" has long been used by the monastic community to mean a turning away from worldly pleasures. However, Steindl-Rast reminds us that it was originally used in Latin to refer to *"the workout by which athletes kept themselves in good shape."*[6] It is fair to say that in most of our lives of spiritual distraction and complacency, a good workout may be just what we need.

Steindl-Rast uses this analogy to present concepts for spiritual transformation. He reminds us of the need for spiritual attentiveness, gratefulness, and obedience as helpful and necessary tools in our efforts to grow in spiritual awareness.

## A PRACTICAL APPROACH TO BEING "AT HOME" IN THE PRESENT MOMENT

How is it then, that we can "put more life in our days," as Kathleen Norris describes in the following?

> Gradually my perspective on time had changed. In our culture, time can seem like an enemy; it chews us up and spits us out with appalling ease. But the monastic perspective welcomes time as a gift from God, and seeks to put it to good use rather than allowing us to be used up by it. A friend who was educated by the Benedictines has told me that she owes to them her sanity with regard to time. "You never really finish anything in life," she says, "and while that's humbling, and frustrating, it's all right. The Benedictines, more than any other people I know, insist that there is time in each day for prayer, for work, for study, and for play. Liturgical time is essentially poetic time, oriented toward process rather than productivity, willing to wait attentively in stillness rather than

always pushing to 'get the job done.' Living at St. John's, I was surprised to discover how much the monastic world was giving me a new perspective on many aspects of my life, not only time, but marriage, family, living in a small town, clothing…"[7]

Most of us will never participate in the monastic life formally. But each one of us can acquire and practice the attitudes and disciplines which lead to being "at home" in the "Present Moment," for the monastic life has much to teach us. I have learned much from the work by Brother David Steindl-Rast entitled *A Listening Heart*, from which I will later be quoting generously.

*The Perspective of the Moment.* This involves developing a meaningful perspective on this gift we call time. It is to appreciate the profound significance of spiritual movements within the banal of each day, as well as the mountain-top experiences. You may have heard the expression that a person was "so heavenly minded, that he was no earthly good," which reminds each of us of the value of a balance in devotion and action. But there needs to be an attentiveness to our moments in time; a perspective of God's presence sanctifying the moment, so that we may consecrate the moment…transforming barren land into holy ground.

In the "Present Moment," time moves more slowly as we become more attentive to spiritual presence. Ann Voskamp[8] describes it this way (I quote selections at length):

> Time is a relentless river. It rages on, a respecter of no one. And this, this is the only way to slow time: When I fully enter time's swift current, enter into the current moment with the weight of all my attention, I slow the torrent with the weight of me all here.
>
> And blind eyes see: It's this sleuthing for the glory that slows a life gloriously…: Giving

thanks for one thousand things is ultimately an invitation to slow time down with weight of full attention. In this space of time and sphere, I am attentive, aware, accepting the whole of the moment, weighing it down with me all here.

Thank God for the time, and very God enters that time, presence hallowing it. True, this, full attention slows time and I live the full of the moment, right to outer edges. But there's more. I awake to I AM here. When I'm present, I meet I AM, the very presence of a present God. In His embrace, time loses all sense of speed and stress and space and stands so still and … holy.

Thanksgiving makes time…
Give thanks …slow time down with all your attention—and your basket of not-enough-time multiplies into more than enough time…
The real problem of life is never a lack of time…
The real problem of life—in my life—is lack of thanksgiving…
Thanksgiving creates abundance; and the miracle of multiplying happens when I give thanks—take the just one loaf, say it is enough, and give thanks—and He miraculously makes it more than enough…
I redeem time from neglect and apathy and inattentiveness when I swell with thanks and weigh the moment down and it's giving thanks to God for this moment that multiplies the moments, time made enough…

*The Attitude of the Moment* is to develop a sensitivity and awareness of spiritual movements within our daily lives. It is to develop our senses to appreciate and enjoy the gifts of each day with gratefulness. Steindl-Rast reminds us that perception begins with spiritual insight and spiritual listening through the attitudes of openness and surrender:

*Spiritual Insight*

> The path to God starts at the gates of perception…
> Most people's gates of perception creak on rusty hinges. How much of the splendor of life is wasted on us because we plod along half-blind, half-deaf, with all our senses throttled, and numbed by habituation.[9]
>
> Wakeful attention makes us aware of facts we had overlooked in a more superficial contact with reality; the fact, for instance, that in a real sense we become that to which we give ourselves with all our senses.[10]

Steindl-Rast challenges us to practice what he calls the *"custody of the eyes"* in order to reap *"the harvest of the quiet eye."* Taken literally, it means guarding our eyes from sights which distract or distort; those which are illusory to genuine spiritual meaning. He states it this way: *"the goal of media fasting is not to see less, but rather to look at less so as to see more."*[11]

Furthermore, he suggests that a person use the same attentiveness as one uses for spiritual reading, or the monastic practice of *lectio divina*, to envision the true character of that which is observed, be it a text, object, or person.

> What makes it sacred is not what, but how we read. What matters is a quiet, unencumbered mind that allows blessing to rise from the page, "and through the eye correct the heart" (David Garrick, 1717-1779). In fact, this kind of read-

ing is not restricted to books…With this attitude we need also to read "the signs of the times" (Matthew 16:3).[12]

When we learn to look through the eye, we will be able to "look through" in still another sense: to look through surface appearances to the heart of people and to the core of things and events. We will see what needs to be done. When we see signals for action, and—most important—respond, then and only then will blessing flow not only in through our eyes, but also out into the world.[13]

*Spiritual Listening*

Steindl-Rast continues with the following notes on the importance of "spiritual listening":

> How can we expect to hear in all things God's voice of silence, unless we stop producing a din that drowns out silence?[14]

> [T]rue listening takes all of you. It might not seem difficult to give ourselves to the rapture of beauty. Yet, out of it emerges a Presence, a Voice, name it as you wish, that goes beyond aesthetics, and makes existential demands: "You must change…"[15]

> There is, however, an aspect of ascetic obedience—its most important one—…obedience listens to the Voice within the voices…
> To distinguish the genuine voice from distracting voices takes practice. Guidance comes to the obedient heart from the heart of reality

> itself, as we face it with trust and courage and wide open senses.[16]

> ...in a spirituality faithful to Jesus Christ, sensuousness is not suspect but sacred. A listening heart recognizes in the throbbing of reality pulsating against all our senses the heartbeat of Divine life at the core of all that is real.[17]

*The Ownership of the Moment* means responsibility and action, setting aside time.

Like God parting the Red Sea for the Israelites to pass safely on dry land from bondage toward the Promised Land; we must part *chronos* time in order to provide the space for *kairos* to be appreciated. We must set aside the time for solitude and silence in which to become surrendered in a spirit of gratitude and obedience, so that God's presence may be revealed and His will be done. The work of the Present Moment can then call us to responsive actions of grace and compassion.

*The Dance of Gratitude and Obedience*

Lastly, Brother David Steindl-Rast describes his vision of our responsive actions that are intimately tied to both gratitude and obedience.

> Alert responsiveness is the essence not only of gratefulness but also of obedience. Obedience? We do not normally pay attention to the fact that obedience and gratefulness are simply two faces of the same coin. Response is the key word that links the two. Both gratefulness and obedience are essentially response, the human heart's response to the heart of reality. When we realize that everything in this given world is a gift,

the heart's fitting response is gratefulness. And when we realize that through everything in life "God speaks" to us, the fitting, the wholehearted response is obedience.

Obedience in the full sense is a mature human response: the heart's willing reply to the call of a given moment.

If our gratefulness is genuine it will be obedient...In obedient gratefulness we listen to reality more than to our wishful thinking; we keep our eyes on the Giver more than on the gift. In turn, if our obedience is genuine it will be grateful...[18]

*The Work of the Moment*: Action

The dance of gratitude and obedience invariably calls for an action of spiritual response.
Actions:

- Awaken with gratitude in your heart. May your first thoughts be "Thank you, Lord" for the rest of the past night and the promise of another day.
- Reflect upon your experience of "Being" today; before jumping into your tasks of "Doing."
- Reflect upon being open to the spiritual movements (those moments of *kairos* time) in the Present Moments that present themselves to you.
- Before checking your cell phone or computer for messages and news, stay unconnected for at least the first thirty minutes of each day. Use the time for personal reflection and prayer instead.
- Consider developing the habit of taking a spiritual word, a song (psalm), and a gift (an act of kindness) into each day as a means of spiritually grounding oneself.

- "Unplug" from the busyness of the day for a few restoring moments of solitude and silence, providing the opportunity to prayerfully perceive the gentle whisper of the Spirit's voice.
- At the close of each day, consider an event or person to hold to the light of spiritual insight, and reflect what opportunities or needs they may have. Say a word of prayer for them…practice empathy and compassion as an evening closure for each day.

Prayer of the Present Moment

The secret of life is quite simply to live it. The present moment holds inexhaustible richness. Attentiveness is the key to living profoundly. This depth is not confined to an esoteric sphere, but is at the heart of the daily round—precisely in its ordinariness.[19](A Carthusian, 99)

---

[1] See contrast between *chronos* and *kairos* under "Season," *Vines Complete Expository Dictionary of Old and New Testament Words*. Edited by W. E. Vine, Merrill F. Unger, William White Jr. (Nashville: Thomas Nelson Publisher, 1985), 554.

[2] Ibid, 554.

[3] Gwendolyn Brooks (source unknown), quoted in Joyce Rupp, *Out of the Ordinary* (Notre Dame, Indiana: Ave Maria Press, 2000), 204.

[4] Jean-Pierre de Caussade, *The Sacrament of the Present Moment*, trans. by Kitty Muggeridge (HarperSanFrancisco, 1989), xiii.

[5] From *A Listening Heart: The Spirituality of Sacred Sensuousness* by Brother David Steindl-Rast, 15. Copyright © 1999. Reprinted by permission of The Permissions Company, LLC, on behalf of The Crossroad Publishing Company, Inc., crossroadpublishing.com.

[6] Ibid, 47.

## SPIRITUAL AWARENESS

[7] Excerpt from *The Cloister Walk* by Kathleen Norris, preface, xix, copyright © 1996 by Kathleen Norris. Used by permission of Riverhead, an imprint of Penguin Publishing Group, a division of Penguin Random House LLC. All rights reserved.

[8] Taken from *One Thousand Gifts* by Ann Voskamp, 68, 69, 70, 72. Copyright © 2011 by Ann Voskamp. Used by permission of Zondervan. www.zondervan.com.

[9] From *A Listening Heart: The Spirituality of Sacred Sensuousness* by Brother David Steindl-Rast, 27. Copyright © 1999. Reprinted by permission of The Permissions Company, LLC, on behalf of The Crossroad Publishing Company, Inc., crossroadpublishing.com.

[10] Ibid., 42.
[11] Ibid., 61.
[12] Ibid., 63.
[13] Ibid., 63.
[14] Ibid., 66.
[15] Ibid., 39.
[16] Ibid., 51–52.
[17] Ibid., 45.
[18] Ibid., 51.
[19] Quoted in "*Seeds of the Spirit.*" Edited by Richard H. Bell (Louisville, KY: Westminster John Knox Press, 1995), 37.

# 8

## *Practicing Praxis*
## *Intentionality, Affirmation, Choice*

As the "Work of the Moment" calls us to action, I am reminded of one of my favorite Southern expressions, "I'm afixin' to…" It generally means one is "thinkin'" about doing something or other, but probably not doing so very soon, if at all. Yet it gives the impression that the action is under some kind of consideration, for a while anyway.

We use this notion frequently in our spiritual lives as well. The concept of a decision and action within the work of the Present Moment may be interesting and challenging, but perhaps a little bit too "close to home" for actual daily living.

But truth be told, this is the easy way out of action; a procrastination in disguise. Not surprisingly, most of us are quite good at this. Unrecognized amidst the clamor of "Not enough time," "Sometime," "I really ought to," lie the still quiet moments of spiritual participation for which we were intended. These are the moments of actualization, in the Work of the Present Moment, that allow us to grow as genuine human beings as well as destined spiritual beings. It is in these opportune and formative moments, shaped by our subsequent choices, that we fashion the path of our spiritual authenticity. For this reason much attention has been spent in this discussion upon developing an awareness of the spiritual significance of both the attitudes and Work of the Present Moment, these moments of *kairos* time.

However, to leave this insight to apprehension only would be a great disservice. For in this glimpse of time, these moments of *Kairos* time, the Present Moment is a Beckoning…a clarion call for choice and action. It is not a request "to reckon" or to consider. Rather it is a demand for decisive action. William Barclay, in his commentary on *The Gospel of John* challenges us:

> "How a person responds to an essential truth or value is a judgment upon that person. Truth confronts a person's values…and demands a response"[1] (Barclay, *The Gospel of John*).

Herein lies one's choice.

## CHOICES[2] AND DECISIONS

Man forever stands at the crossroads of impending decision. Choice beckons a person this way or that, often with little regard or reflection upon the consequences which accompany that decision. Sometimes it is a matter of simply not being able to see into the forest deeply enough; at other times, it may be because one's desire obscures the path of insight that lies ahead.

Few poems portray this imagery more poignantly that Robert Frost's "The Road Not Taken."

The Road Not Taken
by Robert Frost

Two roads diverged in a yellow wood,
And sorry I could not travel both
And be one traveler, long I stood
And looked down one as far as I could
To where it bent in the undergrowth;
Then took the other, as just as fair,
And having perhaps the better claim,
Because it was grassy and wanted wear;
Though as for that the passing there
Had worn them really about the same,

## PRACTICING PRAXIS: INTENTIONALITY, AFFIRMATION, CHOICE

> And both that morning equally lay
> In leaves no step had trodden black.
> Oh, I kept the first for another day!
> Yet knowing how way leads on to way,
> I doubted if I should ever come back.
> I shall be telling this with a sigh
> Somewhere ages and ages hence:
> Two roads diverged in a wood, and I-
> I took the one less traveled by,
> And that has made all the difference.[3]

Gently reflective, Frost considers the uncertainty of choice...its mystery and its permanence. Certainly, there are the "little choices" of tastes and preference, but there are also irretrievable decisions, made within the moment at the crossroads, which will define our future, and likely the futures of others as well. Those choices will be the ones to make "all the difference."

Yet a word of caution. It is to be remembered that these moments of decision cannot be individually created or contrived. Rather, they are Divine moments given to us as gifts. Our role is only to be open and surrendered in order to properly receive those gifts. It is to be attentive to spiritual movements, and to act in spiritual obedience to them with a spirit of gratitude.

## PREPARING THE HEART

We have discussed the preparing of the heart extensively in the previous chapters on humility, openness, surrender, sensitivity, awareness...so we will not reiterate those concepts again here. Suffice it to say that they are fundamental and essential to any meaningful spiritual encounter with which the Lord blesses us. However, this chapter is to focus on the concepts of intentionality and affirmation as they relate to our responsiveness of choice and action. Spiritual exercises have long been used to help one prepare the heart and will for a heightened sense of spiritual sensitivity and service. A few examples are listed here, which are more completely discussed in Appendix I:

## SPIRITUAL AWARENESS

*Spiritual Awareness Activities:* These are not meant to be "formulas" or "requirements," but rather "tools" for spiritual growth. They *sensitize* the soul for spiritual communion and insight. They serve as "preludes" to our lives of Christian service.

1. Spiritual exercises of St. Ignatius
2. *Spiritual Disciplines* by Richard Foster
3. *Disciplines of the Spirit* by Dallas Willard
4. Lectio Divina
5. *Doors into Prayer* by Emilie Griffin
6. "Daily Rule"
7. Pray a Psalm
8. Write a Psalm
9. Pray scriptural phrases—see *Imitation of Christ* by Thomas a'Kempis as an example
10. Practice seeing the "spiritual content" of events and people
11. Honor the Sabbath day, and create "Sabbath moments" throughout the week
12. *Practicing the Presence of God* by Jan Johnson
13. "A Word, A Prayer, A Gift"
14. "Spiritual investing in the lives of others"—making spiritual "deposits" of hope and encouragement in the lives of others
15. Practicing "No Little People"—none should be overlooked or slighted.
16. Meditating on the Westminster or Heidelberg Catechism
17. Meditate on an element of the Lord's prayer
18. Meditate on an element of the Ten Commandments
19. Francis Schaeffer—read a Proverb in the morning and Psalm at night to "bookend" his day
20. "Open" and "Close" your day with the Lord—Psalm 3/ Psalm 4
21. Write a "life prayer"
22. Meditate on a portion of the Sermon on the Mount each day and the thoughts it represents.

## PRACTICING PRAXIS: INTENTIONALITY, AFFIRMATION, CHOICE

## PREPARING THE WILL

One's will is a "cantankerous" fellow…strong and stubborn; always wanting to have his way. Like a bucking bronco, he will jump and kick in order to toss off any attempt to control his desires. As in so many things, there is the good and the bad of such. Certainly, a firm and steady will is essential to one's well-being and proper decision-making and conduct. Efforts to control this wild and willful part of oneself can be a challenge, but not to do so, only leads to more rebellion and disruption. Still as one moves from the willful and spontaneous outbursts of childhood into the arena of adulthood, one may possibly discover a bridled and saddled stallion, standing solidly, ready for a ride by a faithful friend. That certainly is not to imply a suppression or stifling of the will's innate desires for expression or creativity or spontaneity. It is merely a redirection of those wonderful qualities in a beneficial direction. For in doing so, we get where we need to go.

The manner in which we do so is to practice the discipline of intentionality. Intentionality is the process in which we purposefully and consistently develop the focus of intended action. It is more than "a fixin' to." It is a sincere and deliberate attempt to focus our attentions toward a specific person or state of affairs. We do so through the process of choice. We "choose" to act rather than to delay, to affirm rather than degrade, to obey rather than rebel, to seek out rather than hide away, to give rather than to take, to believe rather than to deny. We encounter these choices every moment of every day. Herein lies the work of taming our wills in order to purposefully engage with one another in a meaningful and beneficial manner.

Intentionality is a process. A process that involves first developing our priorities and goals. It involves exercising some restraint on our distractions and desires in an attempt to arrive at a measure of focus upon those priorities we have chosen. As a corollary, though, this also involves allowing our awareness to appreciate the spontaneous and serendipitous openings of need that we encounter in the lives of others in a way that we can respond with acts of compassion. We can never allow ourselves to become so narrowly focused on our priorities that we neglect the Present Moment's intrusions into time, creating *kairos* time of spiritual opportunity and actualization. This discernment is refined and matured as a person establishes the habit of consciously choosing to view the events and persons of encounter in a spiritual light. The repeated and consistent process of spiritual perception heightens our awareness of spiritual movements both within our personal priorities, and also beyond them. As a process, this journey is never over. Sometimes it can be a rough ride through unintended and pathless forests. At others, it can open into meadows of clarity and assurance.

## PURE INTENTIONS: RIGHT VS. SIMPLE INTENTIONS

From time to time it may be helpful for one to take a step back from one's intentions to view the motivations contained within them. A person's motivations for intending an action can be drawn from a crowded basket. Some motivations may seem innocent or benevolent enough, only to be rooted in a hidden shadow of pride or conceit. One's ego thrives on attention and recognition, the lack of which may lead to an attitude of displeasure or irritation. For most people, it can be quite challenging not to at least have some "ownership" in the result of a benevolent act. Thomas Merton describes this by making these distinctions in our intentions. First, he describes the difference between "impure" and "pure intentions."

Impure Intentions

> An impure intention is one that yields to the will of God while retaining a preference for my own will. It divides my will from His will. It gives me a choice between two advantages: one in doing His will and one in doing my own. An impure intention is imprudent, because it weighs truth in the balance against illusion; it chooses between a real and an apparent good as if they were equal.[4]

Pure Intentions

> "A pure intention sees that the will of God is always good…
> Only a pure intention can be clear-sighted and prudent."[5]

Thomas Merton then goes on to further distinguish the forms of Pure Intention: those of "right intentions" and "those of "simple intentions"; two concepts that he attributes to Johannes Tauler.

> When we have a right intention, our intention is pure. We seek to do God's will with a supernatural motive. We mean to please Him. But in doing so we still consider the work and ourselves apart from God and outside Him. Our intention is directed chiefly upon the work to be done. When the work is done, we rest in its accomplishment, and hope for a reward from God.
> But when we have a simple intention, we are less occupied with the thing to be done. We do all that we do not only for God but so to speak in Him. We are more aware of Him who works in us than of ourselves or of our work…[6]

> [T]he man of simple intention works in an atmosphere of prayer: that is to say he is recollected. His spiritual reserves are not all poured out into his work, but stored where they belong, in the depths of his being, with his God. He is detached from his work and from its results. Only a man who works purely for God can at the same time do a very good job and leave the results of the job to God alone.[7]

With a right intention, you quietly face the risk of losing the fruit of your work. With a simple intention you renounce the fruit before you even begin. You no longer even expect it. Only at this price can your work also become a prayer.[8]

Simple intention is a Divine medicine, a balm that soothes the powers of our soul wounded by inordinate self-expression...for a simple intention manifests the presence and action of Christ in our hearts. It makes us His perfect instruments, and transforms us into His likeness, filling our whole lives with His gentleness and His strength and His purity and His prayer and His silence.
Whatever is offered to God with a right intention is acceptable to Him.
Whatever is offered to God with a simple intention is not only accepted by Him by reason of our good will, but is pleasing to Him in itself. It is a good and perfect work, performed entirely by His love. It draws its perfection not from our poor efforts alone but from His mercy which has made them rich. In giving the Lord the works of a right intention I can be sure that I am giving Him what is not bad. But in offering Him the works of a simple intention I am giving Him what is best. And beyond all that I can give Him or do for Him, I rest and take my joy in His glory.[9]

Whether one can make such distinctions between our intentions can be argued, but nonetheless, the point to be made is that pride can easily meld within one's motivations for doing even Christian acts of charitable service. Hidden within one's efforts can remain the desire to make the work one's own, to be designed and accomplished according to one's personal plan and desired result. And of course, a little reward of acknowledgment would be nice as well. Perhaps a simpler way of examining one's motivations is found in the letter to the Philippians, where Paul shares his view of guarding our hearts and minds from pride of self.

> Let your gentle spirit be known to all men. The Lord is near. Be anxious for nothing, but in everything by prayer and supplication with thanksgiving let your requests be made known to God. And the peace of God, which surpasses all comprehension, will guard your hearts and your minds in Christ Jesus. Finally, brethren, whatever is true, whatever is honorable, whatever is right, whatever is pure, whatever is lovely, whatever is of good repute, if there is any excellence and if anything worthy of praise, dwell on these things. The things you have learned and received and heard and seen in me, practice these things, and the God of peace will be with you. (Philippians 4:4–9 NASB)

## DISCOVERING NEED: AFFIRMING VALUE

In some ways intentionality can be viewed as prospecting… looking for the golden nuggets of opportunity within the cold hard stone of life. It requires a persistence of inspection and the insight of awareness to discover those persons of great need. It requires a discernment to cast aside the "fool's gold" of our superficiality from that of the genuine. Like the tough miner, we slowly chip away at the rough moments of life, laboring hopefully, inspecting attentively, discerning the true from the false, seeking to impart some value amidst the worthless debris of life.

This is not seeking for value in a material sense or one which is attached to appearance or prestige. Instead it is an attentiveness to those who are in need…of a smile, of a chat, or of a miracle. It

# SPIRITUAL AWARENESS

is a search mission as such, looking to reconnect and to reaffirm. Sometimes it will be with those with whom we are familiar; at other times not. But it will always be a search for the lost sheep, the lost coin, or the wayward son (Luke 15).

The gem discovered within intentionality is that of an opportunity to affirm another. Affirming means "equipping another" with understanding, compassion, and hope. While affirmation has to do with an *acknowledgment* of value; it also involves *equipping* and *actualizing* value in the life of another person. Intentionality means purposefully choosing to respond with empathy and compassion to the spiritual movements of this "Work of the Present Moment" in a manner which gives the gift of appreciation and value to a life. It becomes a mission of *restoration*.

## THE LANGUAGE OF AFFIRMATION

- You know, I really appreciate…
- What can I do to "make your day?"
- Do you know what makes you so special?
- Comment on a facial characteristic: "I love your dimples." "You have such pretty hair."
- Compliment a "checkout" person at the grocery or retail store, or wait staff at a restaurant regarding their effort or good service.
- Tell a spouse or child how much you love them, and add a compliment.
- "Listen" as another speaks; be attentive; maintain eye contact.

## ACTS OF KINDNESS

- Create a smile in another.
- Send a handwritten friendship note.
- Teach a skill.
- Share a favorite song, poem or story.
- Establish a tradition of anonymous giving.

## PRACTICING PRAXIS: INTENTIONALITY, AFFIRMATION, CHOICE

- Read a child a story and discuss its meaning.
- Bake some bread or cookies for someone.
- Send a favorite book to someone as a gift.
- Send a gift (anonymously?) with a prayer note enclosed.
- Practice gifting undergirded with a prayer.
- Send a comfort note to a person who has lost a loved one within the past year (especially at holiday time, and on dates of previous anniversaries and birthdays).
- Send a Christmas card in July—with a handwritten prayer and note.
- Volunteer to work in a soup kitchen or homeless shelter.
- Spend an afternoon in a portion of your city of the underprivileged and underserved to observe their lives and needs. Respond in some tangible way.
- Volunteer to tutor a child.
- Volunteer to mentor a young married couple.
- Practice "gifting"—simple acts of kindness.

But sometimes the will remains untamed. There are times that I feel the Spirit's gentle nudge to send a card, or make a call, or give a "gift," and I find myself suppressing that impression… perhaps out of distraction or laziness, perhaps out of apathy or rebellion. Nonetheless, I find those gentle nudges keep returning ever more frequently and forcefully until I ultimately surrender to His will, and I am reminded, once again, of the importance of *listening* and *responding*.

It should be noted that some of these acts of kindness require only a brief commitment of time or energy; while others require a longer period of commitment when in the service of tutoring, or of ministering to a struggling young couple. One is confronted with the question, "How much can I give within my frenzied life?"

Most of us raised in the church can recall a Sunday School teacher who had been teaching the second grade boys class for thirty years…and probably loved every (almost?) moment of it. To many, this exemplified the "gold standard" of Christian service, both by means of its consistency and its longevity. Those were the folks others respected, and those upon whom the church relied, whether as ushers, teachers, or song leaders. Those are who I will call the "Lifers." Sincere and devout, they sacrificially, yet joyfully gave time and energy for the benefit of Christ's kingdom.

But in truth, there are others of us, whom I will refer to as the "Timid." Likewise sincere and devout but afraid of the "Five Year Contract." Our thinking goes something like this. Once I get started (ushering, teaching, singing) they (church leaders) will want me to do it all the time. I'll get locked into it for five years or more, and if I decide to quit, I'll be regarded as a "lukewarm" Christian. No, it's better if I not get started at all. And we know how to tactfully back away from service with the well-worn phrases: "It's not my thing." "I'm no good with people." "I'll think about it. Maybe, in the future." Sadly, fear of service expectations torpedoes any further involvement.

Nonetheless, there is hope for those of us who are timid of tenure! Intentionality does not mean a ten-year indenture. Practicing praxis does not compel prolonged church positions. But our faith does demand that we serve others, and that can be done in all sorts of ways. Keep in mind that the New Testament church was much different than that which we are accustomed to today.

In this regard, a certain parable comes to mind in reference to caring for one another, for that is a mission for each one of us, is it not? Once a Jew well-versed in the law asked Jesus, *"What shall I do to inherit eternal life?"* Jesus answered, *"What is written in the Law?"* To which the man responded, *"You shall love the Lord your God with all your heart and with all your soul, and with all your strength, and with all your mind; and your neighbor as yourself."* Jesus said to him, *"You have answered correctly, do this and you will live."* Then the lawyer asked Jesus further, *"And who is my neighbor?"* (Luke 10:25–29 NASB)

In response, Jesus then launches into the Parable of the Good Samaritan (Luke 10:30–37 NASB). A man was beaten, robbed, and left upon the rocky road from Jerusalem to Jericho. A priest and Levite both passed by without offering any help. A Samaritan traveler found the man, and *"felt compassion"* for him, dressed his wounds, took him to an inn, and paid for his care until he had recovered. Jesus then asked the lawyer, *"Which of these three proved to be a neighbor to the man who fell into the robbers' hands?"* To which the lawyer responded, *"The one who showed mercy toward him."* The Jesus said, *"Go and do the same."*

Many commentators, and many sermons have described the value of this Parable of the Good Samaritan. But in the context of this treatise on the intentionality of service, only several of the ones most germane will be mentioned.

- No mention is made of the Good Samaritan's name, yet he was compassionate in the face of need. He cared for the beaten man personally, generously, and without acknowledgment or reward. He gave anonymously. We can all "do the same."
- The Good Samaritan was not confined by rigid, predefined principles for giving or serving. He responded spontaneously and immediately to the needs of another in the moment of decision. We can all "do the same."
- Though undoubtedly ostracized as a Samaritan, one of a different culture, he considered the beaten man a "fellow traveler" despite those differences in culture, and treated him with respect and "mercy." We can all "do the same."

So I would maintain, as admirable as a long-term commitment to a specific act of Christian service may be; there is also the oft-neglected aspect of Christian service that is spontaneous and unconditional and anonymously given. This is certainly not to imply that one type of service or gifting is in any way "better" than another. However, it is an appeal to allow the Holy Spirit to move us according to the Lord's will. For at one time the Spirit may lead us to a brief, but powerful act of benevolence, and at another, the Spirit may lead us to make a sacrificial long-term commitment to His cause. Of additional note is to consider the freeing effect that an attitude within a Christian community free from others' "expectations" may have. As one ponders these thoughts, it may sometimes be helpful to envision the following possibilities:

1. Do "something"—even though it may be of a more limited capacity, it is to give at least a morsel of goodness to another; it is better than nothing at all. God will still use it for His purpose and His glory: Remember Jesus taking the offered five loaves and two fish, and having blessed them, fed the five thousand? (Matthew 14:14ff)
2. This spontaneous and often times serendipitous act may lead one to another area of service of which you are currently unaware, or other persons of need, whom you may be able to serve in a different manner.
3. By starting with a spontaneous act of compassion, it may blossom into an eventual fulfilling and fruitful long-term commitment in your walk with Jesus.

Only our fear holds us back. Practice freedom in the Spirit. Have the courage to step outside the expectations of others, and into the realm of Spirit-guided compassion for others. Allow Jesus to take what you can give, and to bless it, and to feed the masses with His Love for them.

One's fruitful service is a reflection of obedience to God. Words are not enough to claim our ultimate glory. Instead, it is our works of obedience that is the proof of our love for God. William Barclay asks, "Do we confess God with our lips, but deny Him with our lives?"[10]

In the "Work of the Present Moment" we are offered choices which demand a decision. Obedience, Action, Compassion, Encouragement, Generosity, Sacrifice. We encounter these choices every moment of every day. Herein lies the work of taming our wills so that we may affirm and encourage others through obedient actions of compassion and generosity.

Though our choices may be imperfect, they can always be sincere.

Though our views may be shortsighted, they can always be attentive.

Though our insights may be incomplete, they can always be genuine.

Though I am fearful; I can always give a "morsel."

In this regard I am reminded of one of my favorite passages of Scripture found in 1 Kings 17:10–16 (NASB). A great drought and severe famine had covered the land. And as Elijah is hiding in the desert from Ahab, God calls to him and tells him to go to Zarephath (which means "place of refinement") where God has provided a poor widow to care for him.

> So he arose and went to Zarephath, and when he came to the gate of the city, behold, a widow was there gathering sticks; and he called to her and said, "Please get me a little water in a jar, that I may drink." And as she was going to get it, he called to her and said, "Please bring me a piece of bread in your hand." But she said, "As the LORD your God lives, I have no bread, only a handful of flour in the bowl and a little oil in the jar; and behold, I am gathering a few sticks that I may go in and prepare for me and my son, that we may eat it and die."
>
> Then Elijah said to her, "Do not fear; go, do as you have said, but make me a little bread cake from it first and bring it out to me, and afterward you may make one for yourself and for your son. For thus says the LORD God of Israel, 'The bowl of flour shall not be exhausted, nor shall the jar of oil be empty, until the day that the LORD sends rain on the face of the earth.'"
>
> So she went and did according to the word of Elijah, and she and he and her household ate for many days. The bowl of flour was not exhausted nor did the jar of oil become empty, according to the word of the LORD which He spoke through Elijah.

This is a lesson in selfless giving...and God's provision for His people in the midst of suffering. But it is also a lesson in how God uses the simple and seemingly insignificant, when blessed, to have life-changing and life-sustaining results. To further underscore this profound truth, later in the chapter the widow's son dies from a sickness, and then, after Elijah offers up the widow's deceased child in prayer to God, the child's life is restored. What a profound truth... life-changing, life sustaining, life restoring...answers to life, "miracles" even, found in the "morsels" that we offer to God for His blessing and for His glory.

*Knowing the Will of God in Facing Choices and Making Decisions*

When discussing the topic of choices, invariably the question of "God's will" comes up. How do I know what God's will is for this decision I face? What if I make the wrong decision? Perhaps we are too naïve? Some would call this the "dot" concept of understanding God's will as it relates to a person's decision. Within that mindset our challenge is to find the "right dot" amongst the myriad of possibilities of choice, and hope that it is the one that God wanted us to make. This only leads to a frustrating and unhealthy preoccupation of decision-making.

Instead, it may be more helpful to consider our decision-making when we are faced with multiple choices as more like a circuit board. If our motivation or intention is "pure" (Merton's "right or simple"), it will truly become the Lord's work. This task or journey may follow various paths, but if it is offered with sincere intentions, the Lord will accomplish His will even despite our human limitations. Do we truly believe that the Eternal Godhead is limited by providing only one avenue of personal response in order for us to advance toward spiritual intimacy and fulfillment?

In our human finiteness, when faced with spiritual uncertainty, it is in our nature to search for the one true path to spiritual fulfillment. But true spirituality does not work this way. Eternity and infinity do not follow a solitary path. It is not limited by time, place, or our perceptions. Instead, it provides multiple avenues of insight and action that can fulfill the spiritual potential of the moment. Think again of it as a circuit board… from beginning to end…with multiple, but not all, circuits leading to fulfillment. On which circuit we find ourselves does not really matter if that circuit is open to the Spirit's leading. For then the energy flows through the course of greatest power to enlightenment. Do not stress. It is not to us to decide a specific course, only to strive forward and allow the Holy Spirit to work in our lives to direct our paths in such a way leading toward spiritual discernment and fulfillment.

*The Greatest Choice One Will Make*

    Yet there is an even greater decision that each one of us is called to make. This is a decision of monumental significance, with eternal consequences. It is a choice of only one right answer. For what we do with Jesus, who we believe He is, determines our spiritual destiny for all eternity. Think of Jesus as the motherboard upon which all circuits run. For this decision, there are only two possible choices, that of "yes" or that of "no."

    The whole measure of intentionality and praxis rests upon what authority to whom one will yield. It revolves around the question Jesus asked of Peter. *"But who do you say that I am?"* (Matthew 16:15 NASB) And He is still asking each one of us that same question today. It is a matter of belief in the Christ, the Son of the Living God as Lord and Savior.

    So we have had quite a journey. Having tamed the wildness of our will in order to intentionally affirm and equip others, and traversed the crossroads of decision guided by obedient love, we now find ourselves standing upon a promontory called Belief.

1. William Barclay, *The Gospel of John*, revised edition (Philadelphia: Westminster Press, 1975).
2. Any discussion of the concept of choice soon culminates in the contrasting opinions regarding man's free will as opposed to that of a deterministic mindset. Because this debate has not been resolved by philosophers in thousands of pages over hundreds of years, I will forego an extensive discussion of this unresolved issue here. Suffice it to say that I am of the "free will" category, and for the sake of this treatise, my comments will reflect that perspective.
3. Robert Frost, 1915. Public domain
4. Excerpts from *No Man Is an Island* by Thomas Merton, 54. Copyright © 1955 by The Abbey of Our Lady of Gethsemani and renewed 1983 by the Trustees of the Merton Legacy Trust. Reprinted by permission of Houghton Mifflin Harcourt Publishing Company. All rights reserved.
5. Ibid., 55.
6. Ibid., 71.
7. Ibid., 72.
8. Ibid., 74.
9. Ibid., 75–76.
10. William Barclay, unknown source.

# 9

## *Believing the Miraculous Seeing the Unseen*

> Now faith is the assurance of things hoped
> for, the conviction of things not seen.
> —Hebrews 11:1 (NASB)

> Things which eye has not seen
> and ear has not heard
> And which have not entered the heart of man,
> All that God has prepared for
> those who love Him.
> —1 Corinthians 2:9 (NASB)

### GOLDEN CALF OR BURNING BUSH?

People tend to believe many things that are out of the ordinary. There are those who believe that there is spiritual power in crystals, that flying saucers observe our Earth, that a rabbit's foot will bring you good luck... and of course, there are the Ouija boards and "ghosts." But these beliefs are dwarfed in comparison to our beliefs in anti-aging creams, diet pills, and game-day superstitions. Oh, and just one more pull on the slot machine will win that thousand-dollar jackpot! Though we have no way of confirming these convictions, they are easy enough for us to believe. Man's gullibility is without bounds. People choose to believe in the unseen all the time, but refuse to believe in God.

To believe in something extraordinary like God without His visibility seems to be a bit of a stretch. We would prefer to have a visible god of our own making. The Israelites felt that way... so they constructed a golden calf [Exodus 32:1–6]. They fell into idolatry because they wanted a god that they could see and understand, a god they could make which was malleable and fashioned by their own desires and perceptions. In the history of nations there tends to be gods of all kinds, in various shapes and character. Ones that are immaterial, others tangible, some that are fierce, others fertile, benevolent ones, evil ones, and on and on it goes. Every culture it seems shapes their home-grown concepts of reality into the form of an image that can be worshipped. So how is our God, Jehovah, any different?

He is unique in that He reveals His presence and His character in the "miraculous." But we choose not to see. Rather than the burning bush, we choose to worship the golden calf.

> Son of man, you live in the midst of the rebellious house, who have eyes to see but do not see, ears to hear but do not hear, for they are a rebellious house. (Ezekiel 12:2 NASB)

> Now hear this, O foolish and senseless people, who have eyes but do not see, who have ears but do not hear. (Jeremiah 5:21 NASB)

"*Have eyes but cannot see, have ears but do not hear.*" What is really being said is that people can physically see and physically hear, but do not perceive...do not understand...do not comprehend the reality of what is before them. But it's not because God does not reveal Himself to His people. It is because of the blindness caused by idolatry.

The Israelites had a long history of seeing but not perceiving even before they built the golden calf. Within a lifetime God revealed himself to Moses in a burning bush, demonstrated His miracles in the form of Aaron's rod, gave Pharaoh a lesson of the ten plagues, delivered the Israelites on dry land between huge waves of the Red Sea, destroyed the pursuing Egyptian army as He closed the sea… miraculous deeds of Jehovah Mephalte (the Lord our Deliverer). Still, while Moses was later receiving the Law upon Mount Sinai, the Israelites became restless for a god that they could see. They were tired of waiting on Moses (and Jehovah) and wanted a god to "go before" them. So they built one. Out of gold, this god could easily be fashioned and molded to their own design and satisfaction. One that didn't talk back or demand commitment to specific laws or principles. One that they could change if they wanted. They really just wanted their own god like we do today. Their idolatry blinded them to the reality of omnipotence as it presented itself to them within the miraculous. They had eyes but they chose not to perceive.

Later in the Israelites' Exodus, God continued to demonstrate Himself miraculously with signs and wonders leading them within the Shekinah cloud and pillar of fire, His provision of manna for their sustenance in the desert, deliverance from the Canaanites, and establishing the Promised Land flowing with milk and honey. Still Israel clung to her idols. (See first Battle of Ai, Joshua 7 and 8—Achan's sin of idolatry.)

It's easy to criticize the Israelites from our place in history. One is always more wise looking at the past from the promontory of the present. But what Divine miracles are before us today that we do not truly perceive? Do we not cling also to idols for security and comfort, rather than choose to see the spiritual within the secular?

Humanity has been gifted with a tangible, material, four-dimensional world of space and time. Within its predictable movements and form humankind has found a general sense of contentment, for it is in one's nature to find security in that which is familiar, understood and manageable. Moreover, this natural world can be shaped and largely controlled by means of human effort…shelter constructed, sustenance harvested, safety established. Beyond these provisions, a person can discover the fulfillment in relationships, the enjoyment of entertainment, and the means of production. One's senses are stimulated and satisfied on a regular diet of self-gratification. Despite the disparities of benefits within humanity, the "creature" has become well established on this earth.

Yet there remains an often neglected aspect of humanity as "person" having moral capacity and agency and living in a spiritual realm as well. However, the natural world looms large and often draws one's attention away from the spiritual. Our vision is drawn to the immediate and attracted by novelty.

Dallas Willard describes this condition as he shares the difficulty of hearing God's voice amongst the clamor of culture as he describes what he entitles the *"the overwhelming presence of the visible world."*

> The visible world daily bludgeons us with its things and events. ... But instead of shouting and shoving, the spiritual world whispers at us ever so gently. And it appears both at the edges and in the middle of events and things in the so-called real world of the visible...
>
> We are hindered in our progress toward becoming spiritual competent people by how easily we can explain away the movements of God toward us. They go meekly, without much protest. Of course, his day will come, but for now he cooperates with the desires and inclinations that make up our character, as we are gradually becoming the kind of people we will forever be. That should send a chill down our spine.
>
> God wants to be wanted, to be wanted enough that we are ready, predisposed, to find him present with us."[1]

One is reminded in the Book of Acts:

> Go to this people and say, "You will keep on hearing, but will not understand; and you will keep on seeing, but will not perceive; for the

heart of this people has become dull, and with their ears they scarcely hear, and they have closed their eyes; Otherwise they might see with their eyes, and hear with their ears, and understand with their heart and return, and I would heal them." (Acts 28:26–27 NASB)

Yet before the exodus from Egypt is the record of a different response to God's calling and presence within the miraculous. This is the account of Moses tending the flock of his father-in-law Jethro in the sparse desert conditions as a simple shepherd. Having killed an Egyptian overseer and fled, he was hiding in as obscure location as possible, but God encountered him to have a conversation.

It was to be the calling of Moses to lead the people of Israel out of Egyptian bondage, and it was delivered from the confines of a nonconsuming burning bush…the miraculousness of God revealed within the mundane unto a simple shepherd.

Much was disclosed within the conversation between God and man described in Exodus, but several points are worth mentioning here.

- God declares His Holiness.
- God declares His Character.
- God declares His Name.
- God declares His Plan.

As such, God, in a miraculous manner, reveals ultimate spiritual realities within the commonplace experience to a simple person. However, it is to be noted that God chose to do so, only after Moses turned to *see*. "I must turn aside now, and see this marvelous sight." When the Lord saw that he turned aside to look, God called to him, from the midst of the bush and said, 'Moses, Moses.' And he said, 'Here I am'" Exodus 3:3–4 NASB).

Sometimes the biblical account of the Old Testament can seem ancient in time, and that may be so chronologically. But the spiritual truths revealed are timeless and certainly can be applied to our world even today in modern times…if only one chooses to "turn and see."

SPIRITUAL AWARENESS

# THE MIRACULOUS WITHIN THE MODERN: A SPIRITUAL PERSPECTIVE OF FACTUAL INFORMATION

*Spiritual Awareness as Affirming Belief*

Spirituality points, always, beyond: beyond the ordinary, beyond possession, beyond the narrow confines of the self—and above all—beyond expectation. Because "the spiritual" is beyond our control, it is never exactly what we expect.[2]

*The Extra-dimensionality of God*[3]

We live in the spatial three-dimensional world of length, width, and depth, couched within a fourth dimension we call time. Yet we have a notion of God existing beyond the physicality of our three dimensions and the temporality of that of time... within the timelessness of eternity. But somehow we also believe that humankind can relate and live in relationship with Him despite His extra dimensionality. How can this be so?

*The Proposition of Intelligent Design*

A Scientific Perspective

The discipline of physics has long sought an explanation of the universe. From the macro universe of planets and galaxies to the micro universe of subatomic particles, physicists have sought the answers to their many questions of how the universe was formed. What are the material components of our universe, what physical laws does it follow, and how do various forces hold our universe together as it gradually expands? As one examines their efforts, it becomes increasing clear that the more "answers" that are found, a greater number of questions arise. From ever greater complexity of inquiry flows ever greater mystery.

The Holy Grail, if you will, amongst physicists and mathematicians, is to identify and describe a unification view of the various major forces of our universe: gravity, strong nuclear, weak nuclear, and electromagnetic.

This desire has its roots first within Sir Isaac Newton's discovery of gravity. This mysterious force, Sir Isaac Newton discovered, is in some way related to our planet and the surrounding other planets and sun of our solar system. This was, at the time, an astounding discovery. Though he was able to observe and *describe* the existence of gravity, *how* it performed remained a mystery. The answer was left to a later brilliant mind, Albert Einstein. In his identification of general relativity, he described how the movement of our Earth and other planets around the sun moved in a way in which gravity worked within a Space-Time warp. Einstein's discovery of general relativity was a huge jump forward in understanding a force of nature that described with great accuracy the observations of how our macro universe worked. This obviously led to his great notoriety at the time, because this was felt to be a monumental discovery of tremendous significance to an understanding of the universe.

Later, additional forces were discovered. Electromagnetism, and the strong and weak nuclear forces were later identified as even stronger forces which existed in nature. However, there was a problem. The same formula and theory that Einstein used to so accurately describe the gravitational force of the macro cosmos of planets and suns did not seem to work when applied to these micro forces as they related to the atom and its components. There was a stubborn and frustrating disconnect that couldn't be explained or reconciled.

As physicists worked on this problem, quantum theory evolved. This applied more to the micro realm as it related to atoms and specifically protons, neutrons, and electrons. Subatomic particles were identified. And there was the debate between particle and wave theory. All of this led to a great deal of confusion and uncertainty. Nonetheless, quantum theory became recognized as a very precise way of identifying and describing the movements of atomic and subatomic particles. Quantum theory however, contrary to the smooth and structured theory of general relativity brought forth by Einstein to describe the macro cosmos, was a theory that focused on the chaotic and unpredictable realm of subatomic particles. Because of its inherent unpredictability, it could only be described in what the "probability" of subatomic behavior would be. In addition, it was unable to reach outside of the subatomic world and also describe that of the macro cosmos. There still was no unification theory between the macro and micro universe.

Not to be discouraged, physicists have continued to work on this incongruence, and the most recent theory now has been that of "string theory." After years of painstaking calculations, string theorists, mathematically at least, have reconciled the forces of gravity with those of electromagnetism, and the strong and weak nuclear forces. This consists of a theory of extremely tiny strings or loops of vibrating energy that compose the universe.

As before, a further mystery occurred. Their calculations, it was found, were only valid if there existed additional dimensions beyond our four-dimensional world of space and time. For the physicists' calculations supporting string theory to work, there would have to exist a reality of at least six other dimensions. Furthermore, these strings are so tiny, one billionth of a billionth of the size of an atom, that they are unable to be scientifically observed or confirmed by experimentation. So they remain a theory within mystery, which is yet to be resolved.

Could there really be multiple extra dimensions beyond that which we know as height, width, depth, and time? What does that say about the existence of a transcendent God? Can there be any interaction between multiple dimensions outside those of our own? Hugh Ross tells us that man has been specifically designed in such a way that he can only exist within a four-dimensional realm of space and time such as ours.[4] Any other dimensions would have to be much different in physical function because of their required specifications to exist. The current atoms that form our bodies and the material world would not work in other dimensions because of that dimension's necessitated characteristics. Atoms would have to spin in much different directions and paths, which would then make life as we know it to be impossible. Also, changing any one of the nearly two dozen recognized physical constants (i.e., speed of light, gravitational force, etc.) even a miniscule amount, would imbalance our finely tuned cosmos into a realm of chaos and uninhabitability.

A corollary to that of a uniquely posited realm of four dimensions for human existence is that of the Second Law of Thermodynamics. It states that in any closed system such as our four-dimensional realm of space and time, that without an outside force, our world of order will gradually deteriorate into disorder. Structure leads to chaos. So one is forced to ask, "What is it that holds this world together other than perhaps some intrusion from an outside dimension of an intelligent and benevolent being?"

So it would seem, we are uniquely designed and made for our world; or, our world is uniquely designed for human existence. What does that have to say of the plausibility of an intelligent and benevolent God? A Designer of such?

A close and objective observation of our world reveals benevolent design. The intricacies and intent of our world's design consistently reveal a highly intelligent and benevolent Supreme Being. Doesn't this fit our concepts of a Christian God? Though it may not satisfy the scientific demands of physicists with their desire for experimentation and direct observation, this concept of a Supreme Being, of ultimate intelligence and intent, existing in a dimension or transcendent form far beyond ours, yet being able to intrude into our dimension, fits reality much better than mathematical formulas that are becoming cloaked in ever greater mystery.

> The God who made the world and all things in it, since He is Lord of heaven and earth, does not dwell in temples made with hands; nor is He served by human hands, as though He needed anything, since He Himself gives to all people life and breath and all things; and He made from one man every nation of mankind to live on all the face of the earth, having determined their appointed times and the boundaries of their habitation, that they would seek God, if perhaps they might grope for Him and find Him, though He is not far from each one of us… (Acts 17:24–27 NASB)

## SPIRITUAL AWARENESS

*Miracles and Signs of a Miraculous God*

As scientific evidences have unfolded, God continues to reveal himself in miraculous ways by how He allows us to comprehend His intricate and unimaginable design of creation. The "signs and wonders" of modernity are ever before us, but there are those who choose not to see, or seeing, choose not to believe.

Rather than seeing the Divine within the burning bush, they choose to believe in the secular "Big Bang Theory." That is not to say that scientific factual observations are not to be accepted, but rather that they should be seen as they *point to* and *affirm* the reality of design and benevolence of a supreme wisdom and power.

The miraculous is revealed as one examines the factual scientific information within the context of benevolent intelligent design. Can the information we regard as factual be reconciled within a spiritual perspective of a personal and merciful God? Can we believe in an unseen God that is consistent with these scientific facts, but beyond empirical verification? How powerful of a case do these fascinating scientific facts make for the existence of an intelligent and benevolent Supreme Being?

*The Finely Tuned Universe*

The fine-tuning of our universe implies both Intelligence (intricacy) and Intent (design). Intelligence is implied within the intricacy of the material world, and Intent is implied in the design of the universe.

Macro universe:

- Universal Constants:[5] Currently there are nearly two dozen universally accepted physical forces within our universe. These are forces that have been accurately measured and have been found to be stable and unchanging.
  - ➢ The gravitational coupling constant: (force of gravity): it determines what kinds of stars are possible in the universe.

- ➤ The strong nuclear force coupling constant: it holds together the particles in the nucleus of an atom.
- ➤ The velocity of light: 299,792,458 m/s: the slightest variation of which, faster or slower would make our earth and universe uninhabitable.
- ➤ The entropy level of the universe: affects the degree to which massive systems (galaxies and stars) condense.
- ➤ The uniformity of the universe: determines its stellar components.

These are just a few examples of known, scientifically established constants which perform consistently, without variation within our universe. Also, they are intimately interdependent upon one another. If even one of the two dozen or so constants were to vary even the slightest, all life as we know it would perish.

- Earth's finely tuned balance:[6]
  - ➤ Design in the sun-earth-moon system:
  - ➤ Number of stars (our sun) in our planetary system: more than one would disrupt planetary orbits; less than one would produce insufficient heat for life.
  - ➤ Surface gravity: more would retain too much ammonia and methane; less would cause earth's atmosphere to lose too much water.
  - ➤ Earth's axial tilt: if greater or lesser, surface temperature differences would be too great.
  - ➤ Earth's magnetic field: if greater, electromagnetic storms would be too severe; if lesser, inadequate protection from hard stellar radiation.
  - ➤ Oxygen's quantity in atmosphere: if greater, plants and hydrocarbons would burn up too easily; if lesser, advanced animals would have too little to breathe.

Hugh Ross goes on to elaborate a whole host of detailed, finely tuned, and crucial "balances" within our earth's structure, position

# SPIRITUAL AWARENESS

within our solar system, and universe which are essential in order for life to exist.

Micro universe[7]

Michael Behe, PhD, a well-known professor of biochemistry, focuses his attention on the molecular aspects of the biochemical and cellular processes that are necessary for life. In his popular book, *Darwin's Black Box*, he extensively describes the specificity and sophistication of cellular and intracellular processes that make a case for intelligent design; rather than the evolutionary naturalistic theory that time plus chance plus matter form specified complex systems beneficial to life. These systems on the cellular and intracellular level comprise such systems that evolutionary theory cannot explain with any degree of reasonable probability:

- ➢ Informational storage and transfer
- ➢ Functioning codes
- ➢ Sorting and delivery systems
- ➢ Self-regulation and feed-back loops
- ➢ Signal transduction circuitry
- ➢ Myriad of "*complex arrangements of mutually-interdependent and well-fitted parts that work in concert to perform a function.*"[8]

It should be no surprise that the theory for Intelligent Design finds its most vocal critics amongst those defending the evolutionary theory of Darwin. Yet amongst the many other inconsistencies and gaps in Darwinism, is the fact that careful examination of processes on a biochemical or cellular level reveals no substantiation of evolutionary theory. William Dembski shares:

> James Shapiro, a molecular biologist at the University of Chicago conceded that there are no detailed Darwinian accounts for the evolution of any fundamental biochemical or cellular system, only a variety of wishful speculations. It

is remarkable that Darwinism is accepted as a satisfactory explanation for such a vast subject—evolution—with so little rigorous examination of how well its basic theses work in illuminating specific instances of biological adaptation or diversity.[9]

## PATTERNS AND RHYTHMS

Even closer to home are those patterns and rhythms we experience that reveal a finely orchestrated earthly creation. Even casual observation reveals the mystery and magnificence of nature's design within its predictability and consistency.

- Natural Order:
  - Cycles and Rhythms:
    Within the natural order are those cosmic cycles of planetary movement that determine our cycles of time and season upon which we base our various calendars. Our finely tuned earth boasts its unique mechanism of restoration in its cycles of water, carbon, nitrogen, and photosynthesis, without which no life could exist. Circadian rhythm, Neurofeedback circuitry, the seasonal migration of our birds and beasts…all speak to a carefully composed symphony of order and consistency.
  - Patterns:
    Furthermore, there are various patterns which are mysteriously identified within our human experience, sometimes obscure, other times overt. One of the most fascinating patterns is that of "Fibonacci numbers," and those of architectural form and strength.
- Natural Law:
  - Moral Law:
    Natural Moral Law has been described as a set of principles of conduct discerned by reason and pos-

ited within nature. They (i.e., justice, equality, civility) are regarded as universal absolutes, timeless and unchanging, and to be morally extended to every person equitably. Thomas Aquinas was one of the foremost Christian proponents of "natural law."

By now, I hope one can appreciate the abundant evidences of intelligent design in the universe and earth around us, and the purposeful and benevolent will that guides the hand of the Designer. It should be clear that the intricacies of our universe strongly imply intelligence, and the intent of design's many functions imply a benevolent Being. Much of what has been presented is often referred to as the "Anthropic Principle" and has been described thusly:

> The anthropic principle states that in our own universe, all these seemingly arbitrary and unrelated features of the physical world, the distance of the earth from the sun, the physical properties of the earth, the structure of an atom, have one thing in common: they are precisely what is needed so that the world can sustain life. The entire biophysical universe appears to have been thought out and designed, intelligently designed.[10]

William Paley once proposed that where there is a watch, there must be a watchmaker. To carry this concept into contemporary thought, it has been reported that man has now created the most accurate clock ever built. An "optical lattice" clock measures the movement of strontium atoms and is judged to be accurate to within losing only one second every 15 billion years...a time longer than the estimated age of our universe. Would matter plus time plus chance (evolution) be able to construct such a clock, or does its specified complexity demand a designer? Can one fairly ask, "Are the intricacies of our universe and human existence all the result of some accidental event?" I think not.

American astronomer, George Greenstein, is quoted in *The Fingerprint of God*, asking:

> As we survey all the evidence, the thought insistently arises that some supernatural agency—or, rather, Agency—must be involved. Is it possible that suddenly, without intending to, we have stumbled upon scientific proof of the existence of a Supreme Being? Was it God who stepped in and so providentially crafted the cosmos for our benefit?[11]

*A Garden of Creation?*

From what we have just considered, is it too far a stretch to ask if this earth could be for humankind a type of "Garden of Creation?" Could this intricately crafted four-dimensional realm of space and time be the only "paradise" for our safe and beneficial existence? As God's hand fashions the laws of nature and morality that grant stability to our world, does He not also pen the prescriptions for propagation of the species, formation of family and community, and civil relationships between various creeds and races?

However, within this garden are there not also certain pre-established cautions and prohibitions? A special place has been provided by God, a space and time of bounty and relationship with Him, but that which nevertheless still demands a choice of obedience. Humanity, and each of us personally has a choice, a choice that will determine his or her individual destiny. To be granted, our world has suffering as well. Satan still hides in the shadows of this world, tempting man and woman with the lie of skepticism ("for you will not surely die"); with the lie of new knowledge ("to see"); the lie of human autonomy ("you will be like God") [Genesis 3]. Even today, every person faces the same decision of obedience to the Designer's Will and Design.

## MIRACLES

> The experience of a miracle in fact requires two conditions. First we must believe in a normal stability of nature, which means we must recognize that the data offered by our senses recur in regular patterns. Secondly, we must believe in some reality beyond Nature.[12]
>
> —C. S. Lewis

> [I]n all these miracles alike the incarnate God does suddenly and locally something that God has done or will do in general. Each miracle writes for us in small letters something that God has already written, or will write in letters almost too large to be noticed, across the whole canvas of Nature.[13]
>
> —C. S. Lewis

This is not meant to be an exposé on the mystery of miracles, but it is an appropriate time to briefly consider how they may relate to "belief in the unseen." Others have written on the topic in great detail, and I will not attempt to mimic their efforts. Instead, here we will examine miracles in relation to the "ordinariness" of common daily experiences. We will take a small "slice" of the topic of miracles and attempt to understand their significance and purpose within our current personal perspectives.

It is important to remember that it is very difficult to accurately interpret events of others which lie outside of our own personal experience. To do so is fraught with inherent misperception and misunderstanding, even in the best of circumstances. In the realm of apparent miracles, it is even more so.

Miracles have traditionally been understood as a somewhat dramatic break with the commonplace, in such a manner as to transgress the normally expected response to that event. David Hume, a philosopher and skeptic, is quoted as defining miracles as "a transgression of a law of nature by a particular volition of the Deity, or by the interposition of some invisible agent."[14] Other definitions carry this same concept of a supernatural agent intruding into the customary laws of nature.

It is to be acknowledged that our understanding of "laws of nature" may change from generation to generation dependent upon the changes in scientific discovery and evidences. However, I would maintain that true miracles are not only an "intrusion" into the laws of nature, but are in some way a "re-envisioning" of our expectations of natural events and circumstances. Though not "contrary" to natural law, miracles are a "new wrinkle" in how we view reality within our limited understanding of space and time. They are that which are dramatically beyond our normal perceptions, and oftentimes paradoxical to them.

> "To those who first used the word spirituality, it signified 'led by or lived by the Spirit.' Such a life is lived in contrast to a life centered in material reality. It involves a different way of seeing…"[15]

> "Spirituality points, always, beyond: beyond the ordinary, beyond possession, beyond the narrow confines of the self,—and—above all, beyond expectation."[16]

> "Spirituality transcends the ordinary; and yet, paradoxically, it can be found only in the ordinary. Spirituality is beyond us, and yet it is in everything we do. It is extraordinary and yet it is extraordinarily simple."[17]

To perceive the significance of this phenomenon we call "miracles," I would argue, necessitates a life "led by or lived by the Spirit." Limited by one's materialistic perspective only allows for a very narrow and misperceived vision of events outside the normal expectations of our world. We simply choose to view them as coincidences or events peripheral to our orderly lives of fulfilled expectations. Miracles shake us from our complacency and challenge our belief.

So Jesus said to him, "Unless you people see signs and wonders, you simply will not believe" (John 4:48 NASB).

For many of us, the term "miracles" conjures up images of benevolent and miraculous gifts to humankind…miraculous gifts of healing, of provision and providence, of demonstration of spiritual realities. Eric Metaxas suggests that it may be valuable for us to hold the concept of miracles up to include both gift and sign. He says:

> The Greek word for miracle is "simaios," which means "sign." Miracles are signs, and like all signs, they are never about themselves; they're about whatever they are pointing toward. Miracles point to something beyond themselves. But to what? To God himself. That's the point of miracles—to point us beyond our world to another world. They are clues that the other world is not in our imaginations but is actually out there, wherever "out there" actually is. Peggy Noonan once wrote that she thought miracles existed "in part as gifts and in part as clues to that there is something beyond the flat world we see." If miracles exist at all, they exist not for their own sake but for us, to point us toward something beyond. To someone beyond.[18]
>
> Charles Ringma writes, "The ordinary, all the more, needs the eyes of faith to see its value."[19]

We should remind ourselves, that

If we believe in a God who created all the billions of galaxies containing billions of stars and planets…

If we believe in a God who has formed this uniquely habitable earthly realm within a finely tuned universe…

If we believe in a God who desires a personal relationship of redemption with humankind…

Then we can believe in a God who chooses to intrude into our dimension of space and time for His purposes, to give gifts to mankind and to serve as a sign of His reality, mercy, and omnipotence.

> "For now we see in a mirror dimly, but then face to face; now I know in part, but then I will know fully just as I also have been fully known" (1 Corinthians 13:12 NASB).

*Jesus the Miraculous Messiah*

What is it that we actually see within intelligent design?

God's miraculous character. The Alpha and Omega. His omnipotence, omniscience, and omnipresence. His love. Creation and restoration. His mercy. His eternal providence.

What does He ask of us?

To stand before the burning bush and believe. To perceive the light of God's Word as He expresses it to us and reveals the reality of Himself and His Son the Christ.

> *"Believe on the Lord Jesus Christ and thou shalt be saved!"* (Acts 16:31 KJV).

Jesus was, and is, a true Miracle Worker: Feeding the five thousand, healing the blind, the lepers, the lame, turning water into wine. Raising the dead Lazarus. His own resurrection and the visible confirmation of it. A very revealing narrative of Jesus's miraculous healing is described in the Gospel of John.

Healing the Man Born Blind: A Miracle of Jesus

> As He [Jesus] passed by, He saw a man blind from birth. And His disciples asked Him, "Rabbi, who sinned, this man or his parents, that

> he would be born blind?" Jesus answered, "It was neither that this man sinned, nor his parents; but it was so that the works of God might be displayed in him. We must work the works of Him who sent Me as long as it is day; night is coming when no one can work. While I am in the world, I am the Light of the world." When He had said this, He spat on the ground, and made clay of the spittle, and applied the clay to his eyes, and said to him, "Go, wash in the pool of Siloam"… So he went away and washed, and came back seeing. (John 9 NASB)

Those who knew the man quickly came upon him and asked how such miracle could have happened, to which the man responded, "The man who is called Jesus made clay, and anointed my eyes, and said to me, 'Go to Siloam and wash'; so I went away and washed, and I received sight."

Such an event was not to be overlooked by the Pharisees, who had the man born blind brought to them to ask who this person was that had healed him on the Sabbath no less. After explaining to the Pharisees how he had been healed, he responded, "*He is a prophet.*"

Not satisfied with this answer, the Pharisees called the man born blind before them a second time to question him further.

> The man answered and said to them, "Well, here is an amazing thing, that you do not know where He is from, and yet He opened my eyes. We know that God does not hear sinners; but if anyone is God-fearing and does His will, He hears him. Since the beginning of time it has never been heard that anyone opened the eyes of a person born blind. If this man were not from God, He could do nothing." …So they put him out.

Jesus heard that they had put him out, and finding him, He said, "Do you believe in the Son of Man?" He answered, "Who is He Lord, that I may believe in Him?" Jesus said to him, "You have both seen Him, and He is the one who is talking with you." And he said, "Lord, I believe." And he worshiped Him. And Jesus said, "For judgment I came into this world, so that those who do not see may see, and that those who see may become blind." Those of the Pharisees who were with Him heard these things and said to Him, "We are not blind too, are we?" Jesus said to them, "If you were blind, you would have no sin; but since you say, 'We see,' your sin remains."

William Barclay, commenting on John 9:39, writes these poignant words: "Jesus came into this world for judgment. Whenever a man is confronted with Jesus, that man at once passes a judgment on himself. If he sees in Jesus nothing to desire…nothing to love, then he has condemned himself."[20]

This biblical passage hardly needs any commentary, but there are some major points worth revisiting.

- We all are born blind, into a world of sin and darkness.
- Jesus Christ is the "Light of the world," who offers healing and restoration to all.
- Sometimes one's infirmities, one's limitations, one's sufferings help one see Christ. Born of our weakness are the paths leading to a recognition of who Christ truly is, for the Glory of God.
- Humankind, made of the "clay" of the earth, even within our "baseness," can be granted spiritual insight sufficient for belief in the Christ.
- The Anointing by Christ: Note the healing progression of Christ. He applied spittle (felt to have healing properties)

to the ground (sinful man) and covered the man's blind eyes (sin). Then the man was told to wash (image of repentance, forgiveness, baptism), and as the clay fell from his eyes (sin washed away), his vision was restored (redemption).

- Note the progression of the blind man's faith. First he describes Jesus as a "man," then a "prophet," and finally states, "If this man were not from God, He could do nothing."
- Once the blind man's physical sight was restored, his spiritual vision allowed him to see and believe in Jesus, to declare, "*Lord, I believe.*" An important point worth making is the distinction between believing "that," and believing "in." Both the man born blind and the Pharisees believed "that" a miracle had happened, but only the man born blind declared his belief "in" Jesus as the Son of God.
- Jesus came into this world for redemption, but also for judgment of those who choose not to believe. The Pharisees' loyalty was to their positions of authority and influence. Though they stood face to face with Jesus, they chose to worship in the dark shadows of the golden calf. Instead, the healed blind man chose to worship the "Light of the world," before the flames of the burning bush emerging upon holy ground.

"He who believes in Him is not judged; he who does not believe has been judged already, because he has not believed in the name of the only begotten Son of God." (John 3:18ff NASB)

We are moved by the act of God. Omniscience holds no conference. Infinite authority leaves no room for compromise. Eternal love offers no explanations. The Lord expects to be trusted. He disturbs us at will. Human arrangements are disregarded, family ties ignored, business claims put aside. We are never asked if it is convenient.[21]
(Samuel Chadwick, Methodist preacher)

"The fool has said in his heart, "There is no God." (Psalm 14:1 NASB)

Prayer for Insight

"O Eternal God, though Thou art not such as I can see with my eyes or touch with my hands, yet grant me this day a clear conviction of Thy reality and power. Let me not go forth to my work believing only in the world of sense and time, but give me grace to understand that the world I cannot see or touch is the most real world of all. My life today will be lived in time, but eternal issues will be concerned in it. The needs of my body will be claimant, but it is for the needs of my soul that I must care most. My business will be with things material, but behind them let me be aware of things spiritual. Let me keep steadily in mind that the things that matter are not money or possessions, not houses or lands, not bodily comfort or bodily pleasure; but truth and honour and meekness and helpfulness and a pure love of Thyself.

For the power Thou hast given me to lay hold of things unseen:

For the strong sense I have that this is not my home:

For my restless heart which nothing finite can satisfy:

I give Thee thanks, O God.

For the invasion of my soul by Thy Holy Spirit:

For all human love and goodness that speak to me of Thee:

For the fullness of Thy glory outpoured in Jesus Christ:

## SPIRITUAL AWARENESS

I give Thee thanks, O God.

I, a pilgrim of eternity, stand before Thee, O eternal One. Let me not seek to deaden or destroy the desire for Thee that disturbs my heart. Let me rather yield myself to its constraint and go where it leads me. Make me wise to see all things today under the form of eternity, and make me brave to face all the changes in my life which such a vision may entail; through the grace of Christ my Saviour. Amen."[22]

---

[1] Dallas Willard, *Hearing God* (Downers Grove, Illinois; Intervarsity Press, 1999), 217–218.

[2] Excerpt from *The Spirituality of Imperfection* by Ernest Kurtz, 1992 by Ernest Kurtz, Ph.D. And Katherine Ketcham, 31. Used by permission of Bantam Books, an imprint of Random House, a division of Penguin Random House LLC. All rights reserved.

[3] Hugh Ross, PhD, *Beyond the Cosmos* (Colorado Springs, Colorado: NavPress, 1996), 32.

[4] Hugh Ross, PhD, *The Fingerprint of God*, 2nd ed. revised and updated (Orange, California: Promise Publishing Co., 1991), 121–128.

[5] Ibid., 129–132.

[6] Ibid.

[7] Michael J. Behe, Darwin's Black Box (New York: The Free Press, 1996).

[8] William A. Dembski and James M. Kushiner, editors, *Signs of Intelligence* (Grand Rapids, Michigan: Brazos Press, 2001), 11.

[9] William Dembski, *The Design Revolution* (Downers Grove, Illinois: Intervarsity Press, 2004), 214-215.

[10] Ibid., 16.

[11] George Greenstein, *The Symbiotic Universe: Life and Mind in the Cosmos* (New York: William Morrow, 1988), 26–27;

Hugh Ross, *The Fingerprint of God*, 2nd ed. revised and updated (Orange, CA: Promise Publishing Co., 1991), 128.

[12] C.S. Lewis, "Miracles," God in the Dock, ed. Walter Hooper (Grand Rapids, Michigan: William B. Eerdmans Publishing Co., 1970). 27.
[13] *Miracles* by C. S. Lewis, 138. Copyright © C. S. Lewis Pte. Ltd. 1947, 1960. Extracts reprinted by permission.
[14] Excerpt from *Miracles: What They Are, Why They Happen, and How They Can Change Your Life* by Eric Metaxas, 11. Copyright © 2014 by Metaxas Media, LLC. Used by permission of Dutton, an imprint of Penguin Publishing Group, a division of Penguin Random House LLC. All rights reserved.
[15] Excerpt from *The Spirituality of Imperfection* by Ernest Kurtz, 1992 by Ernest Kurtz, Ph.D. And Katherine Ketcham, 31. Used by permission of Bantam Books, an imprint of Random House, a division of Penguin Random House LLC. All rights reserved.
[16] Ibid, 31.
[17] Ibid., 35.
[18] Excerpts from *Miracles: What They Are, Why They Happen, and How They Can Change Your Life* by Eric Metaxas, 16. Copyright © 2014 by Metaxas Media, LLC. Used by permission of Dutton, an imprint of Penguin Publishing Group, a division of Penguin Random House LLC. All rights reserved.
[19] Charles Ringma, "The Ordinary," November 5 meditation, in *Seize the Day with Dietrich Bonhoeffer* (Colorado Springs, CO: Pinon Press, 2000).
[20] William Barclay, *The Gospel of John*, vol. 2 (Philadelphia: The Westminster Press, 1975), 50.
[21] Quotation found in Oswald J. Sanders book, *Shoe Leather Commitment*, 32.
[22] From *A Diary of Private Prayer* by John Baillie, 53. Copyright © 1949 by Charles Scribner's Sons; copyright renewed © 1977 by Ian Fowler Baillie. Reprinted with the permission of Scribner, a division of Simon and Schuster, Inc. All rights reserved.

# 10

## *Suffering and Hope*
## *Light in the Midst of Darkness*

Dad tells us a thousand times the story after dinner, how her eyes were water-clear and without shores, how she held his neck when she hugged him and held on for dear life. We accept the day of her death as an accident. But an accident allowed by God?...

At the grave's precipice, our feet scuff, and chunks of the firmament fall away. A clod of dirt hits the casket, shatters. Shatters over my little sister with the white-blond hair, the little sister who teased me and laughed; and the way she'd throw her head back and laugh, her milk-white cheeks dimpled right through with happiness, and I'd scoop close all her belly-giggling life. They lay her gravestone flat into the earth, a black granite slab engraved with no dates, only the five letters of her name. Aimee. It means "loved one." How she was. We had loved her. And with the laying of her gravestone, the closing up of her deathbed, so closed our lives.

Closed to any notion of Grace.[1]

Can there be a more painful grief than the death of an innocent child? A tiny package of love and happiness and innocence extinguished like a candle's bright flame…to leave only the cold darkness of grief. This heart-rending loss seems a burden too heavy to bear. Death and despair ever haunt our thoughts. Goodness and Hope fade. The whole world turns dim.

It appears we are surrounded with this ever-present threat of loss. Relationships turned bitter by infidelity and rejection, young parents' futures shaken by the sudden peril of cancer, or persons confronted with the slow unrelenting death of ALS. We face too many "I'm sorrys," too many "goodbyes." Then too there are the lonely, the depressed, the underprivileged, and forgotten, and the list goes on and on…murder, suicide, a fatal diagnosis, abuse, drug dependency, stillbirth. From the searing pain, suffering is quick to spawn its minions of grief, anger, bitterness, despair, depression…causing us to ask, "Do we live in a nightmare world?"

And we face the same ever-present question, "WHY?"

It might be well to remember the biblical account of the first "suffering." After violating God's sole moral absolute ("Thou shalt not eat of the fruit of the tree of the knowledge of good and evil"), Adam and Eve faced the judgment of a just God. Now both would face the pain of "labor," Eve in childbirth and Adam in toil. Suffering from then on becomes an inherent experience of humankind.

Even so, the over-arching theme of the entire biblical account is that of a loving and merciful God redeeming and restoring His people unto Himself…into a relationship of loving intimacy. Could it possibly be that our personal, temporal suffering is an inevitable process in restoring our relationship with our Creator? Could pain and grief be a means by which a human soul is prepared for an eternal destiny, like the fire which purifies the dross from the gold? … An eternal destiny that is unseen by us within this earthly existence.

Soren Kierkegaard was a person well acquainted with suffering, and much of his writing dealt with this topic in a very personal and engaging way. He would say that in suffering a person is confronted with a paradox of this earthly existence. Within this crucible of time and place, man and woman are confronted by their limitations vs. their potentialities, by their temporal nature vs. their eternal destiny. It is through this earthly struggle he would say, that one finds his or

## SPIRITUAL AWARENESS

her own authentic being. Suffering confronts us with our vulnerability, our impotence, our despair. Yet hope is discovered in the confidence that on the other side of pain and struggle, one can claim the grace, gratitude, and hope that purifies and transforms.

In her book, *One Thousand Gifts*, Ann Voskamp poignantly shares her personal journey of loss and grief and pain. After the accidental farm death of her four-year-old sister, Aimee, she chronicles her struggle to move from the nightmares of despair and disillusionment in an attempt to find some answer to her haunting question: "Why?" Can there be any purpose to all this grief and pain? Where can one turn to find comfort?

Though each one of us may find our own personal answers, Ann Voskamp describes her individual endeavor to find some meaning within this experience of pain and suffering, but it is a gradual and difficult journey. For her, it becomes a story of discovering and appreciating the "gifts" still present despite her deep grief.

A crucial pivot point occurs in her confrontation with her life of "ingratitude." She shares her insight this way:

> From all of our beginnings, we keep reliving the Garden story. Satan, he wanted more. More power, more glory. Ultimately, in his essence, Satan is an ingrate. And he sinks his venom into the heart of Eden. Satan's sin becomes the first sin of all humanity: the sin of ingratitude. Adam and Eve are, simply, painfully, ungrateful for what God gave. Isn't that the catalyst of all my sins? Our fall was, has always been, and always will be, that we aren't satisfied in God and what He gives.[2]

With this insight, Ann Voskamp reflects upon the awareness which brings her hope.

> But from that Garden beginning, God has had a different purpose for us. His intent, since

> He bent low and breathed His life into the dust of our lungs, since He kissed us into being, has never been to slyly orchestrate our ruin.
>
> His love letter forever silences any doubts: "His secret purpose framed from the very beginning [is] to bring us to our full glory" (1 Corinthians 2:7 NEB). He means to rename us—to return us to our true names, our truest selves. He means to heal our soul holes. From the very beginning, that Eden beginning, that has always been and always is, to this day, His secret purpose—our return to our full glory[3] ...
>
> I wonder too ... if the rent in the canvas of our life backdrop, the losses that puncture our world, our own emptiness, might actually become places to see. To see through to God. That that which tears open our souls, those holes that splatter our sight, may actually become the thin, open places to see through the mess of this place to the heart-aching beauty beyond. To Him. To the God whom we endlessly crave. Maybe so.
>
> But how? How do we choose to allow the holes to become seeing-through-to-God places? To more-God places? How do I give up resentment for gratitude, gnawing anger for spilling joy? Self-focus for God-communion. To fully live—to live full of grace and joy and all that is beauty eternal. It is possible, wildly[4].

In the remainder of her book, Ann Voskamp describes how she carries a word, "Eucharisteo" (meaning "thanksgiving"), into the events of each day...and shares the insights she receives in doing so...how grace allows her to see the many wonders within the commonplace; how gratitude adds a deep insight into our relationship with God, and how joy is the surprise gift of our intimacy with our Lord...how we can now see clearly again.

## SPIRITUAL AWARENESS

Here, in the messy, piercing ache of now, joy might be—unbelievably—possible! The only place we need to see before we die is this place of seeing God, here and now.[5]

I have just one word. A word to seize and haul up out of a terminal nightmare, a word for fearless dying, for saved, fully healed living, a word that works the miracle that heals the soul and raises the very dead to life... Eucharisteo.[6]

Grace, Thanksgiving, Joy: At first glance, they seem like some lost, out of place visitors to this realm of suffering...incongruous to those who are overburdened, those who despair, those who are without hope. But perhaps they are participants of healing in ways which we cannot imagine. Could it be that they are the fruits of our brokenness and pain? Could it be that in the crucible of our suffering we are broken in order to become purified; to be re-formed; to become "new creatures" in Christ? And is it not within our seasons of pain that we find ourselves being called back into a trusting relationship with God? Is it God's way of first getting our attention?

God's Word answers:

"For *who* has *known* the *mind* of the *Lord*, that he will *instruct* him? But we *have* the *mind* of *Christ*." (1 Corinthians 2:16 NASB)

"For now we see in a mirror dimly, but then face to face; now I know in part, but then I will know fully just as I also have been fully known." (1 Corinthians 13:12 NASB)

But *just* as it is *written*, "Things *which eye* has not *seen* and *ear* has not *heard*, and which have not *entered* the *heart* of *man*, *all* that *God* has *prepared* for *those* who *love* him." (1 Corinthians 2:9 NASB)

"But we have this treasure in earthen vessels, so that the surpassing greatness of the power will be of God and not from ourselves; we are afflicted in every way, but not crushed; perplexed, but not despairing; persecuted, but not forsaken; struck down, but not destroyed; always carrying about in the body the dying of Jesus, so that the life of Jesus also may be manifested in our body. For we who live are constantly being delivered over to death for Jesus' sake, so that the life of Jesus also may be manifested in our mortal flesh." (2 Corinthians 4:7–11 NASB)

"Therefore we do not lose heart, but though our outer man is decaying, yet our inner man is being renewed day by day. For momentary, light affliction is producing for us an eternal weight of glory far beyond all comparison, while we look not at the things which are seen, but at the things which are not seen; for the things which are seen are temporal, but the things which are not seen are eternal." (2 Corinthians 4:16–18 NASB)

## SUFFERING

Suffering: "Getting Our Attention?"

He delivers the afflicted in their affliction,
And opens their ear in time of oppression.
—Job 36:15 (NASB)

Both C. S. Lewis and Soren Kierkegaard wrote poignantly about pain and suffering out of their own personal issues.

C. S. Lewis (1898–1963) was to experience the death of his mother at an early age in childhood, and then would later experience the further emotional abandonment of a father who became uninvolved in his life. After enduring the rejection of his academic colleagues at Oxford, he would then witness the terrible ravages of war. Despite these early events, Lewis was to find happiness later in life in a somewhat serendipitous relationship with an American writer, Joy Davidman, whom he would later marry. Tragically, only several brief years after their marriage, she would die after a protracted battle with cancer. His intellectual thoughts described within his book, *The Problem of Pain,* suddenly were challenged by the loss of his beloved wife. His honest and transparent questioning of why God allows for suffering and pain of the innocent is touchingly revealed in his subsequent book, *A Grief Observed.*

Yet after all this he is able to hold true to his earlier convictions as expressed in one of his most quoted passages:

> "Pain insists upon being attended to. God whispers to us in our pleasures, speaks in our conscience, but shouts to us in our pain. It is his megaphone to rouse a deaf world."[7]

Another well acquainted with suffering was the Danish philosopher, theologian, and author, Soren Kierkegaard (1813–1855). Like C. S. Lewis, he began life within a tumultuous childhood. His mother also died when he was a youngster, and he was raised by a stern and very pious father. As a young man he was easily recognized upon the streets of his home town of Copenhagen, as his somewhat deformed hunchback stoop and homely appearance brought him the ridicule of his neighbors and peers. As a philosopher and author, he would initially write pseudonymously in order to avoid the personal rejection of others. He would later regret not marrying the love of his life, Regine Olsen, and would die an early death from his frail health. Known for his somewhat melancholy temperament, he was nonetheless an extremely insightful and prolific writer regarding the human condition. As suffering marked each stage of his life, he would, nonetheless, remain dedicated to his Christian faith, and would pen these words: "Christianity is suffering to the end—it is eternity's consciousness."[8]

Do both C. S. Lewis and Kierkegaard imply that there is some purpose in our pain and suffering? Can it be that a merciful and benevolent God allows for suffering in order to get our attention? Does God cause us to focus attention to our eternal destiny by confronting us with our temporal vulnerabilities? Does He confront us with our helplessness, to then ask us, "In what or in whom do you place your ultimate trust"?

## SUFFERING'S PURPOSE: "BROKENNESS"

> For to you it has been granted for
> Christ's sake, not only to believe in
> Him, but also to suffer for His sake.
> —Philippians 1:29 (NASB)

Ernest Kurtz and Katherine Ketcham describe their reflection upon the purpose of undeserved suffering within the context of our humanity.

> We seek help for what we cannot face or accomplish alone; in seeking help, we accept and admit our own powerlessness. And in that acceptance and admission, in the acknowledgment that we are not in control, spirituality is born. Spirituality begins in suffering because to suffer means first "to undergo," and the essence of suffering lies in the reality that it is undergone, that it has to do with not being in control, that it must be endured. We may endure patiently or impatiently, but because we are human beings, because we are not at each and every moment in ultimate control, we will suffer.[9]

In suffering we are confronted by our lack of control…crushed, overwhelmed and helpless, we struggle with emotions of grief and despair which cloud our perception. For there is nothing we can do to change the circumstances within which we suffer. The past is gone, irretrievable and irrevocable. Raw emotions of fear now stir us from complacency to a confrontation with our vulnerability. Shaken from our casual neglect of deeper realities, we now search for peace and comfort. And from within the crucible of suffering we seek for a source of wholeness and hope.

## SUFFERING: GROWTH IN CHARACTER AND SPIRITUAL MATURITY

> Consider it all joy, my brethren, when
> you encounter various trials, knowing
> that the testing of your faith produces
> endurance. And let endurance have its
> perfect result, so that you may be perfect
> and complete, lacking in nothing.
> —James 1:2–4 (NASB)

Not only does suffering call out to us for our attention to spiritual realities, but it also confronts us with our inability to control our condition. Birthed within suffering are the soils of broken-ness and surrender, from which growth of character and spiritual maturity arise.

Kierkegaard would go a step further to say that we are not only confronted by the inevitability and unavoidability of suffering, but that suffering is a "necessity" for spiritual authenticity and maturity. Because humans are finite and temporal creatures, he would say there exists an existential "necessity" for the transforming work of suffering. Confronted with one's frailty and vulnerability, the person is forced into the action of Choice.

This Choice, like a vanguard, stands before the diverting paths of paradox...finiteness or the infinite, temporality or the eternal, potentiality or actualization. Suffering demands the response of personal Choice: that of bitterness, resentment, and bondage, or that of acceptance, healing, and freedom discovered within the Eternal. By choosing a measure of acceptance of suffering, a newly discovered freedom is birthed toward spiritual transformation. Kierkegaard claims of this choice:

> In like fashion, when a man dares declare, "I am eternity's free citizen," necessity cannot imprison him, except in voluntary confinement.[10]
>
> And when the victim of unavoidable suffering bears it patiently,…
>
> Undeniably he is making a virtue out of a necessity. He brings a determination of freedom out of that which is determined as necessity. And it is just there that the healing power of the decision for the Eternal resides: that the sufferer may voluntarily accept the compulsory suffering…[11]

The acceptance of suffering is not a "giving in" or "giving up" in our seasons of affliction. In choosing to valiantly battle against rejection, grief, and disease, we express our nobility and courage. However, if we accept that suffering can come from the hand of a benevolent and merciful God, we can experience the freedom from despair which restores and preserves genuine hope.

To paraphrase Kierkegaard, bearing suffering patiently is to stand upon the belief that God is still in control and is still good. It is an awareness that our suffering in this life is inevitable, and perhaps necessary in our journey of restoration of intimacy with our Creator. In this recognition is to be discovered the "healing power of the decision for the Eternal" which provides the freedom from despair and the promise of eternal hope.

Yet this "acceptance" is more than an intellectual acknowledgment. It is an experiential reality that allows the light of grace to break into temporal time…enabling one to see the Eternal in the midst of affliction and depression. It is to engage with a spiritual Presence by saying, "Yes, even in my suffering, I will consecrate the experience, as part of my being, to my Creator. I will regard even my suffering as 'holy.'" Then I may say, like Job, "Therefore I have declared that which I did not understand, things too wonderful for me, which I did not know" (Job 42:3b NASB).

This leads us to a consideration of consecration…not only of our blessings, but of our sufferings as well. For it is in doing so, that the experience is "made holy." But one can fairly ask, "What does consecration amidst suffering look like in the here and now of my despair?"

## SUFFERING AS "CONSECRATION"

The word consecration in today's use means "to make holy" or "to dedicate to a higher purpose." In some instances it is "to declare something as sacred." Certain church traditions set aside specific events of dedication (i.e., Baptism, Holy Communion, Marriage, Last Rites, etc.) as Sacraments. Other traditions, like the Quakers, choose not to make such specific distinctions, preferring to regard all of life's decisions and actions as "holy" moments.

In considering the issue of "consecrating" suffering, it is appropriate to ask just how this is accomplished. How, when in the throes of despair, can a person reach beyond the present painful moment? How does one discover hope within the anguish of depression and grief? How does one find light amidst the darkness?

During these times of brokenness, there often arises an innate desire for a grounding in something or someone larger than oneself… for a Presence bigger than our circumstances in which to find comfort. A loving and compassionate "Someone" in whom to place our "ultimate trust." As suffering is accepted as offered from a benevolent God, this newly acquired spiritual freedom springs forth to allow for new and unique avenues in which to find spiritual meaning and purpose. Ann Voskamp found her grounding by intentionally choosing to see God's grace and benevolence in the events of her everyday life. It was, in a very authentic manner, a way of consecrating her life to God's glory. She turned the barren soil of suffering [brokenness] into holy ground.

Thomas Merton and Henri Nouwen share their insights in this regard:

> The Christian must not only accept suffering: he must make it holy[12] (Thomas Merton).

> That is the great conversion in our life: to recognize and believe that the many unexpected events are not just disturbing interruptions on our projects, but the way in which God molds our hearts and prepares us for his return. Our great temptations are boredom and bitterness. When our good plans are interrupted by poor weather, our well-organized careers by illness or bad luck, our peace of mind by inner turmoil, our hope for peace by a new war, our desire for a stable government by a constant changing of the guards, and our desire for immortality by real death, we are tempted to give in to paralyzing boredom or to strike back in destructive bitterness. But when we believe that patience can make our expectations grow, then fate can be converted into a vocation, wounds into a call for deeper understanding, and sadness into a birthplace for joy. (Henri J. Nouwen, *Out of Solitude*)

This leads us to the stark reality that even our pain and suffering can be dedicated to a higher purpose. Is it too much to ask if temporal suffering is worth eternal bliss? Can we accept the position that a benevolent God allows for human suffering in order to redeem souls for eternity? Are His ideas not higher than man's understanding? (Isaiah 55:8–9, 1 Corinthians 2:9, 1 Corinthians 2:16, 2 Corinthians 4:18).

The matter of consecrating our suffering really rests upon our decision upon what to believe and in whom to place our ultimate trust. Am I willing to accept the idea that God is ultimately good and allows my suffering only for my eternal benefit and for His ultimate Glory? Only in doing so, can we find the freedom from despair and the hope of eternity.

## IN OUR SUFFERING, WE ARE NOT ALONE

For the Christian, there is One who has gone before us. One who, in His human form, experienced our fears, our pain, and our despair. He knows what we suffer, because He, too, suffered for each one of us. He knows the sting of ridicule and rebuke. He knows the cold touch of loneliness and depression. He knows the heartache of grief and death.

And having done so, Christ yet remains with us. Out of His everlasting love for us, He participates in each of our struggles and disappointments, our fears and our rejections, our despair and our grief.

I very much appreciate a devotion written by a very close friend of mine, Bill McDonald. Within a Lenten Meditation he wrote these powerful words:

> We are not alone, our suffering is not unnoticed. Our tears, our sorrow, our cries are noticed, noticed tenderly and taken up by another in real existential anguish. He who does that knows what it means to suffer. His existence is marked with deep human anguish so deep and troubling that He sweats drops of blood. He sweats drops of blood in anguish for us. His concern is so great, His love so deep that His anguish is physically manifested in His body for all the broken and frail bodies that find themselves in the depth of human misery…[13]

And it is in this reality, this personal relationship with Christ, our Savior and Redeemer, in which we find hope. In our suffering, we are never alone. Christ knows our pain and sorrow, for He lived among us and suffered for us. And He remains with us still.

> Who will separate us from the love of Christ? Will tribulation, or distress, or persecution, or famine, or nakedness, or peril, or sword? Just as it is written, "FOR YOUR SAKE WE ARE BEING PUT TO DEATH ALL DAY LONG; WE WERE CONSIDERED AS SHEEP TO BE SLAUGHTERED." But in all these things we overwhelmingly conquer through Him who loved us. For I am convinced that neither death, nor life, nor angels, nor principalities, nor things present, nor things to come, nor powers, nor height, nor depth, nor any other created thing, will be able to separate us from the love of God, which is in Christ Jesus our Lord. (Romans 8:35–39 NASB)

## HOPE

Hope springs from the bedrock of Grace and Gratitude. As Grace reveals to us the spiritual realities of this life, Gratitude is our response to the confidence we find in personal relationship with the Eternal One.

By celebrating gratitude amidst our suffering, we step from the bondage of bitterness and resentment. We choose to turn from the burdens of the "self" to discover the freedom of hope found in surrender. Through grace and gratitude, hope is rekindled and coaxed into an eternal flame as our "ultimate trust" is placed in Him that is beyond imagination.

Thomas Merton writes:

> We are not perfectly free until we live in pure hope. For when our hope is pure, it no longer trusts exclusively in human and visible means, nor rests

> in any visible end. He who hopes in God trusts God, Whom he never sees, to bring him to the possession of things that are beyond imagination.
>
> When we do not desire the things of this world for their own sake, we become able to see them as they are.... "Seek ye first the kingdom of God." (Matthew 6:33)[14]

Scripture reinforces that one's hope rests in an understanding that God has provided a release from suffering and an eternal blessing discovered in His great love.

> "These things I have spoken to you, so that in Me you may have peace. In the world you have tribulation, but take courage; I have overcome the world." (John 16:33, NASB)

> "And not only this, but we also exult in our tribulations, knowing that tribulation brings about perseverance; and perseverance, proven character; and proven character, hope; and hope does not disappoint, because the love of God has been poured out within our hearts through the Holy Spirit who was given to us." (Romans 5:3–5 NASB)

We find Hope in the One who scattered the stars across the heavens, who created the fragrance of the rose and the innocence of a newborn baby.

We find Hope in the One who became as man to reveal to us the embodiment of all goodness, mercy, and forgiveness.

We find Hope in the One who suffered for us, who understands our pain and despair, as He has suffered like us…who overcame temptation and sin to claim victory over death.

We find Hope in the One who now reaches from eternity down into this finite realm of ours to offer loving redemption by His gracious hand, and to restore us into intimate relationship with Him for evermore.

> "And He will wipe away every tear from their eyes; and there will no longer be any death; there will no longer be any mourning, or crying, or pain; the first things have passed away" (Revelation 21:4 NASB).

Psalm of Comfort:

> The LORD is my shepherd, I shall not want.
> He makes me lie down in green pastures; He leads me beside quiet waters.
> He restores my soul; He guides me in the paths of righteousness for His name's sake.
> Even though I walk through the valley of the shadow of death, I fear no evil, for You are with me; Your rod and Your staff, they comfort me.
> You prepare a table before me in the presence of my enemies; You have anointed my head with oil; My cup overflows.
> Surely goodness and lovingkindness will follow me all the days of my life, and I will dwell in the house of the LORD forever. (Psalm 23:1–6 NASB)

*The Christian's Response to the Suffering of Others*

> "For He causes His sun to rise on the evil and the good, and sends rain on the righteous and the unrighteous" (Matthew 5:45 NASB).

How is one to deal with the suffering so prevalent within our world? What is the Christian's role and responsibility in responding to the needs of others?

# SPIRITUAL AWARENESS

Our biblical charge is clear:

## The Judgment

> But when the Son of Man comes in His glory, and all the angels with Him, then He will sit on His glorious throne. All the nations will be gathered before Him; and He will separate them from one another, as the shepherd separates the sheep from the goats; and He will put the sheep on His right, and the goats on the left. Then the King will say to those on His right, "Come, you who are blessed of My Father, inherit the kingdom prepared for you from the foundation of the world. For I was hungry, and you gave Me something to eat; I was thirsty, and you gave Me something to drink; I was a stranger, and you invited Me in; naked, and you clothed Me; I was sick, and you visited Me; I was in prison, and you came to Me." Then the righteous will answer Him, "Lord, when did we see You hungry, and feed You, or thirsty, and give You something to drink? And when did we see You a stranger, and invite You in, or naked, and clothe You? When did we see You sick, or in prison, and come to You?" The King will answer and say to them, "Truly I say to you, to the extent that you did it to one of these brothers of Mine, even the least of them, you did it to Me." (Matthew 25:31–40 NASB)

"Caring" is not enough. It must lead to "*action*."

The importance of having an awareness of the suffering all around us seems to be self-evident. However, it is all too easy to become distracted and desensitized by the rapid flow of our busy daily lives. We effortlessly become disengaged from the difficulties that others struggle with, hour by hour, within the confines of their dark despair. Sadly, like a stubborn island within a river, we allow suffering to flow continuously around us, only barely touching the edges of our shores of sensitivity, and we remain unmoved. We do not reach out into the flow of suffering to ease its turbulence, nor allow its movement to shape our shores into beautiful beaches of compassion. So it is with a life, as the currents of suffering allow for a shaping of others and a shaping of oneself.

You may be familiar with the poem, *No Man is an Island* by John Donne.

> No man is an island,
> Entire of itself,
> Every man is a piece of the continent,
> A part of the main.
> If a clod be washed away by the sea,
> Europe is the less.
> As well as if a promontory were.
> As well as if a manor of thy friend's
> Or of thine own were:
> Any man's death diminishes me,
> Because I am involved in mankind,
> And therefore never send to know for whom the bell tolls;
> It tolls for thee.

Steps to Service within Suffering

- ➢ Abandon excuses: Search out opportunities to give comfort and appreciation.
- ➢ Take off your blinders: Remove that which allows us to disregard the suffering around us and within the world. Practice the awareness of a disciple in the wilderness of despair.
- ➢ Take off the insulation of desensitized, calloused hearts: dare to care. Wrapped around us, like so many layers of insulation, are the layers of indifference and self-absorption. Read a book, watch a documentary, DVD, movie

about someone who has suffered much with great inspiration and courage… Viktor Frankl, "The Hidden Place," Carrie Ten Bloom, allow the experience to not only teach you but to sensitize you to the suffering of others…
- Prepare to get messy: Be prepared for different codes of conduct, different expectations, different values than yours.
- Stay grounded in the majors: It's all right to be an amateur. Authenticity states, "I don't have all the answers," but share Christ's healing hope and God's grace discovered in the simple experiences of the everyday. Reach out with a gift to help bear the burdens. Allow for Grace and the Holy Spirit to lead the way.
- Discover the Joy of Mother Teresa

> Joy is a net of love by which we can catch souls. A Sister filled with joy preaches without preaching. Joy is a need and a power for us even physically for it makes us always ready to go about doing good. The best way to show our gratitude to God and people is to accept everything with joy. A joyful Sister is like the sunshine of God's love, the hope of eternal happiness, the flame of burning love.[15]

Be aware/attentive to the needs of one another. Scripture has an abundance of "One another" passages to reflect and act upon:

Romans 12:10: be devoted to one another
Romans 12:16: be of the same mind one to another
Romans 13:8: love one another
Romans 14:19: build up one another
Ephesians 5:21: be subject to one another
Ephesians 4:2: tolerance for one another in love
Ephesians 4:32: be kind to one another
Colossians 3:13: bearing with one another
Galatians 5:13: through love serve one another

Galatians 6:2: bear one another's burdens
James 5:16: confess sins and pray for one another

*The Sacrifices of Caring*

A disclaimer: in serving those who are suffering, it is important to recognize that this is an effort which often yields sparse immediate benefits. The results, if any, of our caring for those who are suffering may never take shape in a tangible way that we can see. We may never have knowledge of the first fruits of our efforts. It is not like baking a loaf of bread and have it resting upon our table as a satisfying reward for our efforts. In that regard, it may be wise to recall Thomas Merton's perspective of our motivations becoming those of "simple intentions"… those being motivations that rest completely within the desires and design of our Lord. All effort to claim acknowledgment or a reward or possession of the end result on our part is a faulty perspective. Only by turning an act of service completely over to the Lord, can the Lord fully bless what little we have to offer, thereby consecrating the act of service to His glory and for His purposes. (Remember the different gifts of Cain and Abel).

Mother Teresa reminds us: "Do small things with great love. It's not how much we do, but how much love we put in the doing; and it is not how much we give, but how much love we put in the giving."[16]

## REACHING OUT: A DELICATE TOUCH

*Attitude Adjustments*

- Be available, but not intrusive.
- Learn Tenderness
- Practice Empathy, Kindness
- Give anonymously.
- Carry someone with you in thought and prayer for a week.
- Examine the attitude of the heart—remember the sacrifices of Cain and Abel. Cain gave begrudgingly out of obligation, but Abel gave sacrifices of genuine benevolence.

It's not necessarily the size or character of the gift given with a sincere heart, but rather God's blessing upon it that determines its fruitfulness. Its benefit and ultimate value to others is conditioned and multiplied by the Lord's blessing.

*Giving Gifts*

- Practice Hospitality.
- Give the gift of your "presence." The ill, the lonely, the widowed, the orphaned, children without families or in single-parent families. Tutoring children. Investing in others' lives.
- Visit a prison, nursing home, hospital.
- Send a random gift to missions.
- Assemble and distribute Care packages of toothpaste, toothbrushes, soap, chocolates, granola bars, fast-food gift card for the homeless and underprivileged.
- Send gifts to servicemen, those affected by natural disasters, the imprisoned, and first responders.
- Create joy in random acts of kindness.
- Send a photo of a happy memory to family or a friend.
- "Carry" someone in thought and prayer with you for a week…send them a note of encouragement.
- Take a meal, bake a loaf of bread, sweet rolls to someone in need.

*Give your gifts accompanied by a prayer of blessing or comfort.*

*Identifying with others*

- Fasting: eating simple foods, "soup day" to identify with those who are without proper food or water. Respond with a specific action to alleviate their need.
- Wearing old clothes: "Patch day" to identify with those who are without satisfactory clothing or shelter. Support

them by sorting your closets and contributing shoes, blankets, coats to Goodwill or charity or Homeless shelters.
- Display the American flag—remember those who are without freedom and who are persecuted or held in prison in foreign countries. Pray for them and their families. Pray for missionaries around the world. Pray for those who defend our country in harm's way.

*Giving with the Proper Motivation*

I have to chuckle sometimes when I read an author commenting that a fictional character in one of his or her books "spoke" to him about the direction of a theme within the plot of the story. Though absurd if taken literally, I find it somewhat refreshing to consider the figurative intent of taking oneself out of the work in order to allow for subconscious musings to find their expression. Though perhaps not a perfect analogy, there is some similarity when we consider the motivations for our giving: often there is too much of "self" in our story.

In our humanness, our giving is many times performed consciously or subconsciously with a few subtle attachments…expectations of appreciation or gratitude. What question first forms in our mind as we consider a gift? "Will they *like* it?" Because if the recipient of our giving does not like our gift, or express profuse happiness, that is a reflection upon *me*. And I want to be liked. I want to be seen as a kind and generous person. It is not so important to me what the person *needs*, but rather that which will ingratiate them to me. Sadly, oftentimes, there is too much of "self" found in the story of our giving.

From a spiritual perspective, it is wise to question our motivations for the benevolence we offer to others. Does pride or self-promotion have a voice within this gift? Do they call for a corresponding response of gratitude? Or can it be truly and freely given?

First of all, it might be wise to remind ourselves that all that we possess are gifts from God. We are only stewards of His benefits to us, and we have the responsibility to use and share these gifts in ways consistent with His will and desires. As we share these God-given blessings with others, we are simply "paying it forward" into the community of need.

Also, honest insight sometimes reveals to us a lingering desire for acknowledgment from God for our efforts. Though our actions are sincere, they are often tainted with an attitude that it is "our work" that we are doing "for God." As admirable as that is, and as much as it pleases God, there remains a sense of ownership in this endeavor of charity…a sense of an effort that is performed with one eye on seeing the fruits of our actions…to find gratification in doing so. As well-intended and valuable as this giving is, sometimes we covertly wrap these gifts with our conditions and expectations.

Thomas Merton does not slight the value of this kind of giving, that which he refers to as those with pure or "right intentions." But he also describes for us a type or work or gift that is given without conditions or expectations…without a sense of ownership…which he calls "simple intentions." This is a giving characterized by an "atmosphere of prayer" and marked by abandoning any sense of ownership of the eventual fruits of our efforts, for it is performed *within* the deep will of God, beyond our understanding. Merton says, "*We are more aware of Him who works in us than of ourselves or of our work.*"[17] Simple intentions then are those in which the "self" fades into the reality of Christ's work through us. He states it this way,

> A simple intention is a perpetual death in Christ. It keeps our life hidden with Christ in God…It prefers what cannot be touched, counted, weighed, tasted, or seen. But it makes our inner being open out, at every moment, into the abyss of Divine peace in which our life and actions have their roots.[18]

*Giving Inconveniently*

It is relatively easy for me to write a check for a cause. I justify that means of giving by telling myself that a financial gift is what is most desired and most needed, but if I am really honest with myself, it is really because this is the most convenient way for me to give. There is no cost of time or comfort; no inconvenience to my daily patterns, no rubbing elbows with those who suffer. Often, I will say a prayer over this financial gift as I place it in its neat envelope, but *I remain unchanged*. That is in no way to deride the generosity of financial giving to needy causes: to aid those children suffering from disease and deformity, those wounded soldiers struggling courageously daily to rebuild their broken lives, those women burdened with the weight of abuse, abandonment, and depression. Yet to do so without personal cost often arouses the reprimand of my conscience whispering, "*too easy.*"

To experience inconvenience is to give a portion of who I am as a person, whether it is of my material possessions in the case of financial contributions or that of loving gifts of clothing or food. It may be gifting of my talents or of my time and energy. More importantly, it is to give attentiveness, concern, and empathy to others. Furthermore, I would make the case that the most meaningful gifting to those suffering are those in which we give a portion of who we are, for in so doing we also are changed. Though not the primary reason to give to others, it still is reasonable to acknowledge the fact that in our sacrificial giving to others, we also enjoy God's gifts to us… in forms of gratification, lovingkindness, and goodness as they flow from our experience of caring for others. It reminds us of our brotherhood and sisterhood with all others, of a community grounded in mutuality and respect for one another.

Mother Theresa responded when once asked if her work among the poor was "easy":

> The poorest of the poor are the unwanted, the unloved, the ignored, the hungry, the naked, the homeless, the addicts in our midst. Christ is hidden under the distressing appearance of the poor…To be able to see and love Jesus in the poor, we must be one with Christ through a life of deep prayer. We need to worship God and

have a spirit of sacrifice. Life of prayer, sacrifice and poverty will lead us to serve the poor.[19]

## Giving Out of Our Poverty

In the book of Luke, we read these words of Jesus:

> And He looked up and saw the rich putting their gifts into the treasury.
> And He saw a poor widow putting in two small copper coins.
> And He said, "Truly I say to you, this poor widow put in more than all of them; for they all out of their surplus put into the offering; but she out of her poverty put in all that she had to live on." (Luke 21:1–4 NASB)

"For they all out of their surplus put into the offering; but she out of her poverty put in all that she had to live on"—these words always touch me deeply, for they convey such a powerful lesson within this simple scene.

The widow's poverty is first demonstrated in her poverty of spirit. For out of her humility flows the recognition that all is from the Lord…and giving becomes an act of submission and gratitude. For us to give out of this kind of poverty implies an awareness that all that one has, even our very lives, are rightfully His. Furthermore, it conveys an attitude of submission to His authority and will.

## Giving Anonymously

Giving anonymously takes ourselves off center stage. Expectations of gratitude and reward are eliminated; only to find a gentle kind of peace in knowing that assistance has been given to another. It is a way of doing for others, without the expectations of acknowledgment. Ruth Calkin's poem challenges us.

## I Wonder[20]

You know, Lord, how I serve You
With great emotional fervor
In the limelight.
You know how eagerly I speak for You
At a woman's club.
You know how I effervesce when I promote
A fellowship group.
You know my genuine enthusiasm
At a Bible study.
But how would I react, I wonder
If you pointed to a basin of water
And asked me to wash the calloused feet
Of a bent and wrinkled old woman
Day after day
Month after month
In a room where nobody saw
And nobody knew.
(Ruth Harms Calkin)

*Giving Consecrated Gifts*

Consecration means dedicating a person, event, or object with special significance. To consecrate an act of giving is to bring those gifts unto God to be used for His purposes and to be multiplied to His glory. For it is only in humbly offering our gifts to the Lord, asking that they be blessed by Him, that they can be most fully received by those in need. It is in His *blessing*, that He amplifies and expands the benefits of our simple offerings into ones of Divine lovingkindness greater than any of our imaginings.

This act of consecration then can become not only a prelude to giving, but an attitude of preparation, of presenting our lives, our everyday thoughts and deeds, unto the Lord to work His will. It becomes a daily dedication of sorts, an act of submission and purpose that adds a significance and perspective to even the most mundane and seemingly insignificant events.

### Prayer for Compassion

O Heavenly Father, give me a heart like the heart of Jesus Christ, a heart more ready to minister than to be ministered unto, a heart moved by compassion towards the weak and the oppressed, a heart set upon the coming of Thy kingdom in the world of men…

Grant, O Father, that Thy loving kindness in causing my own lines to fall in pleasant places may not make me less sensitive to the needs of others less privileged, but rather more incline me to lay their burdens upon my own heart. And if any adversity should befall myself, then let me not brood upon my own sorrows, as if I alone in the world were suffering, but rather let me busy myself in the compassionate service of all who need my help. Thus let the power of my Lord Christ be strong within me and His peace invade my spirit. Amen.[21] (John Baillie)

---

[1] Taken from *One Thousand Gifts* by Ann Voskamp, 11. Copyright © 2011 by Ann Voskamp. Used by permission of Zondervan. www.zondervan.com.
[2] Ibid., 15.
[3] Ibid., 17.
[4] Ibid., 22–23.
[5] Ibid., 33.
[6] Ibid., 41.
[7] *The Problem of Pain* by C. S. Lewis, 83. Copyright © C. S. Lewis Pte. Ltd. 1940. Extracts reprinted by permission.

[8] Soren Kierkegaard, *Papers and Journals: A Selection*, trans. Alastair Hannay (New York: Penguin Books, 1996), 546.

[9] Excerpt from *The Spirituality of Imperfection* by Ernest Kurtz, 1992 by Ernest Kurtz, Ph.D. And Katherine Ketcham, 20. Used by permission of Bantam Books, an imprint of Random House, a division of Penguin Random House LLC. All rights reserved.

[10] From *Purity of Heart Is to Will One Thing* by Soren Kierkegaard, translated by Douglas V. Steere, 175. English translation copyright © 1938 by Harper & Brothers, renewed © 1966 by Douglas V. Steere. Used by permission of HarperCollins Publishers.

[11] Ibid. 174.

[12] Excerpts from *No Man Is an Island* by Thomas Merton, 77. Copyright © 1955 by The Abbey of Our Lady of Gethsemani and renewed 1983 by the Trustees of the Merton Legacy Trust. Reprinted by permission of Houghton Mifflin Harcourt Publishing Company. All rights reserved.

[13] Bill McDonald, *A Lenten Meditation*, April 2, 2019, personal letter (unpublished).

[14] Excerpts from *No Man Is an Island* by Thomas Merton, 14. Copyright © 1955 by The Abbey of Our Lady of Gethsemani and renewed 1983 by the Trustees of the Merton Legacy Trust. Reprinted by permission of Houghton Mifflin Harcourt Publishing Company. All rights reserved.

[15] The writings of Mother Teresa of Calcutta © by the Mother Teresa Center, exclusive licensee throughout the world of the Missionaries of Charity for the works of Mother Teresa. Used with permission.

[16] The writings of Mother Teresa of Calcutta © by the Mother Teresa Center, exclusive licensee throughout the world of the Missionaries of Charity for the works of Mother Teresa. Used with permission.

[17] Excerpts from *No Man Is an Island* by Thomas Merton, 71. Copyright © 1955 by The Abbey of Our Lady of Gethsemani and renewed 1983 by the Trustees of the Merton Legacy Trust. Reprinted by permission of Houghton Mifflin Harcourt Publishing Company. All rights reserved.

[18] Ibid., 74.

[19] The writings of Mother Teresa of Calcutta © by the Mother Teresa Center, exclusive licensee throughout the world of the Missionaries of Charity for the works of Mother Teresa. Used with permission.

[20] Ruth Harms Calkin, *Tell Me Again, Lord, I Forget* (Elgin, Ill.: David C. Cook Pub. Co., 1974), quoted in Charles Swindoll, *Improving Your Serve* (Waco, Texas: Word Pub., 1981), 43–44. Used by permission of Bonnie Knopf.

[21] From *A Diary of Private Prayer* by John Baillie, 59. Copyright © 1949 by Charles Scribner's Sons; and Schuster, Inc. All rights reserved.

# 11

## Grace and Gratitude
## Discovering Peace

Let your gentle spirit be known to all men. The Lord is near. Be anxious for nothing, but in everything by prayer and supplication with thanksgiving let your requests be made known to God. And the peace of God, which surpasses all comprehension, will guard your hearts and your minds in Christ Jesus. Finally, brethren, whatever is true, whatever is honorable, whatever is right, whatever is pure, whatever is lovely, whatever is of good repute, if there is any excellence and if anything worthy of praise, dwell on these things. The things you have learned and received and heard and seen in me, practice these things, and the God of peace will be with you. (Philippians 4:5–9 NASB)

## GRACE

Grace is essentially God's blessing freely bestowed upon undeserving humanity. It is unfortunate that in our English language we have only one word for the multiplicity and multifaceted concepts which we refer to as "grace." That is because, as an instrument of God's lovingkindness, it can be manifested in so many different ways.

Evangelical theology has attempted to describe these various expressions of God's grace by dividing grace into that of Common Grace and Special Grace. Common Grace is God's overarching care for humanity by providing the blessings of *creation*, and the concepts of *civility* and *conscience*. Special Grace is that grace extended to humankind in the act of redemption. It includes *prevenient grace*, that grace that reaches out to every person, beckoning one to relationship with God through the saving work of Jesus Christ; *efficacious grace*, that which effectively works out the will of God to accomplish His desires within the lives of His people; *sufficient grace*, that grace which God extends to His people to give them direction for their earthly responsibilities and strength in their moments of suffering and need, and *irresistible grace*, that which God uses occasionally to actuate His will of redemption by overriding man's free will in order to accomplish His Divine work (Moses, Jonah, Isaiah).

Common Grace[1]: (general, universal)—common to all mankind

    a. Creation
    b. Civility—government, law
    c. Conscience

Special Grace[2]: grace by which God redeems, sanctifies, and glorifies His people

    a. Prevenient grace
    b. Efficacious grace
    c. Sufficient grace
    d. Irresistible grace

*Grace: An Instrument of Lovingkindness*

Grace understood as "unmerited favor" is certainly true as far as it goes. God does express His favor toward mankind despite our imperfections and rebellion. However I like to think of Grace as something more as well…a direct expression of God's will and compassion toward mankind. By Grace God created the heavens and the earth. By Grace God made man "in His image." By Grace God reaches out to redeem His creation. By Grace God intrudes into the events of each day, in the here and now, to aid and direct our paths, and to support us and show us His love for us. Furthermore, Scripture tells us that He is always with us and will never leave us, and that we have a home within His presence. God's Grace is His expression of His lovingkindness to us, and as we experience His grace and lovingkindness in our lives, gratitude is to be our response. As Meister Eckhart once said, our gratitude is how we say "thank you" to God.

> "If the only prayer you said in your whole life was, "thank you," that would suffice."[3]
> Meister Eckhart (1260–1328)

## "CHEAP GRACE"

God's Grace says to us, "I love you so much that I have given my Son to die for you… to pay the penalty of your sin."

> "But the free gift is not like the transgression. For if by the transgression of the one the many died, much more did the grace of God and the gift by the grace of the one Man, Jesus Christ, abound to the many." (Romans 5:15 NASB)

> "If we confess our sins, He is faithful and righteous to forgive us our sins and to cleanse us from all unrighteousness." (1 John 1:9 NASB)

Yet as wonderful as is this gift of grace, we must ask, "Are there times when we accept this gift too casually?" Are we too quick to "soothe" our consciences of the secular, by appealing to God's "grace" like a soothing balm in order to cover our sins without enduring the pain of true brokenness and repentance? Can we honestly ask ourselves, "Do we only want $3 worth of God?" Wilber Rees puts it this way:

$3 Worth of God

I would like to buy $3 worth of God, please, not enough to explode my soul or disturb my sleep, but just enough to equal a warm cup of milk or a snooze in the sunshine. I don't want enough of Him to make me love a black man or pick beets with a migrant. I want ecstasy, not transformation; I want the warmth of the womb, not a new birth. I want a pound of the Eternal in a paper sack. I would like to buy $3 worth of God, please.[4] (Wilber Rees)

Today we live within a predominantly secular culture. It is a culture that values freedom from any moral or spiritual restraint upon individual behavior. Though some may partially accept a message of love and forgiveness based upon a humanistic premise; many would reject any need to acquiesce to any sense of repentance, especially to a notion of a redemptive "God." Instead, morality is self-defined, and grace is little more than a thin veneer of acceptability...

To be clear, God's grace is fully *offered* and *extended* to *all*. But can Divine grace be properly *received* without the conduit of repentance? Jeremiah answers this question in a clear and forceful description of a people's rejection of God's abundant grace.

*God's Redemptive Grace Rejected*

Jeremiah records a similar time and culture as he prophesies to the unrepentant people of Judah. Though God repeatedly extends His free and unmerited blessing upon His people, their lack of contrition and repentance nonetheless calls forth the natural and inevitable consequences of their rebellious desires. Jeremiah records God's powerful warnings of the consequences of the "fruit of their plans" as they reject His grace through acts of rejection and self-determination Jeremiah 6:13–21 (NASB). God speaks to Jeremiah:

> "For from the least of them even to the greatest of them, everyone is greedy for gain, and from the prophet even to the priest everyone deals falsely. They have healed the brokenness of My people superficially, saying, 'Peace, peace,' but there is no peace.
>
> "Were they ashamed because of the abomination they have done? They were not even ashamed at all; They did not even know how to blush. Therefore they shall fall among those who fall; At the time that I punish them, they shall be cast down," says the LORD.
>
> Thus says the LORD, "Stand by the ways and see and ask for the ancient paths, where the good way is, and walk in it; and you will find rest for your souls. But they said, 'We will not walk in it.'
>
> "And I set watchmen over you, saying, 'Listen to the sound of the trumpet!' But they said, 'We will not listen.'
>
> "Therefore hear, O nations, and know, O congregation, what is among them.
>
> Hear, O earth: behold, I am bringing disaster on this people, the fruit of their plans, because they have not listened to My words, and as for My law, they have rejected it also. For what purpose does frankincense come to Me from Sheba and the sweet cane from a distant land? Your burnt offerings are not acceptable and your sacrifices are not pleasing to Me."
>
> Therefore, thus says the LORD, "Behold, I am laying stumbling blocks before this people. And they will stumble against them, fathers and sons together; neighbor and friend will perish."

Though there is much to be explored in this dramatic portion of Scripture, let's unpack it a bit.

- Judah was rampant with greed. (*"Everyone is greedy for gain."*) Materialism had become so immersed into their culture that it was pervasive. People longed for more and more despite having much. Their greed resulted in the rich and powerful preying upon the possessions of others. Never satisfied, care for those less fortunate was abandoned to their hedonistic desires.
- Judah's leaders were dishonest. (*"And from the prophet even to the priest everyone deals falsely. They have healed the brokenness of My people superficially, saying, 'Peace, peace,' but there is no peace."*) Deceit characterized the times, even into the upper levels of religion and government. Like placebos, the people were offered solutions for their conditions that in fact had no real benefit…rather they were only superficial appeasements…(a stronger donkey, a newer abacus… just kidding!). Appeasements designed to comfort but not cure, to distract but not fulfill…deceit and misinformation instead of truth. Promises of peace are proclaimed as conflicts are allowed to grow and divisiveness is fostered. Like sheepskins, leaders' proclamations are cloaked in falsity and manipulation of the masses.
- Judah had no moral compass or grounding. (*"Were they ashamed because of the abomination they have done? They were not even ashamed at all; They did not even know how to blush."*) Forsaking spiritual absolutes, cultural mores had become formed by those in power and by the conventions of the times. Ever shifting attitudes and morals (or lack of) had left Judah at the mercy of its own self-determination. Decisions now revolved around the current popular notions promoted by those of influence. Ethics became culturally defined. The present is regarded as innately better than the past, and the future is believed to be formed and guided by progressive humanistic enlightenments. There are no lon-

## SPIRITUAL AWARENESS

ger any anchors or moral moorings upon which to guide one's ways. We no longer know how to "blush."

- God offers His redemptive grace. (*"Thus says the LORD, 'Stand by the ways and see and ask for the ancient paths, where the good way is, and walk in it; and you will find rest for your souls.'"*) God declares and defines the way back into restoration in relationship with His goodness. There are no platitudes or appeasements. The call is direct. The call is confrontational. The call is to make a choice. The way to personal fulfillment is not through greed or deceitful appeasement or of culturally defined morality, but rather the call is to stand by the ways of the ancients...the paths shaped by universal absolutes, God's design for humankind, His commandments, His truths, and His purpose. Our "rest" lies in our restored loving and forgiving relationship with Jehovah God.
- Judah rejects God's offered grace: (*"But they said, 'We will not walk in it.'... "And I set watchmen over you, saying, 'Listen to the sound of the trumpet!' But they said, 'We will not listen.'"*) God has given to humankind His warnings, demonstrating His expressed will in the written word of Scripture and the Living Word of Christ. If only we would choose to listen! For those who delay the choice or reject His offer of redemptive grace lie the consequences of their own choosing.
- Consequences of rejected grace: (*"behold, I am bringing disaster on this people, the fruit of their plans, because they have not listened to My words, and as for My law, they have rejected it also."*) Attitudes and actions have consequences. Yet our culture chooses to delude itself by disregarding the reality of cause and effect. Rather, it chooses to believe that it can escape the spoiled "fruits" of its unethical and immoral conduct. By ignoring and rebelling against God's Living Word (Christ) and His written law (Scripture), humanity will face the eventual and inevitable judgment of its choices. (*"Therefore, thus says the LORD, 'Behold, I am laying stumbling blocks before this people. And they will stumble against them, fathers and sons together; neighbor and friend will per-*

*ish.'"*) As New Covenant Christians, we know this "stumbling block" to be Jesus Christ. In rejecting the redemptive grace of God, and instead choosing the unrepentant paths or "fruit of their plans," they also are rejecting the redemptive work of Jesus Christ. Matthew 21:42–45 (NASB):

> Jesus said to them, "Did you never read in the Scriptures, 'THE STONE WHICH THE BUILDERS REJECTED, THIS BECAME THE CHIEF CORNER stone; THIS CAME ABOUT FROM THE LORD, AND IT IS MARVELOUS IN OUR EYES'? Therefore I say to you, the kingdom of God will be taken away from you and given to a people, producing the fruit of it. And he who falls on this stone will be broken to pieces; but on whomever it falls, it will scatter him like dust." When the chief priests and the Pharisees heard His parables, they understood that He was speaking about them.

- Superficial worship is not enough: (*"For what purpose does frankincense come to Me from Sheba and the sweet cane from a distant land? Your burnt offerings are not acceptable and your sacrifices are not pleasing to Me."*) Grace is not cheap. Grace cannot be effortlessly appropriated with simple expediencies. It is not in the material or the action, but rather of the heart (Cain and Abel sacrifices). For a genuine acceptance of redemptive grace to occur, a sincere repentance must be first experienced.
- A Cry for Repentance:

> Be gracious to me, O God, according to Your lovingkindness; According to the greatness of Your compassion blot out my transgressions.
> Wash me thoroughly from my iniquity and cleanse me from my sin.

## SPIRITUAL AWARENESS

For I know my transgressions, and my sin is ever before me.

Against You, You only, I have sinned and done what is evil in Your sight, so that You are justified when You speak and blameless when You judge.

Behold, I was brought forth in iniquity, and in sin my mother conceived me.

Behold, You desire truth in the innermost being, and in the hidden part You will make me know wisdom.

Purify me with hyssop, and I shall be clean; Wash me, and I shall be whiter than snow.

Make me to hear joy and gladness, Let the bones which You have broken rejoice.

Hide Your face from my sins and blot out all my iniquities.

Create in me a clean heart, O God, and renew a steadfast spirit within me.

Do not cast me away from Your presence and do not take Your Holy Spirit from me.

Restore to me the joy of Your salvation and sustain me with a willing spirit.

Then I will teach transgressors Your ways, and sinners will be converted to You.

Deliver me from bloodguiltiness, O God, the God of my salvation; Then my tongue will joyfully sing of Your righteousness.

O Lord, open my lips, that my mouth may declare Your praise.

For You do not delight in sacrifice, otherwise I would give it; You are not pleased with burnt offering.

The sacrifices of God are a broken spirit; A broken and a contrite heart, O God, You will not despise. (Psalm 51:1–17 NASB)

Judah seems not so far removed from today!
It might be helpful to remind ourselves of several truths:

- Grace does not lessen the seriousness of sin or its consequences.
- Grace, though freely offered to all, requires genuine repentance (as an opening or conduit) in order to be fully received and Spirit-filled. God does not ask for restitution, only our genuine and sincere repentance.
- Grace allows for *healing from* the consequences of one's sin (redemption)—thereby it restores our designed relationship with God—it redeems us…even in our seasons of sin and suffering.

As wonderful as grace is, it does not protect us *from* sacrifice or suffering. Instead, true grace tends to *reveal itself within our human sacrifice and suffering*, and to draw us into a more intimate and genuine relationship with Jesus Christ.

Dietrich Bonhoeffer cautions us in his work, *Cost of Discipleship*, not to regard this profound gift of God's Grace casually and makes the following distinction between what he calls "Cheap Grace" vs. "Costly Grace."

> Cheap grace is the deadly enemy of our Church. We are fighting to-day for costly grace.
> …Grace is represented as the Church's inexhaustible treasury, from which she showers blessings with generous hands, without asking questions or fixing limits. Grace without price; grace without cost! The essence of grace, we suppose, is that the account has been paid in advance; and, because it has been paid, everything can be had for nothing…That is what we mean by cheap grace, the grace which amounts to the justification of sin without the justification of the repentant sinner who departs from sin and from whom

sin departs. Cheap grace is not the kind of forgiveness of sin which frees us from the toils of sin. Cheap grace is the grace we bestow on ourselves.

Cheap grace is the preaching of forgiveness without requiring repentance, baptism without church discipline, Communion without confession, absolution without personal confession. Cheap grace is grace without discipleship, grace without the cross, grace without Jesus Christ, living and incarnate.

Costly grace is the treasure hidden in the field; for the sake of it a man will gladly go and sell all that he has. It is the pearl of great price to buy for which the merchant will sell all his goods. It is the kingly rule of Christ, for whose sake a man will pluck out the eye which causes him to stumble; it is the call of Jesus Christ at which the disciple leaves his nets and follows him.

Costly grace is the gospel which must be sought again and again, the gift which must be asked for, the door at which a man must knock.

Such grace is costly because it calls us to follow, and it is grace because it calls us to follow Jesus Christ. It is costly because it costs a man his life, and it is grace because it gives a man the only true life. It is costly because it condemns sin, and grace because it justifies the sinner. Above all, it is costly because it cost God the life of his Son: "ye were bought at a price," and what has cost God much cannot be cheap for us. Above all, it is grace because God did not reckon his Son too dear a price to pay for our life, but delivered him up for us. Costly grace is the Incarnation of God.[5]

From an appreciation of this Divine gift of God's grace should blossom forth the beauty of gratitude.

## GRATITUDE

Gratitude is the fairest blossom
which springs from the soul.
—Henry Ward Beecher[6]

The key to life in fullness is gratefulness.
—Brother David Steindl-Rast[7]

Gratitude unlocks the fullness of life. It turns what we have into enough, and more. It turns denial into acceptance, chaos into order, confusion into clarity…. It turns problems into gifts, failures into success, the unexpected into perfect timing, and mistakes into important events. Gratitude makes sense of our past, brings peace for today and creates a vision for tomorrow.
—Melodie Beattie[8]

Gratitude bestows reverence, allowing us
to encounter everyday epiphanies, those
transcendent moments of awe that change
forever how we experience life and the world.
—John Milton,[9] English poet,
historian, and scholar (1608–1674)

As we explore this gift, this notion of gratitude and thanksgiving, it seems important to make the distinction between expressing gratitude "for" and expressing gratitude "to"…Amidst all the wonderful gifts of this life…can one really be truly "grateful for" these gifts without also being "grateful to" the Giver? Does gratitude really have any significance if not directed "to whom?"

"Every good thing given and every perfect
gift is from above, coming down from the Father

of lights, with whom there is no variation or shifting shadow" (James 1:17 NASB).

*Gratitude Is an Intentional Act*

Gratitude is not just some warm and fuzzy emotional response to a specific gift. Rather, it is a process of choosing to see the events and circumstances of our daily lives within a whole overarching perspective of thanksgiving. Gratitude requires intentionality...a conscious choice to find within the mundane, and, yes, even in the suffering of our days, the packaged blessings of God's lovingkindness, freely given, for us to unwrap and experience. Ann Voskamp describes her decision to "do something" by starting to write down her "one thousand gifts":

> Not of gifts I want but of gifts I already have. 1. Morning shadows across the old floors 2. Jam piled high on the toast 3. Cry of blue jay from high in the spruce. That is the beginning and I smile. I can't believe how I smile. I mean, they are just the common things and maybe I don't even know they are gifts really until I write them down. Gifts He bestows. This writing it down—it is sort of like ... unwrapping love.[10]

There is a part of gratitude that yearns to engage and enjoy the grace-filled goodness found in even the simplest and most common...the beauty of the autumn sunset, the fresh fragrance of the springtime rain, the intricacy of the opening rose blossom, the innocence of an infant's first smile.

There is great value in this appreciation of even the commonplace and seemingly insignificant, for it reminds us of the frailty and brevity of these precious moments in time. It teaches us to be attentive to the needs of others and to opportunities that soon pass away forever lost.

Arthur Gordon in his book, *A Touch of Wonder*, describes their family's experience of adopting a frail stray cat, only to have it die after a short time…and the realization of how fragile even the simplest portions of life are sometimes meted out…

> I got in the car quickly and drove away. But not far down the road I stopped the car and put my forehead against the steering wheel and wept. Because she was such a little cat. Because she had tried to tell me that she was sick, that she was in trouble, and I hadn't helped her. Not until it was too late. And I felt the awful emptiness that comes from not knowing how much you love something until you have lost it.[11]

Gratitude also teaches us to enjoy and appreciate each moment in time as though it may never come again. It is to slow time down, to rest in the timelessness of "last moments," perhaps best expressed in a mother's reflections:

> Long ago you came to me, a miracle of firsts
> First smiles and teeth and baby steps, a sunbeam on the burst.
> But one day you will move away and leave me to your past,
> And I will be left thinking of a lifetime of your lasts.[12]

I have heard it said that Satan's most effective temptation of mankind is the phrase, "There is always tomorrow," for it delays decision and deceives us into believing in living an endless series of apathetic days. We believe in the lie that tomorrow will occur much like today, with its similar challenges, opportunities, delights, and disappointments. But someday "tomorrow" will never arrive.

Nicholas Wolterstorff, having lost his young son in a mountain climbing accident, writes these sorrowful words:

> We took him too much for granted. Perhaps we all take each other too much for granted. The routines of life distract us; our own pursuits make us oblivious; our anxieties and sorrows, unmindful. The beauties of the familiar go unremarked. We do not treasure each other enough.[13] *Lament for a Son*

*Gratitude Is Naming the Moments*

Intentionally choosing to seek out and to appreciate the blessings of each day is to allow grace to open one's eyes to a freshly discovered vision. For in discovering delight in the simple and small, the mundane and commonplace, is to welcome a newfound joy in the value of the seemingly insignificant…from which a sense of appreciation and thanksgiving is born.

Yet there is a bit of discipline required in this idea we call gratitude. For we, in our complacency, are quick to blanket these wonderful gifts with a covering of general thanksgiving, like brushing a wooden board with only one thin coat of varnish. Ann Voskamp cautions: "But in this counting gifts, to one thousand, more, I discover that slapping a sloppy brush of thanksgiving over everything in my life leaves me deeply thankful for very few things in my life."[14]

For some, this may begin with a greater appreciation of the delights of our five senses: the cinnamon aroma of freshly brewed coffee, the buttery richness of a chocolate chip cookie, the happy chirps of the birds feeding, the splendor of a sunrise or sunset, and the soft texture of a newborn's hair of silk. In addition, one can consider the gifts of relationships in the devotion and care of an aging parent, the youthful exuberance of a child, the joy of reunion with a friend, and the kindness of a neighbor. Then there are the abstract gifts of love, faithfulness, loyalty, sacrifice…an entire myriad of gifts for which to give thanks, all given by the hand of a gracious God.

Furthermore, Ann describes the profound importance of what she calls as "naming grace moments":

> This act of naming grace moments, this list of God's gifts, moves beyond the shopping list variety of prayer and into the other side. The other side of prayer, the interior of His throne room, the inner walls of His powerful, love-beating heart...To move into His presence and listen to His love unending and know the grace uncontainable. This is the vault of the miracles. The only thing that can change us, the world, is this—all His love.[15]

*Gratitude Flows into Prayer*

Is it any surprise that gratitude and thanksgiving have their culmination in prayer...that intimate and Divine communication with a personal and compassionate God who extends His grace to us? For as we name these moments of blessing, as we grant time both definition and value, our response can only be that of awe and wonder, of inspiration and reverence. Addressing God with gratitude on our hearts is our true act of worship, and to worship is to give glory to God for all that He is, and all that He has done.

*Gratitude Finds Joy and Hope*

It is in this prayerful act of worship that one encounters a Hope for tomorrow. One cannot help but be reminded of the chorus of the once-popular song by Bill and Gloria Gaither, "Because He Lives" in which we are reminded that in Christ the fear of each day can be overcome, that because He governs the future we can face each tomorrow with the confidence that life is truly "worth the living."

Even within the crucible of suffering, a profound Joy and Hope are found in this relationship with Christ, as experienced in the moments of prayerful surrender and worship. For in the incarnation, passion, and resurrection of Jesus Christ, I can now find the grace that grants insight, the gratitude that heals, and the hope that promises a welcomed destiny with Him.

> If we love another truly, our love will be graced with a clear-sighted prudence which sees and respects the designs of God upon each separate soul. Our love for one another must be rooted in a deep devotion to Divine Providence, a devotion that abandons our own limited plans into the hands of God and seeks only to enter into the invisible work that builds His Kingdom. Only a love that senses the designs of Providence can unite itself perfectly to God's providential action upon souls. Faithful submission to God's secret working in the world will fill our love with piety, that is to say with supernatural awe and respect. This respect, this piety, gives our love the character of worship, without which our charity can never be quite complete. For love must not only seek the truth in the lives of those around us; it must find it there. But when we find the truth that shapes our lives we have found more than an idea. We have come upon the action of One Who is still hidden, but Whose work proclaims Him holy and worthy to be adored. And in Him we also find ourselves.[16] (Thomas Merton: *No Man Is an Island*)

1. Walter A. Elwell, *Evangelical Dictionary of Theology* (Grand Rapids, MI: Baker Book House, 1984), 481.
2. Ibid., 481.
3. Meister Eckhart, from *A Listening Heart: The Spirituality of Sacred Sensuousness* by Brother David Steindl-Rast, xiii. Copyright © 1999. Reprinted by permission of The Permissions Company, LLC, on behalf of The Crossroad Publishing Company, Inc., crossroadpublishing.com.
4. Tim Hansel, *When I Relax I Feel Guilty* (Elgin, IL: Chariot Family Publishing, 1979).
5. From *The Cost of Discipleship* by Dietrich Bonhoeffer, translated from the German by R. H. Fuller, with revisions by Irmgard Booth, 43-45. Copyright © 1959 by SCM Press Ltd. Reprinted with the permission of Scribner, a division of Simon & Schuster, Inc. All rights reserved.
6. Henry Ward Beecher Quotes. BrainyQuote.com, BrainyMedia Inc, 2020. https://www.brainyquote.com/quotes/henry_ward_beecher_165302, accessed September 14, 2020.
7. From *A Listening Heart: The Spirituality of Sacred Sensuousness* by Brother David Steindl-Rast, 29. Copyright © 1999. Reprinted by permission of The Permissions Company, LLC, on behalf of The Crossroad Publishing Company, Inc., crossroadpublishing.com.
8. Melody Beattie Quotes. BrainyQuote.com, BrainyMedia Inc, 2020. https://www.brainyquote.com/quotes/melody_beattie_177949, accessed September 14, 2020.
9. John Milton Quotes. BrainyQuote.com, BrainyMedia Inc, 2020. https://www.brainyquote.com/quotes/john_milton_400414, accessed September 14, 2020.
10. Taken from *One Thousand Gifts* by Ann Voskamp, 45. Copyright © 2011 by Ann Voskamp. Used by permission of Zondervan. www.zondervan.com.
11. Arthur Gordon, *A Touch of Wonder* (New York: Jove Books, 1974), 25. Reprinted with permission from the estate of Arthur Gordon.
12. Karen Kingsbury and Gary Smalley, *Rejoice* (Wheaton, IL: Tyndale House Publishers, Inc., 2004), 209–211.
13. Nicholas Wolterstorff, *Lament for a Son* (Grand Rapids, MI: William B. Eerdmans Publishing Co., 1987), 13.
14. Taken from *One Thousand Gifts* by Ann Voskamp, 57. Copyright © 2011 by Ann Voskamp. Used by permission of Zondervan. www.zondervan.com.
15. Ibid., 59.
16. Excerpts from *No Man Is an Island* by Thomas Merton, 9. Copyright © 1955 by The Abbey of Our Lady of Gethsemani and renewed 1983 by the Trustees of the Merton Legacy Trust. Reprinted by permission of Houghton Mifflin Harcourt Publishing Company. All rights reserved.

# 12

## The Tapestry of Prayer
## Prayer within the Fabric of Life

> We sleep, but the loom of life never
> stops, and the pattern which was weaving
> when the sun went down is weaving
> when it comes up in the morning.
> —Henry Ward Beecher, US abolition-
> ist and clergyman (1813–1887)

The ageless, tireless Weaver sets the rhythm of the loom. And as the loom whispers its continuous rhythm, another momentary strand of time is placed upon it…a gentle weaving of spirit and psyche and soul to form the fabric of a life. This rhythm is keyed to a unique signature and meter of time, and the beauty of both melody and harmony flow from this Divinely written score of creation. Planetary orbits, the ocean's tides, the predictable cycle of the seasons and days… instinctual migration and propagation of animals and birds, precise scientific constants of force and movement… all find their established place within this score. It is as though they form the framework of the loom, tightly held together by design upon which to write the opus of humankind.

Within a Personality we are to discover an even deeper purpose for this framework. For the Weaver says much about His character in how He has constructed the framework of His loom… for it is a framework that brings order out of chaos, truth out of fallacy, and hope out of despair… all called forth with His exclamation of eternal lovingkindness for His creation.

As the solid framework is set, the timeless Weaver places the vertical strands of thread upon the loom. This "warp" will be attached tightly to the frame to form the firm structure of fabric upon which to weave the horizontal "weft" of varied color and texture of design.

These vertical strands of warp might be thought of as being composed of eternal principles the Weaver has prepared for humanity upon which to build a meaningful and purposeful life…truth, goodness, freedom, self-sacrifice, equality, justice, responsibility. Though some may perceive these strands of warp as self-evident, each individual can discover these universals as the weft is woven further into the unique fabric of humankind: rational thought, abstract thinking, creativity, empathy, humility, potentiality, faith in the unseen, ethical conduct… tools to equip one with discovery and insight.

The yarn of weft can be envisioned as those events and circumstances within time. The size and color of yarn may vary, and different chapters of life may have an ever-changing or enlarging pattern, but each tapestry of Divine purpose continues to form and grow into a beautiful image of what eternity eventually can be if allowed to be shaped by the Weaver.

As the design emerges, the rhythm of the loom may often change, shifting tempo into an Adagio or Allegro, or the rhythm may become harmonious or discordant. Written upon the score will be the familiar notes of joy and sorrow, hope and despair, confidence and fear. Even so, Divine character and intent gradually form a loving symphony of Divine purpose. Only by submission to this touch of the Weaver can a soul be genuinely formed. However, even when guided by the everlasting hands of wisdom and love, it can be a slow and difficult process.

Beyond this, interestingly, there is an oft-neglected place between the threads of tapestry.

Spirit-filled gaps between the threads of yarn… fenestrations of insight and relationship with Spirit. This is the place where prayer resides. Woven in and out of time, this movement of human and spiritual encounter forms a conversation of relationship and intimacy.

And as each new thread is placed upon the loom of life, another series of timeless openings are created.

This is holy space, where temporal soul encounters timeless Spirit between and within the events and circumstances of the here and now of the "present moment." As such, in a seemingly paradoxical manner, this open space of creature and Creator encounter is the "substance" or binding which holds the design of the tapestry together thereby allowing for its beauty and unique purpose. Unseen at first glance within the beauty of the weave, these openings allow for prayerful Presence to encounter each soul. Yet as each thread of warp and weft are placed upon the loom, there will be those who choose to watch from a distance, finally to turn aside from the Weaver's work… to instead inherit a "cat's cradle" tangle of disorder and despair.

Often overlooked is the fact that it is only because of these spaces, these moments of prayerful communication between soul and Spirit that the fabric of life can move and breathe, then flex and fold into its many forms and dimensions.

Yet there will be a time when the frayed fabric of life will be taken off the loom to be washed with the redemptive mercies of the Weaver, long ago prepared, in which to renew the life as a "new creation" by the Weaver's hand.

Prayer is the conduit by which the Spirit is woven into the fabric of the secular. It is the process in which the Creator touches the creature, where Spirit indwells soul. "Openings" within time and circumstance form the holy ground for which this encounter may occur; and as such, the function of prayer is a sacred Gift, a Divine expression of Lovingkindness.

To write a few pages on such an enormous topic as prayer is an intimidating endeavor, particularly in light of the vast number of books, articles, and treatises written by so many people from so many points of view and religious traditions. For these reasons, this will not be an attempt at a comprehensive reflection upon prayer. Rather, one will find only a collection of fragments or snippets about aspects of prayer that are perhaps less commonly explored and discussed. Since the overall topic of this manuscript is that of spiritual awareness, most of this discussion will focus on the experiential and metaphysical aspects of prayer within the tradition of Christianity. It will be offered as a means to broaden and deepen each individual's prayer life, to live a more "Prayer-Centered Life."

Many of us can still easily recite those childhood prayers we would say at mealtime or at bedtime. They would be uttered innocently and sincerely with a spirit of reverence to a God much bigger than our wildest imagination. Unfortunately, later, most of us would begin to speak those words in a manner of casual repetition, without the focus and reverence of our previous simple, childlike faith. In our adolescent naiveté, we might even begin to consider our prayers like a rabbit's foot, a token for which to obtain "good fortune" for our lives. Or for some, they may become like merit badges, seeking rewards for accomplishing a spiritual good deed. Prayer can easily become primarily asking God for things. "Help me be good. Help Grandma feel better. Please help Daddy or Mommy find a good job. Please have Tommy like me."

Eventually we may be taught the traditional acrostic for prayer… ACTS, in an effort to understand additional aspects of prayer.

> *A* stands for Adoration. Praise is offered to God for who He is and what He has done for us. "Through Jesus, therefore, let us continually offer to God a sacrifice of praise—the fruit of lips that openly profess His name" (Hebrews 13:15 NIV).
>
> *C* is for Confession. Contrition and repentance is offered to God for our sins. David said to Nathan, "I have sinned against the Lord" (2 Samuel 12:13 NIV). (See also Psalm 51.)
>
> *T* represents Thanksgiving. Gratitude is expressed for God's goodness and His benevolence toward us. Appreciation is basic to every relationship. If, when praying for a person, you pray only for his faults or needs, you may develop

a negative outlook. Also pray in thanksgiving for that person's strengths.

> "It is a good thing to give thanks unto the Lord" (Psalm 92:1 KJV). Ephesians 5:20, Philippians 4:6, Colossians 3:17, 1 Thessalonians 5:18

*S* is for Supplication…when we ask God for our desires and needs.
*Personal prayer* (for oneself):

> God knows our every need (Matthew 6:31–32).

*Intercessory prayer* (for others):

> Requests for intercessory prayer: Romans 15:30, 1 Thessalonians 5:25, Ephesians 6:18.
> Examples of intercessory prayer: John 17, Ephesians 3:14–19.

To conceptualize prayer in this manner has the advantage of giving some structure to our prayer life and some insight into broadening our understanding of prayer. It reminds us of the various aspects of our relationship with God and encourages us to envision prayer as much more than "asking God for things."

However, this too runs the risk of codifying our prayer lives into a rather rigid structure that can easily become checking boxes on our "to-do list" of prayer. But it nonetheless serves a purpose by propelling our thoughts and reflections into a more abstract realm. Just what is the purpose of this experience we call prayer? What are the undergirding moorings of how we approach God? Does God really hear me personally and individually? Does God really speak to us? How so? What if God is silent?

The answers to these and other questions about prayer come to different people, in various ways, at multiple stages of life. Though the Bible clearly presents the fundamental foundations of communicating with God in a meaningful way, each person arrives at their awareness of such in a highly personal and experiential manner. Suffice it to say, there are no quick ABC's to acquire a meaningful prayer life. Rather it is a fluid, dynamic growth experience of spiritual awareness and participation. And it truly is participation…no sitting on the sidelines making lists of things for God to do.

Within human nature is also the desire to categorize things. In an attempt to give meaning and order to the myriad of one's experiences and ideas, there is the innate predisposition to analyze, label, and compartmentalize. In doing so, we can begin to understand relationships between concepts in a manner that grants us some sense of security and comfort. Like Aristotle, we develop the process of interpreting each sense experience and thought and placing them in their respective boxes which we have constructed—some boxes have been culturally constructed while others have been personally formed. This process allows us to define and structure our understanding of the internal and surrounding world. Of course, in most cases, this is a very useful process in our effort to understand and discern. However, in a negative form, it also allows us to manage and maneuver these concepts and experiences in ways most beneficial to our own (sometimes selfish) desires. They can easily become self-derived and self-determined. Furthermore, like many others, they can be taken to the extremes of a rigid and confining understanding of the reality which we face.

The concept of Prayer is not exempt from this process within our spiritual lives. Most of us view prayer as one aspect of our spiritual experience, to be defined in various manners and perspectives. But prayer does not like being so confined, and it rebels from within its realm of mystery. Not so easily understood as height and weight and measure, the reality of prayer flows freely, and frequently spontaneously, within the dimension of relationship.

So to begin to understand this concept that we label as prayer is first of all to begin to develop an awareness of an ever-present spiritual conversation. It requires a paradigm shift from viewing everyday experiences often viewed as mundane to one that perceives those same events as ones of spiritual significance and opportunity for encounter… spiritual fenestrations between the temporal and the eternal.

Prayer is the conduit of moments within the fabric of life in which the eternal communes with the temporal. As such, it offers the capacity for spiritual encounter into realms of spiritual union beyond our understanding and human perceptions.

> In the same way the Spirit also helps our weakness; for we do not know how to pray as we should, but the Spirit Himself intercedes for us with groanings too deep for words; and He who searches the hearts knows what the mind of the Spirit is, because He intercedes for the saints according to the will of God. (Romans 8:26–27 NASB)

## QUESTIONS FORM

1. Do we believe in or seek a spiritual encounter beyond the concreteness of this dimension of space and time?
2. Do we believe in intercessory prayer? …prayers which transform the person of prayer and those persons and events for whom we pray…
3. Do we believe in an omnipresent, omniscient, and omnipotent God? If so, how can we not believe in intercessory prayer…and if so, why is our pattern of intercessory prayer so threadbare?

As we begin to seriously explore the various dimensions of prayer, the interrelatedness and culmination of many of the topics already presented in this work on Spiritual Awareness should become more readily apparent.

Attitudes of humility, openness, and surrender prepare the heart for the submission necessary to properly hear God speak. Simplicity, silence, solitude all prepare the groundwork in which God can be heard amidst the clamor of culture in order to generate belief in the unseen and incomprehensible. The present moment creates the conduit within time in which to have experiential encounter with God... out of which flows a sense of awe and wonder. And because of this rich intimate and loving relationship, grace and gratitude can paradoxically flow even out of our deepest pains and sufferings... immersing us in an eternal hope found within the "Living Water" of life.

Like the ever-changing pattern of a kaleidoscope, the experience of prayer is an ever-changing, dynamic, personal relationship of intimacy with Eternal Being. To participate in such is a process of spiritual insight and transformation.

In studying any topic, the natural proclivity is to analyze the subject by dissecting it into its component pieces, then to see how they all fit back together. To do so with the topic of prayer, however, would do a great injustice to the interconnectedness and dynamic dimensions of deep prayer. Instead, though a loose structure will be provided here in an attempt to distinguish various differences amongst some aspects of prayer, the majority of the following discussion will be focused upon reflecting upon the multi-faceted experiences that lead to a truly prayer-centered life.

## GENERAL CONCEPTS OF PRAYER

- *Examine Personal Convictions.* This must be a process of ruthless honesty. Do my beliefs about prayer rest upon the hopes of wishful desires, or rather, upon the strong convictions of faith? Can I offer my prayers to a benevolent God confident that they will be heard? Can I offer those prayers free of my own expectations to an all-knowing God to answer at His own time in His own way with a wisdom beyond my understanding?

- *Establishing the Priority of Prayer.* Do I really want to live a prayer-centered life? Am I sincerely willing to have prayer become the center of my comings and my goings…my choices and my decisions? Am I willing to bear the costs of the responsibilities I may discover within this realm of experience?
- *Overcoming Inertia.* Like so many actions, sometimes the most difficult beginnings are the first two or three steps. The comfort of inactivity placates. At other times, the steady flow of sense experience stimulates our interest and draws our attention. Moving out of comfort and from distraction requires a concentrated effort, a paradigm shift if you will, into the realm of prayer. It is no easy matter to move from the familiar and readily available into an experience that is perceived as much less tangible and certainly much less concrete.
- *Entry into Prayer.* How is it that despite the recognition of the importance of prayer, that it is so easily neglected and marginalized within our busy everyday lives? If prayer is regarded as a person's experience of intimate relationship with Eternal Lovingkindness, how can one allow it to be such a casual aspect of temporal experience? Is it not fair to ask ourselves whether prayer is to be a foundational or peripheral aspect of our spiritual experience?
- *Developing the Discipline of Prayer.* There can be no truly genuine prayer life if prayer is only an afterthought. But for it to become more than that requires a discipline of intentionality, an attentiveness beyond, or perhaps deeper than, the superficial events that scream from moment to moment. Perhaps in some ways it might even be regarded simplistically as an intentional creation of doors leading into spiritual experience—"openings" of a such that *allow for*, but do not force, or in any manner create, an experience of intimate relationship with Ultimate Being. To be clear, it is a discipline for *providing an opportunity* when the Eternal may be perceived within our dimensions of time

and space. It is to genuinely allow for a Holy Place of spiritual encounter.
- *Self-examination:* role of solitude and surrender and repentance.

Jan Johnson shares these views of the benefits of solitude:

> In solitude, our character defects come to the surface. Solitude can make us painfully aware of our tendency to grasp at things and strut our egos across the stage of life. Solitude trains us to quiet our cravings and still our distractions, so that in all of life we can be more attentive to God and listen for God to speak.[1]
>
> Solitude provides a groundedness in God that keeps us from being victims of other people's opinions.[2]

So it is fair to ask then, "How can one best make this transition from a life of episodic prayer to one of a "life of prayer" or what some would call a "prayerful life?"

Several guidelines may be helpful. First of all, let go of the need to accomplish or perform. Secondly, develop an attitude of submission and simply pray what is on your heart and allow the Holy Spirit to guide and direct your thoughts and meditations. Thirdly, don't expect "results" in the manner of "rewards." The primary purpose of prayer is to commune with God. Any blessings of a life of prayer will manifest themselves on the Lord's timetable and according to His will, not ours. Jan Johnson explains:

> Instead performance is replaced by surrender, and self-consciousness gives way to self-forgetfulness. Enjoying God's presence means we stop trying to prove ourselves to God and decide to love Him and enjoy Him forever.[3]

## CONVERSATIONAL PRAYER

*Spontaneous and Intentional*

One of the ways to weave prayer into the everyday is that of what some would refer to as conversational prayer. There are those who may argue that the notion of "conversational" prayer runs the risk of perceiving prayer too casually or in a self-manipulated manner. It may become a simple speaking to oneself without attention to spiritual significance, or furthermore, may even become a measure of personal control.

On the other hand, it may serve as an antechamber to a deepening life of prayer. To see the simple events of each day, the simple tasks of daily living, current relationships and new ones, all in light of a prayerful awareness of a dimension or aspect of the Divine, serves as an ever-growing sensitivity and appreciation for spiritual breathings... to do so returns reverence to life. One may loosely envision conversational prayer in two forms: (1) Spontaneous prayer, which consists of spontaneous prayerful responses to everyday events and (2) Intentional prayer, which involves some sense of preparation or focus of this mode of prayer.

*Prayers of Spontaneity*

There are several notes worth sharing in regards to spontaneous conversational prayer. First of all, spontaneous prayer reinforces the awareness of a moment-by-moment companionship with God.

> Developing eyes for things eternal helps us understand that even, when nothing is supposedly happening, God is delighting in us and working His redemption in us...
> 
> As we become more conscious of God's companionship, we pay more attention to the present moment. Our problem is not lack of time, but failure to value the moment and to see God at work in it.[4]

Secondly, prayer resets priorities. Instead of each day beginning with personal desires, it can begin with a heightened attentiveness to those persons and experiences around us… spiritual listening to others' needs and to God. Perspective shifts from "me" to "you."

Thirdly, spontaneous prayer establishes the habit of "prayerful response" to persons and events that may previously have seemed inconsequential or commonplace. In this way, spiritual awareness leads to active prayerful response in the moment. These points are certainly not exhaustive of the value of conversational prayer, but only serve as adding some perspective to its role in integrating prayer into the everyday events of our lives. Jan Johnson shares some thoughts on how this can best be accomplished.

> As seekers, we become deliberate and aware, we pay attention to God's unfolding presence in every situation: What is God saying? What is His will here?… This involves training the eye to see and trusting that it will find something to appreciate. The more we train ourselves to see, the more we see…
>
> In this way we learn the art of attentiveness, of leaning into the situation or relationship with alert eyes.[5]

One of the characteristics of conversational prayer is that of often being a spontaneous response to a person or circumstance. It involves an awareness of spiritual movements and a sensitivity toward others. It furthermore requires a degree of "seeing" and "hearing" from a spiritual perspective. Because of the clamor of culture, as an ever urgent and boisterous calling for attention, it becomes difficult to experience a life of prayer that is insightful and purposeful. For many, the discipline of using personal or event "triggers" has been helpful in appreciating and responding to the opportunities for prayer in a moment-by-moment manner. Emilie Griffin calls these triggers "Doors into Prayer."[6] They consist of taking a relationship or event and conditioning a spiritual response of prayer. Those responses will be precipitated and guided by the Holy Spirit in such a way that personal "effort" has little to do with the results of the prayer. The praying person has only to offer up to God that His will be done, and to surrender the results of that prayer to God. That is not to say that one should not actively assist in helping another person, rather it is important to do so, but to desire to be in control of or rewarded for the result is misguided.

An additional benefit of conversational prayer practiced in this manner is that of an ever-increasing sensitivity and empathy brought about by the attention to and awareness of spiritual opportunities for encounter and prayerful intercession. It becomes an aspect of spiritual transformation in the praying person's life.

> "And do not be conformed to this world, but be transformed by the renewing of your mind, so that you may prove what the will of God is, that which is good and acceptable and perfect" (Romans 12:2 NASB).

*Spontaneous Prayers of Personal Encounter*

As prayer is considered in the context of personal encounter, it becomes apparent that this requires a great deal of attitude change. It involves changing the way we choose to perceive others. For to earnestly pray for another person is to cushion that prayer in a bed of empathy, which runs counter to the way most of us function in the midst of our busy lives. Usually, as we encounter another person we are constantly, and often subconsciously, observing another's demeanor, posture, expressions, by which we evaluate and judge what they are all about. Out of this we form an "image" or impression of that person, whether true or not, but nonetheless painted by our opinions of what we have observed. Personal encounters then elicit a personal response of thoughts and emotions from which our attitudes are formed resulting in indifference, likes, and dislikes. These encounters are especially prominent in those interactions with others that generate a strong emotion or are experienced in a dramatic fashion. Unfortunately, empathy is often left on the sidelines of the portraits we form of others.

To pray for others, however, is to first break through this wall of opinion-constructed image and search for and develop a strong sense of empathy. Spiritually listening instead of evaluating and judging. Sensitivity rather than indifference. Caring enough to see beyond the casual masks we each wear. It involves an understanding and perception that *all* people carry their individual wounds and burdens. And it requires a genuine desire to understand and perhaps even imagine the needs and wounds of others. Only then can we begin to develop the spiritual insight and awareness which constitute meaningful prayer for others.

Empathy begins by caring enough to try to see. To imagine. To reach out in prayer to benevolently touch another spiritual being by some mysterious manner. It begins by seeing beyond the crustiness of our masks to identify with and participate in those burdens.

Richard Foster, in his work, *Freedom of Simplicity,* describes it this way:

> I became more collected within, then, as I went through the routine of my day. I sought to beam prayers at each one I met. I asked for discernment to perceive what was in people, invited Christ to comfort those who seemed hurt, encourage those who seemed weary, challenge those who seemed indifferent. It was a wonderfully happy day.[7]

As we interact with others, we learn to pray for them. For some reason, we seem to envision that this must be a fifteen-minute exercise, but it can be as simple as a one-sentence prayer: (Hebrews 10:24).

Thought Prayers:

"Lord, awaken me from my indifference."
"Thank you for this person (or experience)."

"Help me be an encourager to…"

"Father, please show me how to best reach out to Susan during her time of trials."

"Dear Father, please show me Your message and grace in going through this difficult time."

"Lord, help me be a light in the life of John…"

"Dear God, take what little I have to give, bless it and use it to Your Glory."

Praying well for others, in the midst of our own personal preoccupations is the first step to a meaningful understanding of genuine intercessory prayer. This involves intentionally conditioning ourselves to perceive through the lens of spiritual awareness, to find empathy, and to respond with conviction to the cries of needs around us.

*Spontaneous Prayers within Life Experiences*

Life tends to rough us up. Fear, anxiety, depression, loneliness, rejection, pain all batter against us—threatening to overwhelm us and to defeat us. Yet amidst even the most difficult clouds of suffering there beams the light of Eternal Hope. And we have a conduit to this sense of hope through our relationship with the Eternal One. Prayer forms this conduit to this hope and to the assurance of things we have not yet seen (Hebrews 11:1).

However, we must be intentionally aware of the movements of the Holy Spirit in the moment-by-moment presence of God. It is an essential truth of which to remind ourselves over and over and over. One of the ways that we can build this awareness is within the mundane tasks of our everyday lives. Brother Lawrence is said to have prayed even while washing dishes.

Another way to integrate prayer within our life experiences is to respond in a prayerful mode even in moments of irritation and pain. Moments of temptation and weakness. Moments of uncertainty. Moments of anger. Moments of despondency. We can bring to mind portions of Scripture or say a brief thought prayer as a means to refocus and reconfirm the reality of God's promises to us. These are times where we can re-examine our priorities of life and the reality of our convictions. These are moments we can practice repentance and re-consecration. These are moments where we can open our eyes to the presence of God by our side.

*Spontaneous Prayers of Worship: Praise and Thanksgiving*

Another way in which conversational prayer can be enjoyed is in the spontaneous expressions of praise and thanksgiving: expressing gratitude, and in acts of worship: singing hymns, repeating and memorizing Scripture, and praying a Psalm.

These responses of prayer to our personal encounters and life experiences require some *conditioning*… an almost automatic sense of spiritual awareness, conviction, and responsiveness. Practiced regularly, we soon find ourselves becoming more sensitive to the wonder and beauty within each day's encounters, and the desire to respond to God with spontaneous exclamations of praise and thanksgiving.

## PRAYERS OF INTENTIONALITY

While we have just focused on how spontaneous prayers of a conversational mode can be used to integrate prayer into everyday experiences, there is another dimension of prayer to which we turn. As conversational prayer implies a brief, spontaneous sentence prayer within the frantic pace of the everyday; intentional prayer implies a more defined and focused form of prayer. Contrary to conversational prayer which is commonly brief and in quick response to the moment, intentional prayer conveys a prayer couched in preparatory movements of the heart. As such, time can be spent in meditation and focus, and there is more opportunity for the movements and direction of the Spirit to be sensed and appreciated. Over-riding emotions and worries can be surrendered to the assurance of Divine Hope within this safe place of prayer. Moment by moment we can be allowed to rest ever more deeply in this encounter with Divine

Love. Yet it is also a place of work, in which our will is to be more completely fashioned by the Divine Will.

> Christian prayer is characteristically a way of speaking to bring our wills into harmony with God's will. Yet, prayer is often distorted, even by Christians, as an effort to bring God's power to bear upon the accomplishment of our will. We decide what is right and good, then we beseech God to bring it about, or at least help us accomplish it. Though the difference between these two approaches may seem subtle in theory, in practice they are often glaringly at odds. In Christian prayer we seek to orient ourselves to the Divine picture of the world. We seek God's perspective—to see ourselves, our problems, our possibilities, our suffering, our dreams through the eyes of Christ.[8] (Maxie Dunham, *Alive in Christ*)

*Rhythms*

One of the most commonly used ways to weave intentional prayers into our daily lives is that of establishing time for morning and evening prayers. By using the rhythm of the day, we are reminded of the need to spend time with the Creator...the One who sets the movements of the sun and the stars (Job 38–39).

Another way is to establish rhythms throughout the day. The simplest and perhaps most neglected is that of praying before each meal. Other times may include those rhythms set by the hour of the day or regular events within each day...all as means of refocusing upon our need to spend prayerful time with God. For example, consider standard prayers of gratitude upon arising each morning, of cleansing and renewal while showering, spiritual preparation for the day's events while dressing, repentance and forgiveness at bedtime...

## THE TAPESTRY OF PRAYER: PRAYER WITHIN THE FABRIC OF LIFE

*Written Prayer*

Though written or formal prayers as liturgy are regarded as somewhat staid by some, two very different writers remind us of the benefits of formal prayer from their perspective.

Evelyn Underhill, who will be frequently referenced later, shares the following

> Therefore those who value the articulate recitation of a daily office, the use of litanies and Psalms, are keeping closer to the facts of existence than those who only talk generally of remaining in a state of prayer. I feel sure that some vocal prayer should enter into the daily rule even of the most contemplative soul. It gives shape and discipline to our devotions, and keeps us in touch with the great traditions of the Church. Moreover, such vocal prayers, if we choose them well, have the evocative quality of poetry: they arouse the dormant spiritual sense, and bring us into the presence of God.[9]

C. S. Lewis certainly more well-known to most, shares his thoughts in his *Letters to Malcolm* about the value of formal written prayers:

> First, it keeps me in touch with "sound doctrine." Left to oneself, one could easily slide away from "the faith once given" into a phantom called "my religion."
> 
> Secondly, it reminds me "what things I ought to ask" (perhaps especially when I am praying for other people). The crisis of the present moment, like the nearest telegraph post, will always loom largest. Isn't there a danger that our

great, permanent, objective necessities—often more important—may get crowded out?...

Finally, they provide an element of the ceremonial. On your view, that is just what we don't want. On mine, it is part of what we want.[10]

A few formal, ready-made, prayers serve me as a corrective..."[11]

Furthermore, other wonderful sources of meditative, written prayers can be found in Thomas A'Kempis's work, *The Imitation of Christ*, in which he beautifully weaves the truths of Scripture into his prayerful reflections:

Lord, for your sake I will gladly bear whatever You shall send to me. From Your hand I will accept gladly both good and ill [Job 2:10], sweet and bitter, joy and sorrow; and for all that may befall me, I will thank You. Only keep me, O Lord, from all sin, and I shall fear neither Death nor Hell [Psalm 23:4]. Do not, I pray, reject me forever [Psalm 77:7], nor blot out my name from the book of life [Revelation 3:5]; then, whatever trials beset me can do me no harm.[12]

Another work of note is that of John Baillie's *A Diary of Private Prayer*. In this little book of his written prayers, one will discover his rhythm of morning and evening prayers for each day, as well as a morning and evening prayer specifically for the Sabbath day. Though the syntax may be a bit archaic, the depth of his devotion clearly shines through. What a wonderful way to start a day with these words:

Almighty God, who of Thine infinite wisdom hast ordained that I should live my life within these narrow bounds of time and circumstance, let me now go forth into the world with a brave and trustful heart. It has pleased Thee to withhold from me a perfect knowledge; therefore deny me not the grace of faith by which I may lay hold of things unseen. Thou hast given me little power to mould things to my desire; therefore use Thine own omnipotence to bring Thy desires to pass within me. Thou has willed it that through labour and pain I should walk the upward way; be Thou my fellow traveler as I go…[13]

*Intentional Prayers of Specific Purpose*

- Divine Dialogue: setting the mind and heart upon God
  - The Prayer of Worship
  - The Prayer of Penitence
  - The Prayer of Lament
  - The Prayer of Relinquishment
  - The Prayer of Praise and Thanksgiving
  - Prayers of Conversation
  - Prayers of Intercession
  - Prayers of Petition
  - Prayers of Guidance

## INTERCESSORY PRAYER: IMMERSING OTHERS IN GRACE BY PRAYER

I am of the conviction that intercessory prayer is one of the most amazing and profound experiences that any person can experience. For what is intercessory prayer if it is not, but for a moment, stepping into infinity or another dimension? To be able to benefit another person or affect a circumstance by participating within some mysterious spiritual realm, with a benevolent and omnipotent Being… how awesome can that be? And furthermore, what kind of spiritual responsibility toward others do we discover in immersing prayerfully within this depth of compassion? Because I have more questions than answers, I will be quoting generously from the works of Evelyn

Underhill, who was a British Christian mystic who wrote a great deal about the topics of the nature of the soul and that of prayer.

To begin, Evelyn Underhill challenges us with these words:

> Now when these thoughts and acts, these ripples on the deep pool of contemplation, are born of that profound feeling of charity and compassion which cannot long remain untouched by our neighbors' needs and griefs, then surely intercession of the very best kind is exercised by us. For intercession is a special and deliberate way of exercising love, in the completest union with the Love of God. And to be in perfect charity with all men is already to intercede for them; to put, as it were, our spiritual weight on their side of the scale.[14]

Intercessory prayer is most mysterious. To think that from the quietness of my moment I can in any way participate in ministering to the needs of others remotely is an idea beyond my comprehension. But if that be true, what a profound process it must be. And I often wonder if a little bit more understanding of intercessory prayer would lend more urgency to that aspect of my prayer life.

Prayer in general is not something "we perform." It is not reciting particular words, praying long enough, or experiencing some emotional high or mental insight. It is not something we come into with an agenda in an effort to control. Rather, like the openings between the weaves of tapestry, prayer is participating in a spiritual fenestration between this dimension of time and place to encounter Spirit, that which is of eternity. Initiated by the great Weaver, He creates this space for encounter and relationship within His loving embrace. As such, it is a Divine gift of Grace offered by the hand of Almighty God. Therefore, humankind's only proper response is to humbly accept and participate within this realm of relationship prepared for us by the sacrificial and redemptive work of Jesus Christ.

This gift of prayer is not only the gift of encounter and relationship, but a gift for spiritual transformation. Humility and surrender are the ingredients which allow the Holy Spirit to prepare and refine the soul. Evelyn Underhill writes, "Humility is the one Grace which gives wings to the simplest prayer."[15]

This refining work of the Holy Spirit prepares the soul to live a sanctified life of surrender, in which the vision of a life consecrated to prayer may form and flourish. Evelyn Underhill describes this work of surrender in this manner:

> For genuine prayer in all its degrees, from the most naive to the most transcendental, opens up human personality to the all-penetrating Divine activity. Progress in prayer, whatever its apparent form, consists in the development of this its essential character. It places our souls at the disposal of imminent Spirit. In other words, it promotes abandonment to God, and this in order that the soul's separate activity may more and more be invaded, transfigured, and at last superseded by the unmeasured Divine action.[16]

Furthermore, the result of this process leads to a consecrated life with a unique perception of Reality. A special personal awareness of the immanence of Spirit now allows for a newly discovered discernment of the world around us. Again, Evelyn Underhill describes this beautifully in the following passages:

> For it (prayer) leads the self into a level of life wholly other than that of Nature; and shows it the rich and mysterious web of existence and spiritual regard. And though this vision is far too great for us, and produces by its very radiance the obscurities of faith, still these humbling disclosures which awe and delight us, these glimpses of the dark mystery of God, do effect first a puri-

fication and then an undreamed expansion and enlightenment of the psyche; making it more supple to the Divine action, more amenable to the creative pressure of the Divine Life. By that inward growth...the human self does more and more transcend the physical. It enters more and more into a richer and deeper knowledge of God, a sense of the profoundly purposive character that inheres in all the movements of the Spirit; whether realized through circumstances, or obscurely felt in the soul.[17]

The mind and soul of a mature man of prayer have simplified their gaze, and deepened and broadened their correspondences with Reality; and the result is seen in a peculiar confidence in the universe, a profound and peaceful acceptance of experience in its wholeness and not only in purely religious regard. Such a soul, though it may and calmly does remain inarticulate as regards its deepest feelings, knows existence, is aware of the mysterious movements and pressure of the Spirit, in a way others do not. Because of its humble and disciplined communion with that immanent Spirit, it has achieved a flexibility which can move to and fro between the inward and the outward finding in both the most actual sense of the presence of a living, acting God. It is this loving discernment of reality through and in prayer,...[18]

In a discussion like this, with a great deal of spiritual language, it is common to become a bit overwhelmed. What do I have to give? For I am a simple soul, barren of talents or acclaim, unadorned with spiritual insights or merits. I struggle and have but a childlike faith... If you feel this way, read Matthew 18:4,[19] then say to Christ, "I have but five loaves and two fish." And remember, after Christ blessed those simple elements, given freely and selflessly, He fed the thousands. Underhill proceeds to expand these thoughts:

> What quality, then, is it in us that can thus become the agent of Divine creativity? Not our intellects, however brilliant; not our faith, however clear and correct; not our active works, however zealous. We may lack all these; and yet through us God's work may be done.
> There is ultimately only one thing in us that can and will be used by God to carry his love and power from soul to soul, and that is the mysterious thing we call a consecrated personality.[20]

She describes the consecrated personality in this way:

> Self offering, loving, unconditional and courageous, is therefore the first requirement of true intercessory prayer. The interceding soul must be willing to go with our Lord to Gethsemane and Calvary, and share with Him the crushing weight of the world's sin, disorder, disease.[21]

The basic prevailing principle is that it is not what we *have*, but rather *that which we freely and gratefully give*, no matter how small, that God uses to His Glory for the benefit of His people.

Remember the widow and the mite? It is not how much we *possess*, but rather *the type of inner person we are* that is of such importance. That is why so much attention in this treatise of prayer has been on growing in our lives of faith and service. So in this discussion of intercessory prayer, it might be helpful to remind ourselves that we do not need to be spiritual "heavyweights" in order to participate in this mysterious way of ministering to others' needs. We do not have to fully understand the mysterious manner in which intercessory prayer reaches out into those persons of need in ways far beyond our comprehension. All the Lord requires is a humble and selfless soul through which to manifest His blessing and benefits. Underhill elaborates:

> We are here the assistants of that Good Shepherd who gives His life for the sheep.
>
> Now, if we are thus to offer ourselves for and in those sick and helpless sheep, we shall not do it only by deliberate religious deeds and thoughts; for no one, without unhealthy strain, can keep all his deeds and thoughts on their religious level all the time. We shall do it as human beings as well as spiritual beings. That is, by more and more giving spiritual and intercessory value to all the acts and intentions of life, however homely, practical and simple; lifting that whole life, visible and invisible, on to the sacramental plane, turning it into prayer.[22]

This is part of the mystery of intercessory prayer. How can so little be transformed into such great benefit and blessing? A small, simple soul used in some mysterious way to minister comfort and healing into another's difficult life? Ridiculous, but Profound!

One word of caution seems warranted here. That is the danger of being so absorbed in mindful prayerfulness that the actions of benevolent service are neglected. For some, comfortable in their prayer closet, it may become easy to neglect our responsibilities to actively engage and care for the needs of others on the streets and in their homes. The importance of intercessory prayer should not in any way obviate our responsibility to lead lives of sacrificial service to others. We must "walk the talk."

> For the real worth of intercessions does not consist in the specific things we ask for or obtain, but in the channel offered by our love and sacrifice to the creative and redeeming love and will

of God. We open a fresh path to His Spirit; make straight the way along which He reaches a needy soul, a struggling movement, or a desolate corner of life.

Perhaps the contact will be made through some act of loving service on our part. Perhaps it will be our disciplined spirit of joy and peace which reaches out to those who most deeply need that inner tranquility. Perhaps the contact will not be made outwardly at all, but secretly in the world of prayer. However it may be made, it is essential to realize that here it is our privilege to minister the supernatural—God, in His richness and wonder; that He is coming through us to other souls in the way in which they can bear it best. The steadfast pressure of the Divine Energy and Love, felt at different levels and in different ways right through creation, is finding in us a special path of discharge.[23]

Conclusion:

Thus we come back again, don't we? to the point at which we began; that the first duty of the intercessor is communion with that Spirit in Whom our being is. Thus only we build up in ourselves a strong and pure spiritual life; thus we grow, sanctify ourselves for the sake of our work. It is for this work that we must keep the sense of wide horizons; our prayers will not escape religious pettiness unless we can do this. And it is for this that we must have spiritual food and fresh air, and receive in prayer the supernatural sunshine; not so much for the sake of its consoling warmth and light, as for the powerful but invisible chemical rays which give us spiritual vitality.

> We must keep ourselves sensitive to the Eternal, delicately responsive to God.
> This is a thing, we know, which no human creature can achieve by its own anxious efforts. It is given from beyond ourselves; but given to those who look steadily in the right direction, and accept the inward discipline which is the only preparation of peace. Thus adoring, self-oblivious vision, confident and unbroken interior communion with God, secret and tranquil renunciation, remain our first duties; for these are the real source and support of the devoted energies of the true intercessor, and of all those who offer themselves for the furtherance of God's work in our world of prayer.[24]

And so it is, that the Weaver uses those surrendered to His use, consecrated to His will and dedicated with compassion toward others to stitch together the frayed and broken threads of pain and sorrow, loneliness and rejection, grief and hopelessness. We are to be the earthly strands upon the loom used by the Weaver's hand to bind up the brokenhearted and to show hope to those in despair. Small pieces, to be sure, often only fragments or remnants of prayerful intercession, but desperately needed ones still. A knot here, a small portion of thread replaced there, prevents the frayed from unweaving and destroying the beauty of the tapestry's design.

## CONTEMPLATIVE PRAYER

> To pray is to descend with the mind into the heart, and there to stand before the face of the Lord, ever-present, all-seeing, within you.[25]
> —Theophan the Recluse

At the risk of oversimplification, the Christian tradition describes two general types of prayer. The first being that of conversational prayer, which has been discussed previously, in which there is actual dialogue, or words expressed, and the second being that of contemplative prayer or deep wordless prayer. Now we move to examine the metaphysical aspects and the personal experiential aspects of contemplative or deep prayer.

Before doing so however, it is important to make a clear distinction between the traditional prayer of contemplation within the Christian tradition, as opposed to the mystical prayers practiced by other religious traditions.

Mystical prayer outside of the Christian faith, especially within the far-eastern traditions, involves an "emptying" of mindfulness and rational thought. Their goal is to become immersed in a meditative state of placidness upon which insight will spontaneously intrude. It is this "enlightenment" that validates the presence of true knowledge and genuine spiritual ascent. Impersonal in nature, spiritual ascent is experience in alternate states of consciousness or ecstasies.

On the contrary, the tradition of Christian contemplative prayer is based upon a specific spiritual entity, whether it be Christ or Jehovah God. It is of its nature a personal, intimate dialogue (often wordless) between man and God that strives for greater loving knowledge of God, or what some would call "union" with God. This process has been described by some to involve several stages of experience: (1) Awakening, (2) Purgation or Self-denial, (3) Illumination, (4) Surrender or Dark Night, and (5) Union. These spiritual movements are not self-generated, and though not irrational, can often be regarded as "beyond" rational definition or description.

Contemplative prayer can be roughly divided into either the apophatic or kataphatic approaches. Both are ascetic in nature and share some common characteristics, but differ in their approach to contemplation.

The apophatic approach is based on "negation." That is to say that any means to deeply contemplate prayerfully upon God by means of words, ideas, icons only limits one's understanding of God. Because of the radical differences between Creator and creature, any focus upon things of this world are too confining and only serve to distract attention from the movement toward God in deep prayer.

Therefore, apophatic prayer has no specific content, and consists of emptying the mind of words and images and simply resting in the presence of God. It uses "negative" terminology to describe what the Divine is *not*. "Centering Prayer" is a form of apophatic prayer as is found in John of the Cross's "*The Cloud of Unknowing.*" Following is an excerpt from his *The Spiritual Canticle*:

> When a soul has advanced so far on the spiritual road as to be lost to all the natural methods of communing with God; when it seeks Him no longer by meditation, images, impressions, nor by any other created ways, or representations of sense, but only by rising above them all, in the joyful communion with Him by faith and love, then it may be said to have found God of a truth, because it has truly lost itself as to all that is not God, and also as to its own self.[26]

Kataphatic prayer, on the contrary, *emphasizes* the similarity that exists between Creator and creature. Because God's design can be seen in His creation, and His character revealed as such, this forms the focus of kataphatic contemplative prayer. It uses "positive" imagery to refer to the Divine by using words, images, ideas, symbols, songs, icons, and Scripture. Ignatius's prayer is kataphatic. *The Spiritual Exercises of St. Ignatius* is a prime example of the kataphatic tradition.[27]

> "All the things in this world are gifts of God, created for us, to be the means by which we can come to know him better, love him more surely, and serve him more faithfully."[28] (Ignatius of Loyola)

Deep prayer is stepping into and participating in a deeper realm of reality. By doing so, there is an acknowledgment of something or someone far beyond our full understanding or comprehension. That acknowledgment is also the submission to a higher Authority and a relinquishment of my own sense of control. And it extends beyond this moment of time to experience He who is timeless and eternal.

Is there time in our prayer life to add a contemplative component? A time to listen rather than list our concerns and appeals to God? A time to rest in the presence of God and open our spirits to the movements of His Divine Spirit? A time for Him to speak to us in the quietness and solitude?

> The ageless, tireless Weaver sets the rhythm of the loom. And as the loom whispers its rhythm of continuous movement… one strand at a time is placed upon it… this gentle weaving of spirit and psyche and soul to form the fabric of a life.

Within the strings and strands of people and events are quiet places, holy places. Existing both within and beyond time, they form the "breathings" of a spiritual life. In and out the Spirit moves within these slivers of Reality, to bridge an encounter between God and man. Within these openings, established by the Weaver, deep spiritual awareness is formed, and out of the ashes of our fallen nature, we discover with delight the beauty of awe: an unrelenting Hope, unconditional Love, everlasting Forgiveness. Intimacy with Almighty God is reaffirmed. This is that which we know as "prayer."

---

[1] Some content taken from *Enjoying the Presence of God: Discovering Intimacy with God in the Daily Rhythms of Life* by Jan Johnson, 127. Copyright © 1996. Used by permission of NavPress. All rights reserved. Represented by Tyndale House Publishers, a Division of Tyndale House Ministries.
[2] Ibid., 128.
[3] Ibid., 17.
[4] Ibid., 69–70.
[5] Ibid., 51–52.

[6] Emilie Griffin, *Doors into Prayer: An Invitation* (Brewster, Massachusetts: Paraclete Press, 2001).
[7] Richard Foster, *Freedom of Simplicity* (San Francisco: Harper and Row, 1981), 84.

Jan Johnson, *Enjoying the Presence of God* (Carol Stream, Illinois: Tyndale House Publishers: NavPress, 1996), 20.
[8] Maxie Dunham, *Alive in Christ: Workbook* (Nashville, Tennessee: Upper Room Books, 1984), 117.
[9] Evelyn Underhill, *Guild of Health*, 1922
[10] *Letters to Malcolm* by C. S. Lewis, 12. Copyright © C. S. Lewis Pte. Ltd. 1963, 1964. Extracts reprinted by permission.
[11] Ibid., 13.
[12] Thomas A' Kempis, chapter 17, "How We Must Place our Whole Trust in God," in *The Imitation of Christ* (New York, NY: Penguin Books, 1952), 115.
[13] From *A Diary of Private Prayer* by John Baillie, 85. Copyright © 1949 by Charles Scribner's Sons; copyright renewed © 1977 by Ian Fowler Baillie. Reprinted by permission of Scribner, a division of Simon & Schuster, Inc. All rights reserved.
[14] Evelyn Underhill, Guild of Health, 1922.
[15] Ibid.
[16] Evelyn Underhill, Expository Times, 1931.
[17] Ibid.
[18] Ibid.
[19] "Whoever then humbles himself as this child, he is the greatest in the kingdom of heaven." (NASB)
[20] Evelyn Underhill, An address given to the Fellowship of Prayer, Church of Scotland.
[21] Ibid.
[22] Ibid.
[23] Ibid.
[24] Ibid.
[25] Theophan the Recluse, *The Art of Prayer: An Orthodox Anthology*, ed. Timothy Ware (London: Faber & Faber, 1966), 110.

Henri Nouwen, *The Way of the Heart* (San Francisco: Harper San Francisco, 1991), 76.
[26] John of the Cross, *Cántico Espiritual (The Spiritual Canticle)*. Note to Stanza 29, Part 8), 1622.
[27] Other resources for *The Spiritual Exercises of St. Ignatius* can be found in the following works: Josef Neuner, S. J., *Walking with Him*; Louis J. Puhl, S. J., *The Spiritual Exercises of St. Ignatius: Based on Studies in the Language of the Autograph*; David M. Stanley, S. J., *A Modern Approach to the Spiritual Exercises*.
[28] Ignatius of Loyola (unknown source).

# Conclusion

Many are those who experience simple, wonderful Christian lives of faith…they demonstrate their trust resting clearly upon the benevolence of Almighty God. A certain gentleness and kindness mark their steps, and in their love for others we see Christ…gratitude shines forth in both their quiet sufferings and in their celebrations of joy…their decisions and conduct are shaped by ultimate truths… One Faith, One Hope, One Lord.

This book as such would have little benefit to them, for to them only one Book is necessary, and it is sufficient…but there are others of us who still seem to errantly muddle through life…our journeys are marked with uncertainty and confusion. We discover we have chosen the wrong markers along the way. We often find ourselves on the wrong path, and we search for redirection and insight. It is for those of us who struggle in this matter of finding a deeper spiritual life, that this book is written. It is a work focused on developing a spiritual awareness to the spiritual movements of our moment-by-moment lives which grant us insight for spiritual transformation. Hopefully, it provides guideposts of attitudes and activities which can assist in guiding our way.

Between its covers, you will find the wisdom of many other people who like us have strived to draw closer to Christ within the chaos of their everyday lives. To those I am deeply indebted…I hope you will avoid the temptation of trying to master all of the thought and practices offered here. But I hope that you can find some value within this work, in which to draw deeper in your faith and closer to our Lord Jesus Christ. May your faith shine out into the world to touch others with the redeeming hope provided by our Lord and Savior.

> Therefore I urge you, brethren, by the mercies of God, to present your bodies a living and holy sacrifice, acceptable to God, which is your spiritual service of worship. And do not be conformed to this world, but be transformed by the renewing of your mind, so that you may prove what the will of God is, that which is good and acceptable and perfect. (Romans 12:1–2 NASB)

> Therefore, since we are surrounded by such a huge crowd of witnesses to the life of faith, let us strip off every weight that slows us down, especially the sin that so easily trips us up. And let us run with endurance the race God has set before us. (Hebrews 12:1 NLT)

# Appendix I

## *Spiritual Awareness Exercises Sensitizing the Soul*

There are times in each Christian's life when he or she finds themselves confronted by a "staleness" of the soul. Our daily demands and responsibilities become rituals of obligation, rather than opportunities of service. Our routines become dulled by the covering of monotony, and our attentiveness to the sacred is lost in the fog of complacency. The spiritual vitality of our souls seems far removed.

During these times, we seek a renewal of soul…a "re-sensitizing" if you will to the sacred within the secular, the spiritual within the temporal. Through the guiding presence of the Holy Spirit each person eventually walks their own path to spiritual renewal. But one has to question whether there may be reflections and actions which can help provide assistance in doing so.

This discussion of what I refer to as "Spiritual Awareness Exercises" is offered with a clear understanding that there are many others not described below. However, these few are offered in the hope that they will stimulate one to formulate their own personal exercises that resonate most in tune with their personality and spiritual needs. Some no doubt will be drawn more to those activities which are focused primarily on reflection of Scriptural truths; while others are drawn to patterns of worship or prayer. In any case, they are meant as activities to enhance our awareness of the spiritual dimension of our lives…to add insight and vitality into the events and relationships which we encounter in our commonplace lives.

## SPIRITUAL AWARENESS

In contrast to "Spiritual Disciplines" which are considered to be most beneficial when practiced in a regular and consistent manner; rather, these "Spiritual Awareness Exercises" are focused upon episodic, brief, and spontaneous ways in which to apprehend and appreciate the spiritual dimensions of everydayness. They are meant to sensitize, to arouse, to stimulate…a "tenderizing" of the soul which enhances our communion with the Lord. Hopefully, they become ways of not only sensitizing the soul, but conduits of conversation with God that refocus and revitalize our days.

You will no doubt notice that some activities are also claimed by the "Spiritual Disciplines." This overlap is to be expected, as many worthwhile practices can still find immense value in their use even in an abbreviated manner.

- *Practice "Sensual Spirituality"*

    "Sensual Spirituality" is a way of discovering spiritual awareness through one's senses of touch, smell, sight, hearing, and tasting. It involves the practice of experiencing these senses within the everyday activities of our lives in a way that encourages a greater appreciation and wonder of each experience…take a sense and enjoy it for a week at a time…perhaps one week, then a month. Allow it to become a worshipful experience on the magnificence of God's provision for us.

    When was the last time you *slowly* ate an apple, to hear the crunch of it from your first bite and felt its roughened texture upon your tongue? When have you last noticed its drips of nectar easing down your chin and tasted the teasing play of sweetness and tartness dance together? When have you truly tasted life, and given thanks to God for the bounty and beauty of His creation all around us?

- *Pray a Psalm*

    Select a Psalm, either one that is familiar to you, or one that is not, and pray the psalm as a song unto the Lord. Whether of praise or lament, focus on the key words and concepts of the psalm and add your expressions of gratitude or doubt to those. This is like an abbreviated *Lectio Divina*, but can be done in just a few moments; *Lectio Divina* is best experienced when one has the benefit of more time for prayerful reflection.

- *Lectio Divina*
    This involves:

    > *Lectio*—Reading the Bible passage gently and slowly several times. The passage itself is not as important as the savoring of each portion of the reading, constantly listening for the "still, small voice" of a word or phrase that somehow speaks to the practitioner.

    > *Meditatio*—Reflecting on the text of the passage and thinking about how it applies to one's own life. This is considered to be a very personal reading of the Scripture and very personal application.

    > *Oratio*—Responding to the passage by opening the heart to God. This is not primarily an intellectual exercise, but is thought to be more of the beginning of a conversation with God.

    > *Contemplatio*—Listening to God. This is a freeing of oneself from one's own thoughts, both mundane and holy, and hearing God talk to us. Opening the mind, heart, and soul to the influence of God.

    Lectio Divina is discussed more extensively in the Appendix II on Spiritual Disciplines.

- *Meditating on Doctrinal Truth*

    Choose a selection from the Lord's Prayer and live with it throughout at least a week. Meditate on its truths and how it undergirds your personal perspectives and priorities. The same can be done with a phrase of one of the Ten Commandments, a selection from the Westminster or Heidelberg Catechism, or a phrase from the Apostle's Creed. The principle is to focus and reflect upon a spiritual truth in a manner that grounds a person within their life of faith. It serves to recollect the principles of faith upon which our ethical and moral convictions rest. By doing so, one often is blessed with a greater appreciation of how God's law works in a dynamic way to safeguard and encourage one even within the storms of life.

- *Practicing "No Little People"*

    Establish the practice as viewing others as on a level playing field, all as fellow creatures made in the "image of God." Make a concerted effort to avoid the judgmental thoughts that so easily enter into our thought lives, "He's too fat," "She needs to dress better," "He just needs a stronger faith"—all those thoughts which feed our pride. Put them aside and focus on how we can appreciate the complementary way in which we are so uniquely created. Consider what it means to live together within the community of faith and that of our global community. How can we value one another's unique gifts to live together in harmony?

- *Pray with Scriptural Phrases*

    Perhaps the best way to express this practice is by quoting a prayer of Thomas A'Kempis, from his classic work, *The Imitation of Christ*. You will readily see how naturally he weaves Scriptural truths within the context of his prayers. How meaningful it is to be able to call to mind the truths of God's Word as one communes in prayer with God. What a profound experience to have the enlightening (and correcting) work of the Scriptures intermingle with the discerning and guiding work of the Holy Spirit as one enters the presence of the Holy One in prayer.

> Thus, O Lord my God, it comes about that, while I inadvertently delight in your law[1], and know Your commands to be good, just, and holy,[2] both for the condemnation of all evil and the avoiding of sin, yet in my body I serve the law of sin,[3] and obey my senses before my reason. Hence, while I indeed possess the will to good, I find myself powerless to follow it.[4] In this way, I make many good resolutions, but, through lack of grace to support my weakness, any small obstacle causes discouragement and failure. This, too, I know the way of perfection, and see clearly enough what I ought to do; but I am borne down by the burden of my own corruption, and advanced no nearer to perfection. Lord, how urgently I need your grace if I am to undertake, carryout and perfect any good work! Without it, I can achieve nothing; but in you and by the power of Your grace, all things are possible.[5],[6]

- *Honor the Sabbath*
    Keeping Sabbath is discussed at length in the Appendix II on Spiritual Disciplines, and describes the two-fold value of "remembering" and "resting" in regarding the Sabbath day as a special day established as part of God's design. But one can also set aside "Sabbath moments" throughout the week; brief moments of rest and remembering the benevolence of God our Creator.

- *Write a "Life Prayer"*

    By "life prayer," I am referring to a prayer constructed by a person which reflects his or her most basic concerns and forms of worship. It is the prayer that is said each day (preferably in the morning) as a prelude of worship and preparation for the day. It is simply your way of saying "Good morning" to God. Each person will discover the prayer most meaningful for them; usually as a slowly evolving process of adding, modifying, and deleting certain elements. Usually a person will arrive with a prayer that resonates deeply with what one feels is most important in their time alone with God…and the Holy Spirit will lead him or her to that place. That is not to say modifications will not occur, but the basic elements remain.

    Over the years, I have found a prayer that I open the day with consistently. It includes elements of worship, repentance, intercession, and protection. It is a purely discursive prayer, as opposed to the "listening prayer" of contemplation, yet even with the form of this prayer, the Holy Spirit intrudes with thoughts of insight and direction. Let it be so…then return to the place in your prayer where you left off.

    In forming my prayer, I desired to begin with an acknowledgment of my sin and that of my family, and to pray for forgiveness each day. I also wanted phrases that praised the Godhead of Father, Son ("Lord and Savior") and Holy Spirit. In the tradition of centering prayer, I recite each phrase three times in an effort to avoid distractions and to focus clearly upon the content of my prayer. After this, I request peace, patience, Godly devotion, strength, and spiritual discernment for me and my family, before praying specifically for each family member. Then I pray for those suffering physically, and finally I pray for my friends. In conclusion, I pray for the mental, physical, and spiritual well-being of myself before finalizing my prayer with the Sign of the Cross.

## APPENDIX I

December 12, 2018

Jesus Christ, my Lord and Savior, have mercy upon me and my family, all sinners.

Jesus Christ, my Lord and Savior, have mercy upon me and my family, all sinners.

Jesus Christ, my Lord and Savior, have mercy upon me and my family, all sinners.

Hallelujah, Emmanuel

Hallelujah, Emmanuel

Hallelujah, Emmanuel

May your Holy Spirit find some measure of openness and surrender of my still small being, that You might shape me and mold me into the soul You would have me be. May Your Spirit lead me upon the warp and weft of your will this day in a way that would be pleasing to You; and glorify You in thought and deed.

For me and all my family I pray:

For the peace which surpasses all understanding that can only come through our relationship with You,

For the patience to see Your will worked out in my individual life and in the world at large.

For our dedication and devotion to You to be the bedrock upon which our choices and decisions rest.

For the strength, perseverance, and discipline to run the race and finish the course of this life in a way that glorifies You.

For spiritual discernment to live a life of the Spirit in this fallen world.

Prayers for immediate family: After praying for the specific needs of each member of our immediate family, I conclude with the following request for each family: Please protect them from all manner of harm: from sickness, disease, injury, mood disorders, and temptation. May they experience Your love for them and our love for them each day.

Prayers for other family members…

Prayers for those with serious health issues…

Prayers for friends…

Please heal my mind and body and soul; that I may be an instrument of Your lovingkindness in the lives of others to Your glory.

I pray this in the name of the Father, and the Son, and the Holy Spirit. (Sign of the Cross)

May Your name be praised!

Amen

- *"Open" and "Close" Your Day with the Lord*

    Morning Opening: Psalm 1, Psalm 3:1–8, Psalm 5:1–3, Psalm 90:12–17, Psalm 92, Psalm 108

    Evening Closure: Psalm 4:4–8, Psalm 51, Psalm 61:1–4, Psalm 95:1–7, Psalm 103, Psalm 121

- *"Bookend Your Days"*

    Francis Schaeffer is said to have read a Proverb in the morning and Psalm at night to "bookend" his day.

- *Practice Seeing the "Spiritual Content" of Events and People*

    Establish the practice of spiritual awareness and insight into the events of each day. Search and celebrate moments of grace you discover in the day's events. Find yourself asking, "Is there any spiritual content or significance to this event or circumstance?"

    As one learns to visualize the events of the moment with "spiritual eyes," one gains a greater understanding of the call to spiritual participation. It becomes a call which leads to a discernment that gently compels one to compassionate actions of benevolence and service toward others.

- *"Spiritual Investing in the Lives of Others"*
    This involves making spiritual "deposits" in the lives of others. A corollary to that of the practice of spiritual "seeing" is that of "acting." This is the call to responsiveness with intentional gifts of attentiveness, encouragement, empathy, and compassion. Like placing a bank deposit, we place something of value (a smile, an encouraging word or note, cookies!) into needy and impoverished lives.

- *Write a Psalm*
    Like David, there will be seasons of our lives of wondrous gratitude, and others filled with the lament of discouragement and despondency. At times like these, we sometimes find a desire to express our emotions with the songs of praise or lament. A practice that can be helpful is to compose your own personal psalm unto God. Express your thanksgiving and joy in a psalm filled with praise (e.g., Psalm 100, Psalm 103) or in your valley of fear or insecurity, cry out your pain in a psalm of lament (e.g., Psalm 102).

- *"Daily Pattern": "A Word, A Prayer, A Gift"* (actualizing spirituality)
    Not many days start out as planned. We get up late for work. Unexpected intrusions disrupt our schedule. Misunderstandings cause emotional turmoil and regret. The "to do list" has grown longer. At the end of the day, we are commonly chagrinned in realizing how little spiritual content was considered or even contemplated upon throughout the rapid paced movements of events and relationships. Prayers unuttered. Good intentions undone. Spirituality sacrificed to the urgent moments.
    "A Word, A Prayer, A Gift" is an attempt to establish a pattern of spiritual participation within this whirlwind of daily activities. Though brief and simple, they serve as pivot points in our days to recollect, to refocus, and to reset our

attentions and affections. If practiced regularly, they form a flexible spiritual structure of awareness and action…simple as they may be. I like to think of it as carrying three colorful packages into that day's events: "a word," "a prayer," and "a gift."

- A Word: by "a word" I mean any positive word of significance that one can recall easily throughout the day…kind of like a walking mantra…upon which to focus. That may be a word (or phrase) from Scripture, words of a favorite song or hymn, a psalm, or an attitude to strengthen.
- A Prayer: by "a prayer" I mean an appeal to God for His participation…a sentence or two at most. It may be a thought prayer for myself, "Lord, help me be patient today," or for others, "Lord, please be with John today during surgery." They may be repeated throughout the day as many times as the need comes to mind.
- A Gift: by "a gift" I mean an offering for another. A gift in this sense is a tangible, concrete act of compassion and service. It can be as simple as bringing a smile to the face of one discouraged or fearful, sending a card of encouragement or comfort…any manner of depositing goodness into the life of another person…openly or anonymously.

It should be emphasized that this approach works best if allowed to be flexible and personalized for each person. It is only a suggested way of integrating spiritual awareness into the temporal demands of culture. For some individuals, changing their word-prayer-gift daily may work just fine; while others may find their own modifications to this approach. I honestly haven't had much luck changing my pattern from one day to the next. I simply do not have that much intentionality to do so consistently. A weekly change in pattern seems to work better for me. And furthermore, the frequency of changing one's pattern probably doesn't matter all that much as long as it is practiced as a daily effort. Because the purpose is only to link oneself to that which is deeper than the secular and superficial, in order to appreciate and actuate spiritual content in the present moment.

As an example: I may choose to carry the following into each day of this week:

My Word: Empathy: I will try to understand the situations of others.

My Prayer: Lord, safely guard Patricia today as she travels.

My Gift: I want to make the grumpy checkout person at the grocery smile today as I shop.

Your word-prayer-gift may be as simple or profound as the Holy Spirit leads you, but you will soon find that spiritual "openings" are sensed with ever-increasing frequency. At the end of each day one can then honestly pray, "Lord, burn away the dross of the efforts of this day to reveal the spiritual content of Your presence and purpose." (Psalm 119:11, Psalm 119:105.)

- *Close the Week* with prayers of forgiveness, thanksgiving, and provision/protection for the week ahead. Each Sunday evening, as a way of closure of the past week, and a preparation for the week ahead, set aside a quiet time when distractions are at a minimum (9:00 p.m.?) and focus on three prayers. A prayer asking for forgiveness for the events of the past week, prayers of thanksgiving, and prayers for provision and protection in the week to come. Some may also participate in their own home Communion service at that time, as a means of repentance and consecration.

- *Intersperse Prayer Throughout Each Day:* This is described eloquently in *Practicing the Presence of God* by Jan Johnson.[7]

## SPIRITUAL AWARENESS

[1] Romans 7:22.
[2] Romans 7:12.
[3] Romans 7:25.
[4] Romans 7:18.
[5] Philippians 4:13.
[6] Thomas A' Kempis, *The Imitation of Christ* (New York, NY: Penguin Books, 1952), 172–173.
[7] Jan Johnson, *Practicing the Presence of God* (Colorado Springs, CO: NavPress, 1996).

# Appendix II

## *Spiritual Disciplines*

> I go through life as a transient on his way to eternity, made in the image of God but with that image debased, needing to be taught how to meditate, to worship, to think.[1]
> —Donald Coggan,
> Archbishop of Canterbury

It is fitting to begin a discussion of Spiritual Disciplines with the following quotation by Richard J. Foster from his classic work, *Celebration of Discipline*, in which he frames the contemporary need for all to live deeper spiritual lives within the routines of the everyday.

> Superficiality is the curse of our age. The doctrine of instant gratification is a primary spiritual problem. The desperate need today is not for a greater number of intelligent people, or gifted people, but for deep people.
>
> The classical Disciplines of the spiritual life call us to move beyond surface living into the depths. They invite us to explore the inner caverns of the spiritual realm. They urge us to be the answer to a hollow world. John Woolman counseled, "It is good for thee to dwell deep, that thou mayest feel and understand the spirits of people."[2]

## SPIRITUAL AWARENESS

> We must not be led to believe that the Disciplines are for spiritual giants and hence beyond our reach, or for contemplatives who devote all their time to prayer and meditation. Far from it. God intends the Disciplines of the spiritual life to be for ordinary human beings: people who have jobs, who care for children, who must wash dishes and mow lawns. In fact, the Disciplines are best exercised in the midst of our normal daily activities. If they are to have any transforming effect, the effect must be found in the ordinary junctures of human life: in our relationships with our husband or wife, our brothers and sisters, our friends and neighbors.[3]

If what Richard Foster says is true, the Disciplines provide an avenue or channel of sorts in which each one of us, regardless of where we are in our spiritual journeys, can avail ourselves to the spiritual within the ordinariness of our commonplace lives. It should be stated, however, that many Christians already use these exercises within their lives, though not in such a formal manner. This discussion is for those who still search for ways to deepen their spiritual lives.

Before proceeding with the discussion, it may be wise to remember several principles:

- *No Resume Required:* The Spiritual Disciplines are for anyone seeking a closer relationship with Christ, and a more intimate Spirit-led experience of daily living…no matter how briefly or long ago one has accepted Christ as their Lord and personal Savior. Open and available to all…no "credentials" are required.
- *No 1, 2, 3 to Eternity:* The Spiritual Disciplines are not a simple three-step program of attaining salvation or spiritual maturity. They are not a manner of "climbing up" a ladder of spiritual accomplishments, nor are they meant to be a

form of spiritual "advancement" in the sense of becoming "more spiritual" than another. They are only instruments for one's own personal spiritual transformation within the body of Christ.
- *No "Quick Fix" Program:* The Spiritual Disciplines aid in our walk toward spiritual maturity, but they are not a rapid short cut to it. The gradual work of the Holy Spirit will guide and direct our course in a timeliness only known to God. We must be willing to exercise patience in the days which the Lord gives us.
- *No Room for Legalism:* The Spiritual Disciplines are not a rigid, strictly to be followed set of rules for gaining spiritual maturity. They must not be experienced as required practices to be mastered, nor a set of rituals codified into stone. Available to all, but required by none…for the Holy Spirit works in many ways not known to man.

In their simplest form, the Spiritual Disciplines serve to provide various ways to remove the encumbrances to our spiritual growth and to enhance our relationship with God. They provide a quiet dimension of receptivity in which the Spirit can more fully be perceived…they provide the spiritual focus and attentiveness necessary to appreciate and respond to spiritual movements even in the everydayness of our chaotic life.

Spiritual Disciplines strive to establish both an open awareness and a spiritual grounding for spiritual transformation, and attitudes which allow for spiritual reflection and growth. When repeated regularly, they establish a pattern for spiritual growth in an intentional and purposeful manner. They are different than Spiritual Awareness Activities in that they are best experienced as a consistent part of our devotional life as a means to heighten our spiritual awareness and insights. Whereas, Spiritual Awareness Activities are more typically single, episodic and spontaneous acts of appreciation and benevolence.

The distinction between Spiritual Awareness Activities and Spiritual Disciplines is certainly somewhat arbitrary. But I envision the Spiritual Awareness Activities tending to be a bit more superficial than the Spiritual Disciplines. They are like cracking the shell of a nut or breaking through the veneer of the woodwork, breaking through our preoccupations, insensitivities, and pride. They tend to be episodic, spontaneous, and sometimes even serendipitous. The Spiritual Disciplines, rather, tend to be a process that is best done in a regular and repeated manner, which establishes the habit of growing deeper and more consistent in our spiritual awareness and devotion. They require a different type of focus and intentionality. We might say that one breaks through the crustiness of our lives while the other allows us to eat of the deeper morsels of spiritual nourishment. I would offer that both are purposeful, but one is more reflexive while the other is more rhythmic in character. The intent of both, however, is to eliminate the many encumbrances we face to spiritual transformation as we seek spiritual insight and growth.

In any discussion of the Spiritual Disciplines, it is necessary to first consider the underlying principles that make the use of these disciplines purposeful and meaningful. It is tempting not to refer to these practices as "disciplines" to, instead, soften their concept with words like "habits" or "experiences," but to do so would seriously undermine their true character. These concepts are referred to as "disciplines" because they do require an intentional, and hopefully consistent, "setting aside" in order to create the necessary margin in our lives to be available for spiritual movements. Our word "discipline" comes from the Greek word *gumnasia*, which means "to exercise" or "to discipline."

Any cursory examination of the topic of Spiritual Disciplines soon reveals a multiplicity of various spiritual practices and various categories. Richard Foster speaks of the Inward Disciplines of Meditation, Prayer, Fasting, and Study; the Outward Disciplines of Simplicity, Solitude, Submission, and Service; and the Corporate Disciplines of Confession, Worship, Guidance, and Celebration. Donald Whitney would add those of Stewardship and Journaling; while Ruth Haley Barton describes those of Honoring the Body, Self-examination, Discernment, Keeping Sabbath, and Cultivation of a

"Rule of Life." Ernest Boyer applies the Spiritual Disciplines to family life by examining ways of promoting spirituality with the family.

Few musicians can play all the instruments in a symphony orchestra with any significant expertise…so it is with the Spiritual Disciplines. Each one of us will find disciplines that seem to resonate most clearly and in tune with that which we need for a specific season of life…different disciplines may be most appropriate at various times in our lives and during various circumstances. Therefore, we should grant ourselves the freedom of flexibility to pursue those disciplines which speak to us most clearly and meaningfully.

Also, there will be those disciplines that we use for longer or shorter periods of time. One may participate in a two-week retreat focused on solitude and simplicity, or one may develop a discipline at noontime each day to carve out fifteen minutes of quietness and attentiveness to the spiritual movements of the day. The Holy Spirit will be our guide into the spiritual disciplines most needed for our respective individual lives.

Though these "disciplines" are many and varied, they all share common characteristics.

Fundamentally they all share a sincere desire for a deepened spiritual experience in general, and a closer life in Christ specifically. Superficiality is not enough. More of "this or that" will never be enough. Instead an innate urging calls for a step back from our momentary gratifications and into a quiet place in which one can experience the Eternal. You may notice that most Disciplines are two-fold in nature: the first being an aspect of "turning aside from" or an act of asceticism, and the second an aspect of "refocusing" or attentiveness to a spiritual truth or reality of Divine presence.

Finally, a practical point. If there is a predictable time or circumstance of temptation within one's days or evenings, try precluding that event with an aspect of a Spiritual Discipline …conceptually stepping away to refocus. Fasting: portion control for overindulgence; Simplicity: giving away two objects before buying another; Silence: unplugging from social media or TV for one day in order to avoid distractions; Scripture memorization for moments of sexual temptation; Examination of conscience for times of self-absorption and pride…

## SPIRITUAL AWARENESS

As noted above, the Spiritual Disciplines can be categorized in various ways, and are abundant in number. The list following is neither exhaustive of all the types of Spiritual Disciplines that exist, nor extensive in describing all the subtleties of how the Spiritual Disciplines are experienced. Both are better left to those who address the Spiritual Disciplines in greater detail. Therefore, for the purpose of this discussion, I will only discuss several of the more commonly mentioned and utilized ones, and will group them in the following manner:

- Awakening the soul:
    o Solitude: being alone; free from the distractions and demands around us; alone before God
    o Silence: being quiet; quieting the "noise" and "voices" calling out; receptive to the Spirit's leading
    o Simplicity: developing a sense of sufficiency and stewardship
    o Listening Prayer, Meditation: being attentive; listening to God's "still small voice"; assuming an attitude of relinquishment and surrender.
    o Fasting: being detached; stepping away from immediate gratification, materialism
    o Scripture study and meditation (*Lectio Divina*): being focused upon absolute truths; finding instruction for attitudes and actions
    o Vulnerability Moments: death, loss, depression—being vulnerable; finding tenderness and compassion within suffering

## SOLITUDE AND SILENCE

Literature describing the Spiritual Disciplines commonly does so as a discussion of solitude and silence together, for they are very intimately interconnected. Though distinct in character, both solitude and silence are experienced in symbiotic relationship. While solitude involves a stepping out from the crowd of expectations; silence involves a stepping out from the noise of culture. Both, however, are necessary to "create space" for God within the daily demands and affections of everyday life. They provide the foundations of receptivity and openness which allow for an attitude of "listening" for that "still small voice" of God which whispers to us amidst the clamor of culture.

That is not to say that we become distanced or isolated from the needs of others within our world. For man and woman were created and designed to live with companionship and within community. It is only within relationship that we experience and understand the value of our humanness, sacrifice, and giving. Yet within this design, there are necessary times for silence and solitude. Jesus in His earthly ministry of teaching and healing would often "withdraw" into the quiet and deeply personal renewing relationship with His Father (Matthew 4:1–11, Matthew 14:13, Matthew 14:23, Matthew 17:1–9, Matthew 26:36–46, Mark 1:35, Mark 6:31, Luke 5:16, Luke 6:12). This example of Jesus demonstrates a two-fold purpose: the first, being freed from the influence of the "crowd," and the second, creating the "space" within time in which to draw closer to God in intimate relationship. It is like stepping from the fog of culture into the sunshine of Divine Presence.

Soren Kierkegaard takes this notion a step further by asking if we can envision our own personal relationship before Almighty God. He poses the question to each of us: *whether you live in such a way that you are conscious of being an "individual?"*[4] What Kierkegaard is attempting to confront each of us with is our desire to find acceptance in conformity within the crowd, rather than face our individual responsibility honestly before God…for that is ultimately how each of us will be judged…one man or one woman accountable to God alone. Silence and solitude help us confront this reality.

One cannot hide within the crowd. Kierkegaard describes this concept eloquently:

> For in the outside world, the crowd is busy making a noise. The one makes a noise because he heads the crowd, the many because they are members of the crowd. But the all-knowing One,

who in spite of anyone is able to observe it all, does not desire the crowd. He desires the individual; He will deal only with the individual, quite unconcerned as to whether the individual be of high or low station, whether he be distinguished or wretched. Each man himself, as an individual, should render his account to God.[5]

...Long ago, Adam attempted this same thing when his evil conscience led him to imagine that he could hide himself among the trees. It may even be easier and more convenient, and more cowardly to hide oneself among the crowd in the hope that God should not be able to recognize one from the other. But in eternity each shall render account as an individual. That is, eternity will demand of him that he shall have lived as an individual.[6]

He proceeds to describe how the "crowd" compromises one's "voice of conscience":

For, after all, what is eternity's accounting other than that the voice of conscience is forever installed with its eternal right to be the exclusive voice?

...it happens all too readily that the voice of conscience becomes merely one voice among many. Then it follows so easily that the isolated voice of conscience...becomes overruled—by the majority. But in eternity, conscience is the only voice that is heard. It must be heard by the individual...[7]

Most people today are familiar with the concept of "groupthink" that characterizes our culture so accurately today. Like a flock of sheep led to the slaughter, contemporary man and woman mindlessly follow the latest fashion, the most popular entertainers, and even the most predominant political media sway. "Political correctness" becomes prevalent, often not because of its innate value, but from the coercion and intimidation of the outspoken crowd. Differing viewpoints are ostracized. Marginalization and vilification soon follow. Others who may stand outside the popular crowd are branded as "offensive" to the minority's sensitivities, and they are intimidated to conform. The path of least resistance soon leads to conformity within the crowd.

This cultural force often conflicts with a person's most fundamental ethical and spiritual principles. Concepts of morality then become shaped by external and societal constructs, rather than internalized moral convictions. The person becomes insignificant within the flow of culture. The "crowd" of culture becomes absolute.

The Spiritual Disciplines can serve as antidotes to the poison of this popular cultural conformity. Particularly, those of solitude and silence serve to take a step away from the influences of expectations and the voices of affections which surround the individual. Ruth Haley Barton describes this process of solitude and silence as "creating space for God."

A measure of ascetic withdrawal from errant popular notions becomes essential; as does a renewal of authentic spiritual intimacy, to find genuine spiritual awareness and truth in relationship with the Divine. "Listening" and "Renewal" become the hallmarks of the Disciplines that have their fruit in love, joy, peace, patience, kindness, goodness, faithfulness, gentleness, self-control.[8]

First of all, this involves "unplugging" from the continual flow of noise around us. Not only from cyber noise, but from the intrusions of outside expectations and commitments. For a "moment," a slice in time, allow solitude to create for you the "safe place" in which you can pause in a vulnerable quietness. Our Lord appeals to us: *"Be still and know that I am God."* (Psalm 46:10 NIV)

This is the place in which we can begin to get in touch with who we genuinely are. It becomes an experience where we can listen honestly to the suppressed voices of our doubts and fears, disappointments and pain, hopes and dreams. It is a place where we can cry out like the Psalmist: *"How long must I struggle with anguish in my soul, with sorrow in my heart every day?"* (Psalm 13:2 NLT). But it is also a place of great comfort and consolation. For God is in the silence as well, and He speaks out of the silence with the comforting words of Scripture, "*I will never leave you, nor forsake you*" (Hebrews 13:5 ESV) Interestingly, in these moments of solitude and silence, we discover a paradoxical companionship and conversation. There is much soul work done in these moments; within the ebb and flow of spiritual interaction between soul and the Divine Presence…the fruits of which are those of restoration and renewal of soul. Here we experience the "*peace that passes all understanding,*" because we know that *Jehovah-shalom,* "the Lord is peace," goes before us.

There are many ways to enter into this experience of solitude and silence. Ruth Haley Barton suggests the following, which is a fairly typical approach:

> Choose a place that feels comfortable and safe to you, a place that allows you to be opened and available to God—a favorite chair at home, your own backyard if it is quiet, or even a nearby chapel if you have access to one. Settle into a comfortable position in your body and sit quietly for a few moments, breathing deeply, becoming aware of God's presence with you and your desire to be present with God.
>
> Sit quietly at the base of the tree that is your life and begin to notice what is true about you these days. Don't rush or try to make anything happen. Let your soul venture out and say something to you that perhaps you have had a hard time acknowledging. Is there a particular Joy you are celebrating? A loss you are grieving? Are there tears that have been waiting to be shed? A question that is stirring? An emotion that needs expression?
>
> Sit with what comes into your awareness, becoming conscious of God's presence with you

in that awareness. Don't try to do anything with what you are knowing except be with it. Feel the difference between doing something with it and resting with it. Feel the difference between trying to fight it and letting God fight for you. What does it mean for you to be still and let God fight for you in this particular area?

Practice this way of entering into solitude regularly until it becomes routine for you to begin your times in solitude by being quiet and letting your soul come out and then rest in God's presence. You will likely be surprised at what your soul wants to say to God.[9]

Steps into solitude:

1. Build a quiet time, in a quiet place into your daily routine.
2. Disconnect for a day, perhaps a weekend day, when you do not use any electronic devices for networking or communications.
3. Occasionally practice a "monastic day" of minimal conversation to provide space for quiet solitude and reflection; prayerful attendance to the beauty of nature.
4. Consider "day retreats" of visiting a library for personal reading and thoughtfulness, or attend a favorite park or nature reserve.
5. Practice minimizing the distractions of "noise"; continuous music, cell phone use, TV, conversations…create "quiet moments" of solitude to "listen."
6. Consider an annual two-day retreat at a cabin or lodge amongst nature to reflect in solitude and quietness the priorities of your life, and goals for the future.

Interestingly enough, as one exercises the personal disciplines of solitude and silence, a sensitivity for others is appreciated, enhanced, and expressed in acts of compassionate service.

Both Richard Foster and Thomas Merton write of their experiences with the disciplines of solitude and silence that demonstrate this heightened awareness of the care for others in need.

> The fruit of solitude is increased sensitivity and compassion for others.[10] (Richard J. Foster).

Thomas Merton writes of his monastic life:

> True solitude is found in humility, which is infinitely rich... True solitude is selfless. Therefore, it is rich in silence and charity and peace. It finds in itself seemingly inexhaustible resources of good to bestow on other people.[11]
>
> True solitude separates one man from the rest in order that he may freely develop the good that is his own, and then fulfill his true destiny by putting himself at the service of everyone else.[12]
>
> Thus we are both in time and out of it. We are poor, possessing all things. Having nothing of our own left to rely on, we have nothing to lose and nothing to fear. Everything is locked away for our sure possession, beyond our reach, in Heaven. We live where our souls desire to be, and our bodies no longer matter very much. We are buried in Christ, our life hidden with Christ in God and we know the meaning of His freedom.[13]

## HELPFUL RESOURCES ON SOLITUDE AND SILENCE

Ruth Haley Barton. *Sacred Rhythms: Arranging our Lives for Spiritual Transformation* (IVP, 2006), Chapter 2

Jeanie Miley, *The Spiritual Art of Creative Silence: Lessons in Christian Meditation*

# APPENDIX II

Morton T. Kelsy, *The Other Side of Silence: A Guide to Christian Meditation*

Richard J. Foster, *Celebration of Discipline: The Path to Spiritual Growth*: (San Francisco: Harper & Row, Publishers, 1978), Chapter 7

Donald S. Whitney, *Spiritual Disciplines for the Christian Life*, Chapter 10

## SIMPLICITY

Freedom from desire

In character, in manner, in style, in all things,
the supreme excellence is simplicity.
—Henry Wadsworth Longfellow

"Enough" is always a little more
than a person presently has.
—Unknown

"We buy things we do not want to
impress people we do not like."[14]

Much has been written about our desire for more…more money, more security, more attention…each of us has our conscious and subconscious lists; as well as those desires that often change in urgency from month to month or moment by moment. Our desires seem natural enough, simply bubbling up out of a sea of daily activities. More time, I need more time…More resources…if only I had more talent, more strength, more wisdom. Life has a way of confronting a person this way. It continually confronts us with the demand for more, faster, bigger, better, then slams upon us a pace and complexity of activity that strikes a person again and again with daggers of desire. We become pierced by our never-ending insatiable appetites. Like a run-away freight train, we seem to be going faster and faster toward an unfortunate ending; with the brakes we are attempting to apply simply not working.

Simplicity is an answer to the demands of "more," because it confronts us with the question of what will ever be considered as "enough." What is it that we genuinely seek? Simplicity's composition is both a sense of "sufficiency" and that of good "stewardship."

Sufficiency speaks to a quieting of the yearning for more, and an acceptance and appreciation for that which we already have. As the Psalmist reminds us, "*The Lord is my shepherd; I have all that I need.*"[15] All too often, in our search for self-gratification, we devalue that which we adequately have in our mad rush for "more." This is no small form of idolatry, which opens the door to greed.

Perhaps it needs to be stated that there is a distinction between "having" vs. "hoarding." The Lord chooses to shower us with His blessings so that we may "have" that which we need. But we must be careful not to attempt to accumulate those blessings in a miserly way. Recall the manna lessons of the Israelites in the wilderness (Exodus 16:14–32, NASB).

> When the layer of dew evaporated, behold, on the surface of the wilderness there was a fine flake-like thing, fine as the frost on the ground.
>
> When the sons of Israel saw it, they said to one another, "What is it?" For they did not know what it was. And Moses said to them, "It is the bread which the LORD has given you to eat.
>
> This is what the LORD has commanded, 'Gather of it every man as much as he should eat; you shall take an omer apiece according to the number of persons each of you has in his tent.'"
>
> The sons of Israel did so, and some gathered much and some little.
>
> When they measured it with an omer, he who had gathered much had no excess, and he who had gathered little had no lack; every man gathered as much as he should eat.

Moses said to them, "Let no man leave any of it until morning."

But they did not listen to Moses, and some left part of it until morning, and it bred worms and became foul; and Moses was angry with them.

They gathered it morning by morning, every man as much as he should eat; but when the sun grew hot, it would melt.

Now on the sixth day they gathered twice as much bread, two omers for each one. When all the leaders of the congregation came and told Moses, then he said to them, "This is what the LORD meant: Tomorrow is a sabbath observance, a holy sabbath to the LORD. Bake what you will bake and boil what you will boil, and all that is left over put aside to be kept until morning."

So they put it aside until morning, as Moses had ordered, and it did not become foul nor was there any worm in it.

Moses said, "Eat it today, for today is a sabbath to the LORD; today you will not find it in the field.

Six days you shall gather it, but on the seventh day, the sabbath, there will be none."

It came about on the seventh day that some of the people went out to gather, but they found none.

Then the LORD said to Moses, "How long do you refuse to keep My commandments and My instructions?

See, the LORD has given you the sabbath; therefore He gives you bread for two days on the sixth day. Remain every man in his place; let no man go out of his place on the seventh day."

So the people rested on the seventh day.

The house of Israel named it manna, and it was like coriander seed, white, and its taste was like wafers with honey.

Then Moses said, "This is what the LORD has commanded, 'Let an omerful of it be kept throughout your generations, that they may see the bread that I fed you in the wilderness, when I brought you out of the land of Egypt.'"

There are many lessons to be placed within our hearts from this portion of Scripture, but I would like to put forward at least these which are most germane to our consideration of "sufficiency" within the discipline of Simplicity.

- The Scripture additionally teaches that we are to *"seek first His kingdom and His righteousness, and all these things will be added to you."* (Matthew 6:33 NASB)
- If our possessions become a barrier to our relationship with God, we are called *"to sell all that we have and give to the poor."* (Matthew 19:21 NLT, paraphrased)
- God provides: *"Do not be anxious about your life"* (Matthew 6:25 ESV).
- Man is not to hoard the blessings of God or to use them in a miserly or selfish manner.
- Greed results in worthlessness and decay.
- God's provision is to be remembered as a testimony of blessing and sufficiency unto the generations.

Simplicity means trusting in the faithfulness and lovingkindness of God, *"El Shaddai,"* the "All-Sufficient One."

Thomas Merton writes these thoughts on the topics of attachment and illusion, vision, and detachment:

> Saint Gregory of Nyssa… which constitute his commentary on Ecclesiastes, observes how

*APPENDIX II*

time weaves about us this web of illusion. It is not enough to say that the man who is attached to this world has bound himself to it, once and for all, by a wrong choice. No: he spins a whole net of falsities around his spirit by the repeated consecration of his whole self to values that do not exist. He exhausts himself in the pursuit of mirages that ever fade and are renewed as fast as they have faded, drawing him further and further into the wilderness where he must die of thirst...

And so, that "vanity of vanities" which so exercised the Ancient Preacher of Ecclesiastes and his commentator is a life not merely of deluded thoughts and aspirations, but above all a life of ceaseless and sterile activity. What is more, in such a life the measure of illusion is the very intensity of activity itself. The less you have, the more you do. The final delusion is movement, change, and variety for their own sakes alone.[16]

All the preoccupation of men with the things of this life [writes Saint Gregory], is but the game of children on the sands. For children take delight in the activity of their play and as soon as they have finished building what they build, their pleasure ends. For as soon as their labor is completed, the sand falls down and nothing is left of their buildings.[17]

Pascal sums up his observations with the remark: "Distraction is the only thing that consoles us for our miseries and yet it is, itself, the greatest of our miseries."[18]

Why? Because it "diverts" us, turns us aside from the one thing that can help us to begin our ascent to truth. That one thing is the sense of our own emptiness, our poverty, our limitations, and of the inability of created things to satisfy our profound need for reality and for truth.

What is the conclusion of all this? We imprison ourselves in falsity by our love for the feeble, flickering light of illusion and desire. We cannot find the true light unless this false light be darkened. We cannot find true happiness unless we deprive ourselves of the ersatz happiness of empty diversion.[19]

Embedded within the Discipline of Simplicity is also the notion of "preservation": both of our personal possessions, and that of the earth's natural resources. Contrary to "hoarding," it is a resourceful care for that which God has already given to us. To conserve resources is to honor their innate value, and an expression of responsible stewardship found within God's design.

Frugality is to use wisely that which we have, before acquiring more than we need. It is a guard against overconsumption and greed. Attitudes of moderation and conservation characterize this form of simplicity. Instead of "use and dispose," a person attempts to "use-repair-reuse." This is also a lesson we should be teaching our children at an early age before becoming shaped by this culture of consumption and waste.

The Spiritual Discipline of Simplicity is in reality a lifestyle. It is an attitude which is ingrained within our comings and goings of the everyday. It is a perspective of *sufficiency* and *stewardship*. In the concreteness of the commonplace, one can strive for a simpler life style of spirituality:

- Attempt to design a life built upon the concepts of *sufficiency* and *stewardship*.
- Ask oneself, "Is what I have sufficient for the tasks of this day or this week?"
- In my purchases, am I motivated by "need" or by "desire" for novelty or social accommodation? One's five-year-old car, with which one has been very satisfied, can suddenly

become quite drab when a neighbor purchases a new vehicle with all the new electronics and features. What once was just fine suddenly becomes undesirable.

- De-advertise your viewing. Design your computer and cell phone to minimize the exposure to advertising and distracting stories of "interest." Consider browsers that do not collect your viewing and purchase habits to feed you additional items of desire. Be cautious in surveying newspaper and magazine ads unless there is something specific for which you are shopping.
- Practice buying things for their usefulness rather than their novelty or attraction.
- Practice "repairing" before "replacing."
- Examine honestly whether one has an "addiction" for certain purchases. Do I really need twenty pairs of shoes or season tickets for sports events?
- Declutter: for each new purchase, consider discarding or donating a similar item. Battle against hoarding.
- Avoid purchases that foster the oppression or subjugation of other persons or cultures.
- For large purchases rarely used, consider sharing it with others as a mutual purchase.
- Practice delayed gratification by avoiding immediate or impulsive purchases.
- Practice daily the discipline of gratitude for what one has rather than dissatisfaction from not having what one desires. Count your blessings every day. Be thankful for the blessings which can't be purchased…one's health, family, love…
- Find appreciation in the full enjoyment of one's senses… try eating slowly to fully taste the flavor and texture of our food, listen carefully to the different chirps of the birds and the whispering of the wind, smell the impending storm or the spice of cinnamon, delight in the varied subtle tones of color within a flower blossom and the softness of its touch against the sharp prick of its thorn.

SPIRITUAL AWARENESS

- Read and meditate upon Matthew 6:19–34 at least weekly, perhaps at the beginning of your week?
- Journal, for one week, your actions which could be regarded as "wasteful."

## HELPFUL RESOURCES ON SIMPLICITY

Barbara DeGrote-Sorensen and David Allen Sorensen, *Six Weeks to a Simpler Lifestyle*

Henri Nouwen, Richard Foster, Cecile Andrews and others, edited and compiled by Michael Schut, *Simpler Living, Compassionate Life*

Peter J. Wicks, *Everyday Simplicity: A Practical Guide to Spiritual Growth*

Richard A. Swenson, MD, *Margin: Restoring Emotional, Physical, Financial and Time Reserves to Overloaded Lives*

Richard J. Foster, *Freedom of Simplicity*

## LISTENING PRAYER, MEDITATION, CENTERING PRAYER

Within the realm of solitude and silence is found a special sense…an attitude of receptivity. Thomas Merton describes the inevitable struggle which confronts human souls:

> Man was made for the highest activity, which is, in fact, his rest. That activity, which is contemplation, is immanent and it transcends the level of sense and of discourse. Man's guilty sense of his incapacity for this one deep activity which is the reason for his very existence, is precisely what drives him to seek oblivion in exterior motion and desire. Incapable of the Divine activity which alone can satisfy his soul, fallen man flings himself upon exterior things, not so much for their sake as for the sake of the agita-

tion which keeps his spirit pleasantly numb. He has but to remain busy with trifles; his preoccupation will serve as a dope. It will not deaden all the pain of thinking; but it will at least do something to blur his sense of who he is and of his utter insufficiency.[20]

Innate to human nature is its attraction to novelty…that which is new and unique. Our affections are shaped around those things which we find desirable.

Contemplative prayer is a prayer of silence, of listening, of receptivity. Its essential character is that of a quiet centering upon the presence of God in the quietness of the moment. *"Be still, and know that I am God"* (Psalm 46:10, NIV).

This type of opening unto the presence of God goes by many names within the Christian tradition. John Main refers to this type of prayer as "meditation," Evelyn Underhill uses the phrase "contemplative prayer" or "prayer of simplicity." Pennington uses "centering prayer," and Dallas Willard describes "listening prayer." Each describes their own personal perspective and experience on what I shall choose to refer to as "deep prayer."

I choose to do so, not from any desire to create a new label of prayer, but rather to avoid mischaracterizing the specific perspectives of those described above. Instead, I will sketch out the essential characteristics of deep prayer with the understanding that this profound type of prayer contains many nuances and personal variations that are unique to each individual as they enter into a deep relationship with God.

One is to be cautioned that deep prayer is not some simply emotional high. Deep prayer is not something a person can conjure up or create within oneself. It is not an experience unmoored from the truth of Scripture, or to be contrived outside the provisions of God's Grace. Rather, it rests clearly upon the doctrinal teachings of the traditional church. Yet it is an indescribable experience of Eternity extending into this dimension of time and space.

Furthermore, it is important to remember that participation in deep prayer is not "working one's way toward heaven." There is nothing that man can do or bring to this unification of spirit. It is only provided and enriched by the initiative and love of God.

Deep prayer is not the kind of prayer in which we "do business" with God. In no way do I wish to minimize the importance of conversational prayer or vocal prayer in which we share with God our worries, our fears, our praise and adoration. Nor do I take lightly the profound importance and mystery of intercessory prayer, in which we lift others up to the Lord for His healing and protection. For these are the prayers in which we begin to know God and understand the aspects of His character, at least in our limited human way. We discover the reality of His lovingkindness. We begin to understand that there is a Divine will and purpose beyond our greatest imaginings. We begin to discern God's design for His creation and for our personal destinies. Furthermore, we discover the dynamic movements of the Holy Spirit within our realm of prayer, guiding and revealing ultimate truth. Within these prayers we find the "safe place" in which we can grow in intimacy with God our Creator because of the redemptive work of Christ our Savior. For now we can humbly present ourselves before the Lord as newly birthed children because all debt for our sins has been paid once and for all time.

As essential and meaningful as these prayers are, deep prayer is yet another level more profound. Instead of speaking to God of our thoughts and desires, we discipline our minds to listen for His still small voice. Instead of considering what we feel we need from God, we assume a spirit of receptivity to His will. Overall there is a sense of relinquishment of our human thoughts and images to enter into a spiritual relationship which is mediated through Divine love. The language spoken here is not that of human words or concepts, but rather that of a spiritual awareness which extends far beyond that which we can grasp in the here and now of temporal life. The contemplatives refer to this state of prayer as "union" or "unification," where we finds ourselves immersed within an ultimate and Eternal Love "*For God is Love.*" (1 John 4:8 NLT).

Of necessity this form of deep prayer demands the requisite simplicity and solitude to step away from the superficial and distracting. Here, one steps away from the phantom promises of self-fulfillment and self-gratification into a realm of truthful reality. It is a realm incapable of being described or even marginally understood, for it is a realm of Spirit. In deep prayer one finds a clearer Way, a genuine Truth, and a vision of eternal Life through the one we know as Christ.

## HELPFUL RESOURCES ON CENTERING PRAYER

Dallas Willard, *Hearing God*
Peter Toon, *Meditating as a Christian*
John Main, *The Way of Unknowing*
M. Basil Pennington, OCSO, *Centering Prayer*

## FASTING

Fasting reminds us of our vulnerabilities and our dependence upon the most basic needs for our sustenance—food and water. Barring disease or injury, it is amazing how well a person can be sustained upon such simple elements. An appreciation for how little we really "need" can form the foundation for severing the bonds of materialism. Fasting then, both literally and figuratively, is an exercise in "appetite control," a stepping away from the immediate gratification of our desires. By fasting, we become more aware of our hunger and thirst for consumption. It serves not only to curb our physical appetites but to modify or mollify our desires for gratification. That is not to imply that everything material is to be denied but rather seen in its proper role and purpose, its context—freedom *from* desire, not freedom *of* desire—desire is now seen in its proper context and its proper form.

Those familiar with the Old Testament can't help but have images of "weeping and mourning" and "sackcloth and ashes" come to mind with the concept of fasting, for it was a common devotional response of the Israelites (and other religions as well) to circumstances of threat and loss. As with so many commandments, fasting became adulterated into a misguided appeal to manipulate a Divine reaction. However, Christ reminds us:

> Whenever you fast, do not put on a gloomy face as the hypocrites do, for they neglect their appearance so that they will be noticed by men when they are fasting. Truly I say to you, they have their reward in full. But you, when you fast, anoint your head and wash your face so that your fasting will not be noticed by men, but by your Father who is in secret; and your Father who sees what is done in secret will reward you. (Matthew 6:16–18 NASB)

Fasting can be exercised in various forms for varying periods. A person's underlying health issues should be taken into account when choosing how to fast. Often consulting a physician is wise to do before a fast, especially a very radical or extended one.

Fasting can consist of exclusively water or juice or, in other cases, omitting certain foods like meat or sweets. Some people will fast for a day, several days, or a week—others may fast a certain day of the week consistently. It is imperative to keep in mind that the "style" of one's fast is not the most important aspect of fasting. The longer or most severe fast is not innately better than a shorter, more flexible one. The fundamental aspect is to keep the *purpose* of your fast foremost in your mind.

Scripture describes multiple purposes and situations in which fasting is valuable. In his book, *Fasting for Spiritual Breakthrough*, Elmer Towns uses the biblical passage from Isaiah 58, to ferret out various purposes for fasting:

> Yet they seek Me day by day and delight to know My ways, as a nation that has done righteousness and has not forsaken the ordinance of

## APPENDIX II

their God. They ask Me for just decisions, they delight in the nearness of God.

Why have we fasted and You do not see? Why have we humbled ourselves and You do not notice?' Behold, on the day of your fast you find your desire, and drive hard all your workers.

Behold, you fast for contention and strife and to strike with a wicked fist. You do not fast like you do today to make your voice heard on high.

Is it a fast like this which I choose, a day for a man to humble himself? Is it for bowing one's head like a reed and for spreading out sackcloth and ashes as a bed? Will you call this a fast, even an acceptable day to the LORD?

Is this not the fast which I choose, to loosen the bonds of wickedness, to undo the bands of the yoke, and to let the oppressed go free and break every yoke?

Is it not to divide your bread with the hungry and bring the homeless poor into the house; when you see the naked, to cover him; and not to hide yourself from your own flesh?

Then your light will break out like the dawn, and your recovery will speedily spring forth; and your righteousness will go before you; The glory of the LORD will be your rear guard.

Then you will call, and the LORD will answer; You will cry, and He will say, "Here I am." If you remove the yoke from your midst, the pointing of the finger and speaking wickedness,

And if you give yourself to the hungry and satisfy the desire of the afflicted, then your light will rise in darkness and your gloom will become like midday.

# SPIRITUAL AWARENESS

And the LORD will continually guide you, and satisfy your desire in scorched places, and give strength to your bones; and you will be like a watered garden, and like a spring of water whose waters do not fail. (Isaiah 58:2–11 NASB)

Towns describes as follows:[21]

- *The Disciple's Fast: purpose*—to loosen the bonds of wickedness (Isaiah 58:6)
- *The Ezra Fast: purpose*—to undo the heavy burdens (Isaiah 58:6)
- *The Samuel Fast: purpose*—to let the oppressed (physically and spiritually) go free (Isaiah 58:6)
- *The Elijah Fast: purpose*—to break every yoke (Isaiah 58:6)
- *The Widow's Fast: purpose*—to share (our) bread with the hungry (Isaiah 58:7)
- *The Saint Paul Fast: purpose*—to allow God's light [to] break forth like the morning (Isaiah 58:8)
- *The Daniel Fast: purpose*—that your recovery will spring forth (Isaiah 58:8)
- *The John the Baptist Fast: purpose*—that your righteousness will go before you (Isaiah 58:8)
- *The Esther Fast: purpose*—that the glory of the Lord will protect us from the evil one. (Isaiah 58:8)

There are many lessons regarding fasting that one can learn from a close examination of Isaiah 58:1–11. First of all, it starts with an admonition regarding a superficial manipulative attitude of addressing Jehovah God. After initially encouraging the Israelites as a "nation which has done righteousness" and "has not forsaken the ordinance of their God," God turns to the adulterated fasting of individuals. Repeating their pleas for attention ("Why have we fasted and You do not *see*? Why have we humbled ourselves and You do not *notice*?" [italics mine]), the Lord responds by describing their *actions* ("on the day of your fast you find your desire, and drive hard all your workers. Behold, you fast for contention and strife and to strike with a wicked fist"). He then goes on to describe the hypocrisy of their passiveness of "spreading out sackcloth and ashes as a bed."

The Lord then proceeds with a clear description of His desired form of fasting. Interestingly enough, it is action-oriented, in stark contrast with the preceding passivity of the traditional form of fasting…*the fast which I choose, to loosen the bonds of wickedness, to undo the bands of the yoke, and to let the oppressed go free and break every yoke? Is it not to divide your bread with the hungry and bring the homeless poor into the house; when you see the naked, to cover him; and not to hide yourself from your own flesh?*

Here we find three components of God's desire for the process of fasting:

1. Freedom from the bondage of sin.
2. Freedom for the oppressed.
3. Provision for the hungry, poor and naked, and for family.

Do we see these elements in our acts of fasting? Is our fasting one of a passive performance or one of authentic action? Here, we must be ruthlessly honest with ourselves. Yes, fasting is a form of stepping away from the bondage of materialism, but it is also a form of refocusing—one in which a person, in poverty of spirit, enters into the suffering and needs of those around them. In prayer and fasting, as we experience hunger and thirst, one is drawn to the deep-seated needs of those around us—those who are the lonely, the homeless, the addicted, the despondent, and globally as well, those without clean water, those persecuted in foreign countries, those oppressed in human trafficking. "Weeping and mourning" are not enough. "Sackcloth and ashes" are not enough. *"Blessed are those who hunger and thirst for righteousness, for they shall be satisfied"* (Matthew 5:6 NASB).

Fasting, in our physical hunger and thirst, leads us to a place of a personal encounter with the righteousness of Christ, in whom we can be satisfied, for the Bread of Life and the Living Water is the only "Sufficient One" in whom to find peace.

## CELEBRATION OF THE FEAST

In contradistinction, one may pursue the discipline of the celebration of the table. In many cultures, a prolonged fast is broken with a celebratory feast. Meals are prepared that celebrate traditional values and aspirations. Foods are selected and prepared that have a special significance of events of the past or present. For example, the Jewish Passover Seder feast features four cups of wine, each representing a stage of the Exodus from Egypt into the promised land: "I will bring out," "I will deliver," "I will redeem," and "I will take." Bitter herbs represent the bitterness of slavery, a roasted shank represents the Pesach sacrificial lamb; the unleavened bread is a reminder of the urgent flight from captivity; and an egg symbolizes the circle of life.

Though the Jews have very long-standing traditions based upon their heritage; nonetheless, each family even today can develop their own traditions of serving and enjoying specific foods and beverages that hold special memories of significance for them.

Helpful Resources on Fasting: Elmer L. Towns,
*Fasting for Spiritual Breakthrough*.

## SCRIPTURE STUDY: LECTIO DIVINA

*Lectio Divina* is Latin for "Divine reading," "spiritual reading," or "holy reading," and represents a method of prayer and Scriptural reading intended to promote communion with God and to provide special spiritual insights. The principles of *lectio divina* were expressed around the year AD 220 and practiced by Catholic monks, especially the monastic rules of Sts. Pachomius, Augustine, Basil, and Benedict.

The practice of *lectio divina* is currently very popular among Catholics, and is gaining acceptance as an integral part of the devotional practices of the Emerging Church. Pope Benedict XVI said in a 2005 speech,

"I would like in particular to recall and recommend the ancient tradition of lectio divina:

the diligent reading of Sacred Scripture accompanied by prayer brings about that intimate dialogue in which the person reading hears God who is speaking, and in praying, responds to him with trusting openness of heart."

The actual practice of *lectio divina* begins with a time of relaxation, making oneself comfortable and clearing the mind of mundane thoughts and cares. Some *lectio* practitioners find it helpful to concentrate by beginning with deep, cleansing breaths and reciting a chosen phrase or word over and over to help free the mind. Then they begin with the following four steps:

*Lectio*: Reading the Bible passage gently and slowly several times. Which passage that is chosen is not as important as the savoring of each portion of the reading, constantly listening for the "still, small voice" of a word or phrase that somehow speaks to the practitioner.

*Meditatio*: Reflecting on the text of the passage and thinking about how it applies to one's own life. This is considered to be a very personal reading of the Scripture and very personal application.

*Oratio*: Responding to the passage by opening the heart to God. This is not primarily an intellectual exercise, but rather is thought to be the beginning of a conversation with God. There is a dialogue of such, back and forth, of thought and emotion.

*Contemplatio*: Listening to God. This is a freeing of oneself from one's own thoughts, both mundane and holy, and hearing God talk to us. Opening the mind, heart, and soul to the influence of God.

The Old and New Testaments are words from God to be studied, meditated upon, prayed over, and memorized for the knowledge and objective meaning they contain and the authority from God they carry, and not for any feelings of personal empowerment, inner peace, or mystical experience that may be produced. Sound knowledge comes first; then the lasting kind of experience and peace comes as a byproduct of knowing and communing with God rightly. This is the approach that Bible-believing followers of Christ have always commended.[22]

## SCRIPTURE STUDY: SPIRITUAL READING

Spiritual reading is a kind of corollary to *lectio divina*, with an emphasis upon the Scriptures as an agent for spiritual transformation. Mulholland in his book, *Shaped by the Word*, makes the case for reading Scripture, not only for "information," but also for "formation." Most of us are familiar with the essential value of reading and understanding the Divine truths revealed in God's Word. In the Scriptures we experience the expressed Divine will of God for all His creation. Care for the earth upon which we live and guidelines for our relationship with Almighty God are dramatically played out in the lives and events of which we read. Many are the themes of truth found in these pages. Themes of man's rebellion and idolatry, God's grace and forgiveness; His overarching plan of redemption despite our failures fill the pages of text. God furthermore demonstrates His Divine character in His acts of creation, judgment, forgiveness, and redemption. His faithfulness and mercy flow from His great love for each of His creation, to grant the light of hope to a darkened world, and His lovingkindness is witnessed in His gift of Christ for the redemption from our sins and restoration of our intimate and eternal relationship with Him.

As valuable and essential as this rational cognitive understanding of Scripture is to our spiritual growth, Mulholland would say there is an additional value of Scripture to be experienced in a type of "formational" approach. This approach centers its focus upon assuming a spirit of receptivity in which the Word of God can work upon one's soul in the act of spiritual formation. Mulholland describes it this way: "this means we come to the text with an openness to hear, to receive, to respond, to be a servant of the Word rather than a master of the text."[23]

That is not to imply that one approach is preferred over the other, nor that they are mutually exclusive. Rather, it is an appeal to experience both the informational truths and the formational insights together, as a dynamic dance of God's grace working toward becoming more spiritually attuned and mature. Mulholland elaborates:

> There is need for balance here. You may start with the informational dynamics but you must be sensitive to the need to move to the formational dynamics of reading. You must allow yourself to become open and receptive to the intrusion of the living Word of God into the garbled, distorted, and debased "word" you are. You must be responsive to the word God is speaking you forth to be in the world. You may start with the formational dynamics but frequently find that you get tripped up on an informational point. You will need to back off momentarily and deal informationally with the text and then move on to the formative mode. There is a necessary interplay between these two approaches to the scripture.[24]

## HELPFUL RESOURCES ON SPIRITUAL READING

Susan Annette Muto, *The Practical Guide to Spiritual Reading*
Michael Casey, *Sacred Reading: The Ancient Art of Lectio Divina*
M. Robert Mulholland Jr., *Shaped by the Word*
Rueben P. Job, *A Wesleyan Spiritual Reader*
Jan Johnson, *Savoring God's Word: Cultivating the Soul-Transforming Practice of Scriptural Meditation*

## EXAMINATION OF CONSCIENCE

The examination of conscience has long been a tradition within the Christian traditions. It involves a deliberate reflection, often within the context of prayer, of one's actions within the day or week. Often, it is comprised by a thoughtful examination of both the blessings and also the failures of our lives. As a Spiritual Discipline though, it is more than a personal meditation for it involves asking some difficult questions of oneself, and honestly answering them. Following is an example of how this may be done.

- *Find a quiet place where you can be alone with God.*
- *Perhaps begin with reading or recalling a Scripture of examine or praying a "thought prayer." "Be still and know that I am God." "Examine my heart, Lord." "Make me aware of Your presence, Father."*
- *Ask how your relationship with God stands...*
- *Review the events of the day or week with a focus upon the choices and decisions you have made and the actions you have performed.*
- *What do these choices, decisions, and actions tell me about my relationship with God and with others?*
    o *What were my attitudes, motivations, and desires?*
    o *What were my omissions and wrongful actions?*
    o *What are the hindrances in my life of faith and service? What should be my response to these?*
    o *What are the encouragements and influences that strengthen my walk of faith and service? How can I appropriate more of the same?*
- *Do I understand that I cannot be all things to all people? What guidelines can I use in which to properly choose those responsibilities which I can accept and those which I cannot?*
- *What values am I affirming with my life?*
- *What kind of person am I becoming as a result of my choices and actions?*
- *What kind of person do I wish to become?*

# APPENDIX II

- *Do I have adequate spiritual and emotional resources and support for the work of spiritual transformation?*
- *In which areas of personal growth do I need God's specific guidance and strengthening?*
- *Are there wounds or harm I have caused in my relationships with others that I must repair? How do I most compassionately do so?*
- *Can I accept a life of humility and submission to spiritual movements within my daily life?*
- *Thank God for all the blessings you have received in the day or week; ask for His continued presence and protection in the everyday moments of living.*
- *Ask for the Lord's grace and guidance for the decisions and actions in the future.*

## SPIRITUAL JOURNALING

Spiritual Journaling can be a wonderful companion to many of the Spiritual Disciplines…especially those of deep, centered prayer, *lectio divina* and examination of conscience. Listening, meditation, and reflection…all contain their moments of insight and correction; of repentance and rededication…but in our humanness, those Divinely crafted moments soon fade from our consciousness into the shadows of the past. Journaling is a way of preserving those moments of awareness and encounter. It is a means of grounding in experience and enlightening one in the hopes for tomorrow.

> A journal is a book in which you keep a personal record of events in your life, of your different relationships, of your response to things, of your feelings about things—of your search to find out who you are and what the meaning of your life might be. It is a book in which you carry out the greatest of life's adventures—the discovery of yourself.[25]

# SPIRITUAL AWARENESS

Ronald Klug in his excellent book, *How to Keep a Spiritual Journal*, later describes ten of the many benefits of spiritual journaling[26]:

1. Growth in self understanding
2. An aid to the devotional life
3. Guidance and decision-making
4. Making sense and order of life
5. Releasing emotions and gaining perspective
6. Greater awareness of daily life
7. Self-expression and creativity
8. Clarifying beliefs
9. Setting goals and managing your time
10. Working through problems

In today's culture "writing it down" becomes "dictate to cell phone."

A teacher of journal writing, Metta Winter, summarizes:

> The personal journal is a private place of quiet and solitude: a place to befriend yourself and to explore the uniqueness of your life's journey. For centuries men and women have written in journals in times of loneliness, crisis, transition, conflict, spiritual quest, physical or intellectual challenge, or serendipitous joy. In these journals, they have found companionship, emotional release, clarification, resolution, the self-affirmation required for courage, the discovery of spiritual resources, and a deeper appreciation of their lives.[27]

Helpful Resources on Spiritual Journaling

Ronald Klug, *How to Keep a Spiritual Journal*

# APPENDIX II

# KEEPING SABBATH

"The Sabbath cannot survive in exile, a
lonely stranger among days of profanity."[28]
—Abraham Joshua Heschel

The dominant biblical accounts of keeping the Sabbath are elaborated most completely in Exodus 20:8–11 and Deuteronomy 5:12–15 but are also featured in Leviticus 23:3; Nehemiah 10:31, 13:15; Isaiah 56:1–8, 58:13–14; Jeremiah 17:19–27; Ezekiel 20:12, 20, 22:8, 26. Their main themes convey the description of a specific time set aside to cease from labor and to celebrate God's deliverance and blessing.

Reading of the childhood memories of the Jewish people as they celebrate the *Shabbat* is inspiring. In their tradition, the Sabbath day is elevated to a day of special significance—truly a day of celebration with special food, special music, and special prayers. The routines of the week become faded as a chosen people recognize their unique relationship with their Lord, Jehovah. Israel's ancient history of the exodus is a story of a people's struggles with persecution and captivity. Within this struggle was a desire to be "like other peoples" with their own land, their own king, their own god…and the idolatry discovered within other cultures often blinded them from their relationship with the great "I AM." But this is our story too, as we all too easily become enculturated to the norms of the modern and the idols of our desire.

Marva Dawn describes how the Sabbath is so very important even in today's Christian struggles with cultural accommodation and compromise.

> We already set ourselves apart from the surrounding culture when we choose not to work in any way on the Sabbath. We further extricate ourselves from society's values if we give up the need for accomplishment and abstain from worry and anxiety about our position. We choose deliberately to be different from our culture if we

> give up our striving to be God and let Yahweh be God instead. We definitely do not conform to our culture if we choose not to be dominated by possessions or by the anxiety to acquire more of them, but decide instead to give away much of what we have and use what we have been given as good stewards who desire to enjoy the things of God for the purposes of God.[29]

Each one of us, Jew and Christian alike, is commanded to *"remember the Sabbath day, to keep it holy."* The Sabbath is to be kept "holy," sanctified, and highly esteemed—as set aside from the profane. The Leviticus passage (Leviticus 23:3 NIV) describes the Sabbath as a "sacred assembly" that is to be practiced "wherever you live." Despite the Sabbath commandment being the longest commandment given, it is perhaps the one taken most casually within Christianity today. How then, does one reclaim the desire for recognizing and celebrating the Sabbath as a holy day of "remembering"?

Remembering the Sabbath is a means of remembering God's acts of *creation* and *deliverance*. It is interesting, and of note, that despite the similarities describing the Sabbath in both the Exodus and the Deuteronomy passages, there is a rather marked difference in emphasis. Both passages require the cessation of work, but each focuses on different observances of God's relationship with mankind. In Exodus, one sees a clear emphasis on God's work of creation, and in Deuteronomy, there is the remembrance of God's deliverance.

> Remember the sabbath day, to keep it holy. Six days you shall labor and do all your work, but the seventh day is a sabbath of the LORD your God; in it you shall not do any work, you or your son or your daughter, your male or your female servant or your cattle or your sojourner who stays with you. For in six days the LORD made the heavens and the earth, the sea and all that is in them, and rested on the seventh day; therefore

> the LORD blessed the sabbath day and made it holy. (Exodus 20:8–11 NASB)
>
> Observe the sabbath day to keep it holy, as the LORD your God commanded you. Six days you shall labor and do all your work, but the seventh day is a sabbath of the LORD your God; in it you shall not do any work, you or your son or your daughter or your male servant or your female servant or your ox or your donkey or any of your cattle or your sojourner who stays with you, so that your male servant and your female servant may rest as well as you. And you shall remember that you were a slave in the land of Egypt, and the LORD your God brought you out of there by a mighty hand and by an outstretched arm; therefore the LORD your God commanded you to observe the sabbath day."(-Deuteronomy 5:12–15 NASB)

Like two pillars, these two similar biblical passages both uphold the fundamental principle of remembrance, pausing to rest in the acknowledgment and confidence of God's works of creation and His merciful acts of deliverance.

In the Christian tradition, both in the acts of creation and in the acts of deliverance from sin (redemption), Christ has an instrumental role. Therefore, as we celebrate our Sabbath day, incorporating the central role of Christ as Lord and Savior has special importance and significance. This can be accomplished in any number of ways… by the celebration of Holy Communion and by reading portions of Scripture that recognize Christ's roles in creation and redemption and special prayers of Christ's life. Marva Dawn describes the early church's solution.

> The earliest Christians at first celebrated both the Sabbath on the seventh day (Saturday),

in keeping with their Jewish heritage, and the Lord's Day on the first day of the week (Sunday), in keeping with their recognition that Christ's resurrection was the major turning point for their faith. The Jews emphasized a Sabbath of resting and thinking about God's creation and deliverance, a seventh day of delight serving as a sign of the covenant. To all this the Christians added their remembrance of the radical reorientation of the Sabbath that Jesus demonstrated, especially in his healing miracles on that day, and they also set apart the day of his resurrection to celebrate his continuing Lordship.

It seems that Sunday became the exclusive day for worship only after persecution in Jerusalem dispersed the Christians...The change was legislated by an edict on Sunday observance issued by the Emperor Constantine in C.E. 321.[30]

*Sabbath Rest*

> There are six days when you may work, but the seventh day is a day of sabbath rest, a day of sacred assembly. You are not to do any work; wherever you live, it is a sabbath to the LORD. (Leviticus 23:3 NIV)

> God admonishes each person to *"cease striving, and know that I am God."* (Psalm 46:10 NASB)

(The Hebrew word *shabbat* means primarily "to cease or desist.")[31]

> *O Lord, thou has made us, and our spirits are restless until we rest in thee.* (St. Augustine)

Celebrating the Sabbath is foremost an act of *worship*. In the "ceasing" and "stillness," one is called to "know" Jehovah as the Lord God Almighty, Maker of heaven and earth.[32] It is to acknowledge His glory and grace, which cause one to break out into expressions of praise and gratitude for who He is.

I rather like the way Ruth Haley Barton describes the delight that culminates in worship and renewal as she experiences the Sabbath day:

> I know what it's like to have rest turn into delight, and delight turn into gratitude, and gratitude into worship. I know what it is like to recover myself so completely that I am able, by God's grace, to enter into my work on Monday with a renewed sense of God's calling and God's presence.[33]

## MY THOUGHTS FOR A PERSONAL SABBATH

- My Saturday night preparation
    - Lighting of the two candles: "Observe God's creation" and "Remember God's deliverance"
    - "Worthy are You, our Lord and our God, to receive glory and honor and power; for You created all things, and by Your will they existed, and were created" (Revelation 4:11 ESV).
    - Psalm 63
    - Prayer of thanksgiving
    - Prayer of relinquishment
    - Blessing the children (and grandchildren), parents, spouse by name individually

> The Lord bless you and keep you;
> The Lord make His face to shine upon you,
> And be gracious to you.

## SPIRITUAL AWARENESS

      The Lord lift up His countenance upon you,
      And give you peace. (Numbers 6:24–26 ESV)

- o  Hymn: "Guide Me, O, Thou Great Jehovah"

- My Sunday morning preparation
  - o  This is the Lord's Sabbath rest, rejoice and find your peace in Him.
  - o  Early morning Psalm and prayer
    Psalm 92, 93, 100, 126
    Hymn: "Great is Thy Faithfulness" (Lamentations 3:22–23)
  - o  Holy, Holy, Holy, Lord God Almighty; heaven and earth are full of Thy Glory; glory be to Thee, O Lord Most High.

O God, I crave Thy blessing upon this day of rest and refreshment. Let me rejoice to-day in Thy worship and find gladness in the singing of Thy praises. Forbid, I beseech Thee, that only my body should be refreshed to-day and not my spirit. Give me grace for such an act of self-recollection as may again bring together the scattered forces of my soul. Enable me to step aside for a little while from the busy life of common days and take thought about its meaning and its end. May Jesus Christ be to-day the companion of my thoughts, so that His Divine manhood may more and more take root within my soul. May He be in me and I in Him, even as Thou wert in Him and through Him mayest be in me and I at rest in Thee.

O Thou who art the Source and Ground of all truth, Thou Light of lights, who hast opened the minds of men to discern the things that are, guide me to-day, I beseech Thee, in my hours of reading. Give me grace to choose the right books and to read them in the right way. Give me wisdom to abstain as well as to persevere. Let the Bible have proper place; and grant that as I read I may be alive to the stirrings of Thy Holy Spirit in my soul.

I pray, O God, for all human hearts that to-day are lifted up to Thee in earnest desire, and for every group of men and women who are met together to praise and magnify Thy name. Whatever be their mode of worship, be graciously pleased to accept their humble offices of prayer and praise, and lead them unto life eternal, through Jesus Christ our Lord. Amen.[34]
(John Baillie, *A Diary of Private Prayer*)

- My Sunday afternoon meditations
    - Focus on an attribute of God
        - Righteousness of God
        - *Hesed*: steadfast love
        - Study the Hebrew names for God and their respective meanings.
    - Enjoy music, art, nature
    - Self-examination
        - Dis-embedding from culture: John 17:15–16
        - Celebrate discovery, creativity, music
        - Honestly re-examine priorities
    - Examine relationships: praying for and helping others, building and strengthening relationships, giving/gifting with intentional affirmation.

- My Sunday evening
    - Devotions: lighting of the candle
        - Prayer of Thanksgiving

- Prayer for Forgiveness
- Communion
- Prayer of Protection and Provision for the coming week
- Prayer of Closure

Holy Spirit of God, Thou who art a gracious and willing guest in every heart that is humble enough to receive Thee, be present now within my heart and guide my prayer.

For all the gracious opportunities and privileges of this day, I give Thee thanks, O Lord:

For the rest I have this day enjoyed from the daily round of deeds:

For thine invitation to keep thy holy day to Thyself:

For the house of prayer and the ministry of public worship:

For the blessed sacrament in which, as often as we eat and drink it, we remember our Lord's death and taste His living presence:

For all the earthly symbols by which heavenly realities have to-day laid firmer hold upon my soul:

For the books I have read and the music which has uplifted me:

For this day's friendly intercourse:

For the Sabbath peace of Christian homes:

For the interior peace that has ruled within my heart.

Grant, O heavenly Father, that the spiritual refreshment I have this day enjoyed may not be left behind and forgotten as to-morrow I return to the cycle of common tasks. Here is a fountain of inward strength. Here is a purifying wind that must blow through all my business and all my pleasures. Here is a light to enlighten all my road. Therefore, O God, do Thou enable me so to discipline my will that in hours of stress I may honestly seek after those things for which I have prayed in hours of peace.

Ere I lie down to sleep, I commit all my dear ones to Thine unsleeping care; through Jesus Christ our Lord. Amen.[35] (John Baillie: *A Diary of Private Prayer*)

- Singing of the *Gloria Patri*

"Glory be to the Father and to the Son and to the Holy Ghost; as it was in the beginning, is now, and ever shall be, world without end. Amen. Amen."

## HELPFUL RESOURCES ON KEEPING SABBATH

Ruth Haley Barton, *Sacred Rhythms* (IVP, 2006), Chapter 8
Dorothy C. Bass, *Practicing our Faith* (San Francisco: Jossey-Bass Publishers, 1997)
Marva J. Dawn, *Keeping the Sabbath Wholly* (Eerdmans, 1989)
Tilden Edwards, *Sabbath Time* (Nashville, Upper Room Books, 1992)
Abraham Joshua Heschel, *Sabbath*
Karen Burton Mains, *Making Sunday Special* contains many suggestions for making Sunday special for children and families.
J. I. Packer, *Knowing God* (Downers Grove, Illinois: IVP, 1973)
Kay Arthur, *Lord, I Want to Know You* is an excellent book for studying the names of God and knowing more fully Who He is

## IN COMMUNITY

The Spiritual Disciplines discussed previously are primarily ones utilized by the individual in privacy. However, there are also those which are to be practiced within the environment of family and religious community. Richard Foster, in the later section of *Celebration of Discipline*, describes the "Corporate Disciplines" of confession, worship, guidance, and celebration. Ernest Boyer, in *A Way in the World: Family Life as Spiritual Discipline*, focuses upon establishing a sense of spirituality of the family. This occurs by means of placing special significance upon common family activities of helping and caring for one another and in serving others as a collective family ministry. Relationships are thereby valued, enriched, and deepened as the family interacts and reaches into the community at large. Many are the various ways in which a person, inspired and led by the Spirit, can experience intimacy with God, alone or within a spiritual community.

## HELPFUL RESOURCES ON THE SPIRITUAL DISCIPLINES

Richard J. Foster, *Celebration of Discipline*
Richard J. Foster, *Prayer*
Dallas Willard, *The Spirit of the Disciplines*
Dallas Willard, *Hearing God*
Donald S. Whitney, *Spiritual Disciplines for the Christian Life*
Oswald Chambers, *Christian Disciplines*
John Ortberg, *The Life You've Always Wanted*
Ruth Haley Barton, *Sacred Rhythms*
Ernest Boyer Jr., *A Way in the World: Family Life as Spiritual Discipline*
Louis J. Puhl, S. J., *The Spiritual Exercises of St. Ignatius: based on studies in the language of the autograph*
Josef Neuner, S. J., *Walking with Him*—this is a thirty-day devotional patterned after the *Spiritual Exercises* of St. Ignatius of Loyola.
David M. Stanley, S. J., *A Modern Scriptural Approach to the 'Spiritual Exercises'*

# APPENDIX II

1. Quoted in Richard J. Foster, *Celebration of Discipline: The Path to Spiritual Growth* (San Francisco: Harper & Row, Publishers, 1978), 1.
2. John Woolman, *The Journal of John Woolman* (Secaucus, New Jersey: The Citadel Press, 1972), 118.
   Richard J. Foster, *Celebration of Discipline: The Path to Spiritual Growth* (San Francisco: Harper & Row, Publishers, 1978),
3. From *Celebration of Discipline* by Richard J. Foster, 1. Copyright (c) 1978, 1988, 1998 by Richard J. Foster. Used by permission of HarperCollins Publishers.
4. From *Purity of Heart Is to Will One Thing* by Soren Kierkegaard, translated by Douglas V. Steere, 184. English translation copyright © 1938 by Harper & Brothers, renewed © 1966 by Douglas V. Steere. Used by permission of HarperCollins Publishers.
5. Ibid., 184.
6. Ibid., 185.
7. Ibid., 186.
8. Galatians 5:22–23 (NASB).
9. Ruth Haley Barton. *Sacred Rhythms: Arranging our Lives for Spiritual Transformation* (Downers Grove, Illinois: InterVarsity Press, 2006), 43–44.
10. From *Celebration of Discipline* by Richard J. Foster, 95. Copyright (c) 1978, 1988, 1998 by Richard J. Foster. Used by permission of HarperCollins Publishers.
11. Excerpts from *No Man Is an Island* by Thomas Merton, 248. Copyright © 1955 by The Abbey of Our Lady of Gethsemani and renewed 1983 by the Trustees of the Merton Legacy Trust. Reprinted by permission of Houghton Mifflin Harcourt Publishing Company. All rights reserved.
12. Ibid.
13. Ibid., 253.
14. Arthur G. Gish, *Beyond the Rat Race* (New Canaan, Connecticut: Keats Publishing, Inc., 1973), 21.
    Richard Foster, *Celebration of Discipline: The Path to Spiritual Growth* (San Francisco: Harper & Row, Publishers, 1978), 70.
15. Psalm 23:1 (NLT).
16. Excerpts from *The Ascent to Truth* by Thomas Merton, 23. Copyright © 1951 by The Abbey of Our Lady of Gethsemani and renewed 1979 by the Trustees of the Merton Legacy Trust. Reprinted by permission of Houghton Mifflin Harcourt Publishing Company. All rights reserved.
17. Saint Gregory of Nyssa, *Homily I on Ecclesiastes*, PG 44:628. Excerpts from *The Ascent to Truth* by Thomas Merton, 23-24. Copyright © 1951 by The Abbey of Our Lady of Gethsemani and renewed 1979 by the Trustees of the Merton Legacy Trust. Reprinted by permission of Houghton Mifflin Harcourt Publishing Company. All rights reserved.

[18] Blaise Pascal, *Les Pensees* (Paris, Ed. Giraud, 1928), 67. Excerpts from *The Ascent to Truth* by Thomas Merton, 25. Copyright © 1951 by The Abbey of Our Lady of Gethsemani and renewed 1979 by the Trustees of the Merton Legacy Trust. Reprinted by permission of Houghton Mifflin Harcourt Publishing Company. All rights reserved.

[19] Excerpts from *The Ascent to Truth* by Thomas Merton, 25. Copyright © 1951 by The Abbey of Our Lady of Gethsemani and renewed 1979 by the Trustees of the Merton Legacy Trust. Reprinted by permission of Houghton Mifflin Harcourt Publishing Company. All rights reserved.

[20] Ibid., 24-25.

[21] Elmer L. Towns, *Fasting for Spiritual Breakthrough* (Ventura, California: Regal Books, 1996), 20–23.

[22] http://www.gotquestions.org/lectio-divina.html.

[23] M. Robert Mulholland Jr., *Shaped by the Word: The Power of Scripture in Spiritual Formation* (Nashville, Tennessee: The Upper Room. 1985), 54.

[24] Ibid., 59.

[25] Harry J. Cargas and Roger J. Radley, *Keeping a Spiritual Journal* (Garden City, NY: Doubleday, 1981), 8.

Ronald Klug, *How to Keep a Spiritual Journal* (Minneapolis: Augsburg Books, 1993), 12.

[26] Ronald Klug, *How to Keep a Spiritual Journal* (Minneapolis: Augsburg Books, 1993), 18–26.

[27] Metta Winter, *Pendle Hill Bulletin* No. 322 (October 1981), 6.

Ronald Klug, *How to Keep a Spiritual Journal* (Minneapolis: Augsburg Books, 1993), 13.

[28] Quoted in Dorothy C. Bass, *Practicing Our Faith*, (San Francisco: Jossey-Bass Publishers, 1997), 77.

[29] Marva J. Dawn, *Keeping the Sabbath Wholly* (Grand Rapids, MI: William B. Eerdman's Publishing, 1989), 43–44.

[30] Ibid., 42–43.

[31] Ibid., 3.

[32] J. I. Packer, *Knowing God* (Downers Grove, Illinois: InterVarsity Press, 1973).

[33] Ruth Haley Barton, *Sacred Rhythms: Arranging our Lives for Spiritual Transformation* (Downers Grove, Illinois: InterVarsity Press, 2006), 137.

[34] From *A Diary of Private Prayer* by John Baillie, 133. Copyright © 1949 by Charles Scribner's Sons; copyright renewed © 1977 by Ian Fowler Baillie. Reprinted by permission of Scribner, a division of Simon & Schuster, Inc. All rights reserved.

[35] Ibid., 135.

## About the Author

Larry E. Maugel, MD, grew up in the small town of Farmer, Ohio; he received his BS from Bowling Green State University and his MD from the Medical College of Ohio at Toledo. After practicing family medicine for thirty-six years, he retired and began writing about his lifelong passion of philosophy and theology.

Despite these interests, he is a firm believer that the best things in life are the simple things—a bowl of pasta and a glass of wine on the deck with his lovely wife Laurel, or a steaming cup of freshly brewed coffee and a good book in the chill of autumn.

Larry and Laurel live in Charlotte, North Carolina.